IMAGES
of America

DELAWARE TOWNSHIP

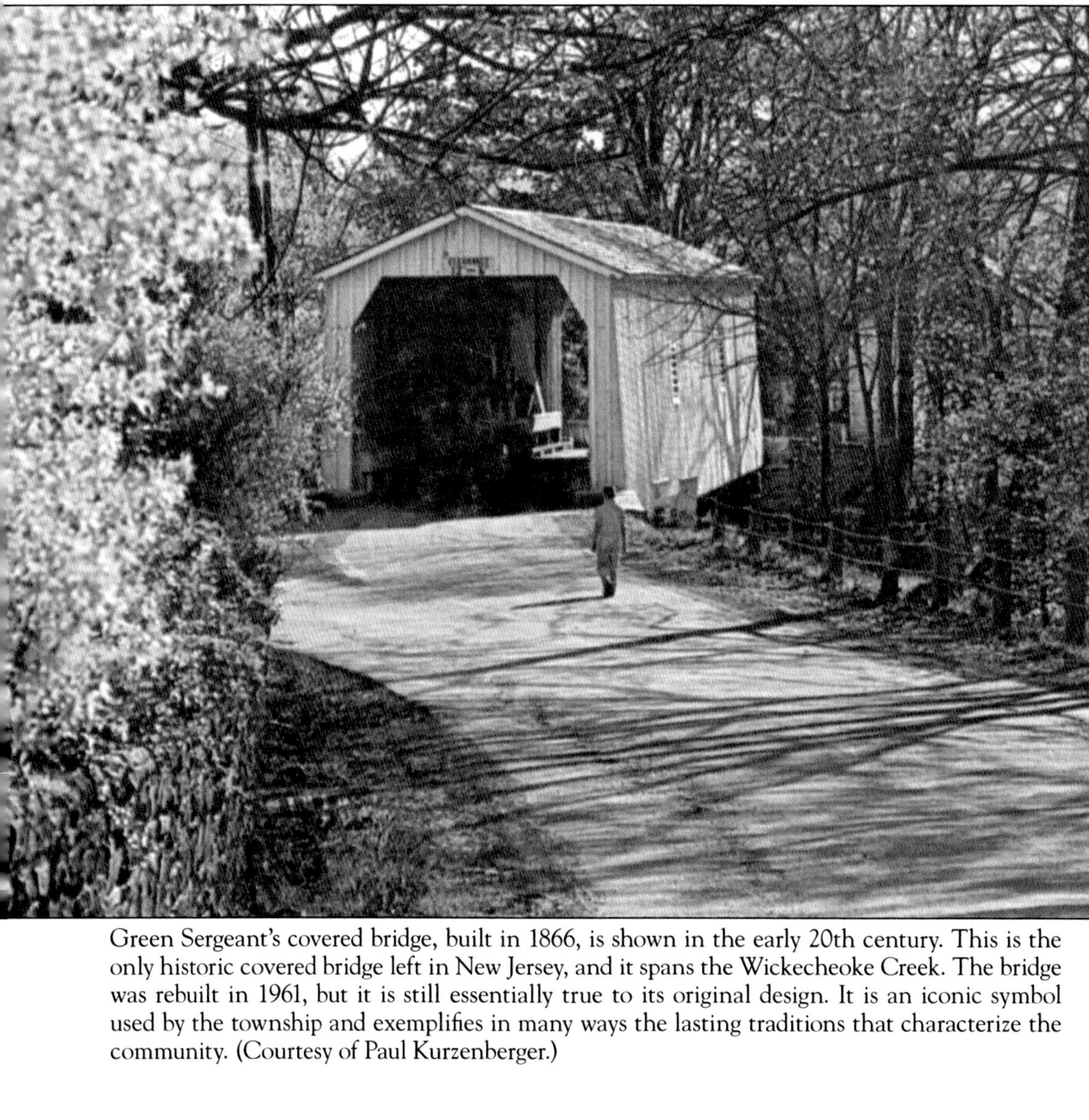

Green Sergeant's covered bridge, built in 1866, is shown in the early 20th century. This is the only historic covered bridge left in New Jersey, and it spans the Wickecheoke Creek. The bridge was rebuilt in 1961, but it is still essentially true to its original design. It is an iconic symbol used by the township and exemplifies in many ways the lasting traditions that characterize the community. (Courtesy of Paul Kurzenberger.)

On the cover: This photograph was probably taken about 1920 and shows a cross section of the township citizenry in front of the Sergeantsville House during the annual town meeting. Babies in arms are on the porch as well as many of the wives and mothers. After the meeting, they traditionally stayed together for dinner, a strong indicator of the cohesive nature of community in Delaware Township that reached back in time to the early 1700s. (Courtesy of Paul Kurzenberger.)

IMAGES
of America

DELAWARE TOWNSHIP

James Drummond

ARCADIA
PUBLISHING

ISBN 978-0-7385-7215-4

Published by Arcadia Publishing
Charleston SC, Chicago IL, Portsmouth NH, San Francisco CA

Printed in the United States of America

Library of Congress Control Number: 2009929570

For all general information contact Arcadia Publishing at:
Telephone 843-853-2070
Fax 843-853-0044
E-mail sales@arcadiapublishing.com
For customer service and orders:
Toll-Free 1-888-313-2665

Visit us on the Internet at www.arcadiapublishing.com

To Paul Kurzenberger, Blanche Carl, and Dave Bond, the longtime Delaware Township citizens who made this study flow

Contents

Acknowledgments

A great and heartfelt thank-you is owed to Paul Kurzenberger. Without his more than 30 years of dedication to collecting pictures of life in Delaware Township, there would not have been a book. He not only had a great collection, which he was willing to share, but he faithfully met day after day to explain the meaning of the pictures.

Blanche Carl, the historian in residence at the Amwell Church of the Brethren, was always available, gathered pictures, shared stories, and gave her time to the project.

Both Kurzenberger and Carl opened avenues of approach to others in the community because of their lifelong residence and wide contacts within the township.

Dave Bond, farmer and entrepreneur extraordinaire, went out of his way in a busy schedule to share pictures and stories that gave very practical insight into the ways of life in the township.

Carla Mackey, Gary Hinesley, and Maggie Clare all shared scrapbooks that were left behind as people departed the township. Frank Barlow, president of Holcombe-Jimison Farmstead Museum, provided information and insight into Delaware Township's farming history. Roger Byrom, the current, caring owner of Headquarters Farm, also provided good background and encouragement.

Susan Lockwood, former mayor and current township committee member, gave support and official encouragement from the very beginning of the project. The historical society provided a good impetus in brainstorming possible approaches at the very beginning of the study.

Many others gave of their time and materials, including Charles Higgins, former fire chief; Bruce Mast, chief of police; and Judy Allen, township clerk.

Erin Rocha, my Arcadia Publishing editor, was extremely helpful and available with directions, advice, and encouragement along the way.

Finally, I am so grateful to my wife, Veda Mathis Drummond, for her support, expert technical input, and long hours of labor getting the rough copies into final form. As always through these many years together, I could not have done it without her.

It almost goes without saying that any mistakes in the account are mine, even though I have had such wonderful guidance from these longtime residents. The 300 years of township history will take a lifetime for me to put together, but the journey is worth the effort to begin understanding this garden spot and its story.

Unless otherwise noted, all images appear courtesy of Paul Kurzenberger.

Introduction

Notable 1930s historian Carl Becker published a provocative book titled *Everyman His Own Historian* in which he called for an approach that involved having people develop their own histories. By this approach, individuals would look around their own environment and create a view of change over time, that is, history based upon their own lives and interests.

That was considered a radical move by many in the discipline of history (the professionals), who would lose control over the stuff of history by such an approach. They often considered local history topics antiquarian and less than acceptable academically.

Paradoxically by the 1960s, Becker's focus became one of the main currents of academic historical endeavor with social history developing many of the topics of local history that were the very heart of life as lived by everyman.

Delaware Township is the perfect place to practice Becker's call to develop the history of those things around us. Here there is actually a road that George Washington traveled, and, to this day, the local residents tell stories of Washington watering his horse at a spring along that road. True or not, it is part of the lore and history of Delaware Township.

From the standpoint of history as lived by regular people with regular common sense needs, Delaware Township is an exciting place worth preserving and getting to know in all of its rich historical dimensions.

Delaware Township was officially separated from the township of Amwell on February 23, 1838, at the first annual town meeting held at the inn of Henry Wagner within the village of Sergeantsville. However, settlers had been in the township as early as 1695, and quite substantial stone houses date to the early 1700s. By 1880, the population of Delaware Township had reached 3,092 with 366 farms.

Life in the township in those early days centered upon the farms, the numerous churches (with some having congregations numbering in the hundreds), and the compact local schools located strategically throughout the thriving township. Finally economic and social activity also focused on a number of small, scattered villages or hamlets sprinkled in a regular pattern a few miles apart.

Delaware Township in many respects looks very similar today to how it did 100 or 200 years ago. In collecting vintage pictures for this book, scores of town studies having a similar theme and approach were consulted, and very few appear today as they did even 20 years ago. The drama of change over time was often quite striking in those other towns, but picture after historical picture of Delaware Township almost seemed current because one could just look about town and easily recognize today the scenes from the past. Delaware Township has a rich history that can be seen in its people, its physical structures, its natural environment, and its cultural and organizational approaches; this does show up strongly in the vintage pictures.

The township has been a very vital and dynamic place, from its original settlement up to the present day. This seems to have been its destiny since it lies close to the exact center of the eastern megalopolis, that amoebic growth of the giant and almost solidly grown modern city that lies between Richmond, Virginia, in the South and extends to Boston, Massachusetts, in the North. From its beginning, the township was greatly affected by its locale since it also lay halfway between the two largest American cities, Philadelphia and New York City. It is a minor miracle of planning and simple luck that it has not become just another commercial strip and commuter dormitory connecting those monoliths to the north and the south, as has happened to most of the surrounding Garden State. The importance of location for the historical development of Delaware Township cannot be overstated since it lies in the center of the shortest route for movement up and down the East Coast of America.

The geographic placement of Delaware Township has meant that it would be an important nodal point on any movement along the whole eastern seaboard of America from Native American times right up to the present. Consequently, geese fly a route over the township, airplanes are directed in a stream overhead, and the Big Inch and Little Big Inch pipelines flow underground right alongside the township.

The shortest and most vital connecting link between New York City and Philadelphia even in early America was the Old York Road, with Delaware Township situated near the halfway point along the journey. The route of the road through a corner of the township proceeded south out of Ringoes on Boss Road, turned left on the present Garboski Road, and went left again on Bowne Station Road. At Mount Airy-Sandy Ridge Road (Queens Road), the old route turned left again and crossed the Alexauken Creek on its way up the hill to Mount Airy.

The total route of the road was almost identical to the Lenni-Lenape trail and had originally been built right over the old Native American path that started at Front and Vine Streets in Philadelphia and connected the Neshaminy River with the Raritan River near New Brunswick. In Delaware Township, the road was laid out exactly over the Native American path and accounts for its twisting character.

Prior to 1710, Hunterdon County was an "undefined wilderness," according to one witness, and the Old York Road helped shape Delaware Township's early character with its first farm being purchased and settled along the route near the Alexauken Creek. That township portion of the road remained a notoriously difficult stretch to navigate, as it took four to six horses to pull through a quite rutted and twisting route. Passengers often had to walk the section between Mount Airy and Ringoes as wagons broke down.

Traffic on the Old York Road was primarily associated with movement involved in the westward migration, but it also had heavy usage by stagecoaches plying their way between Philadelphia and New York City. Two companies competed for passengers along the road: the Swift-Sure Line and the Philadelphia Mail Stage. The stage drivers congregated at John Ringoes Tavern (the present bank building in Ringoes), and it was said among those in the Hunterdon countryside that a stage driver could knock a fly off the lead horse's hip with his whip and a casual flip of the wrist. The stages were Troy Post coaches, which were built broad and high, with the body mounted on leather straps; the swaying motion often made passengers land sick. The Philadelphia Mail Stage left Philadelphia three days a week at 8:00 a.m. and arrived in New York City the following day. Because of the rough section through Delaware Township, passengers were many times stranded at Ringoes and stayed over in John Ringoes Tavern.

One of the most historic happenings along the old road was on April 25, 1740, when the great evangelist George Whitefield came from Philadelphia over the Old York Road and preached to 5,000 people in an open-air meeting just outside Ringoes near the church (just beyond the present-day Dunkin' Donuts at Route 202 and the Old York Road). Whitefield's voice could carry to a huge crowd without amplification; Benjamin Franklin testified to his persuasiveness when he attended one of Whitefield's meetings in Philadelphia and found himself giving money in the collection plate, even though he was skeptical of Whitefield's message. In general, as was true of all America, this evangelistic activity is a strong indicator of the great influence these early itinerant preachers had in the formation of local cultures both nationally as well as locally. It is also quite indicative of the influence that travel on the old road had locally as various cultural influences flowed along the artery and came to affect aspects of life in Delaware Township. Five thousand people in attendance had to be practically every person for miles around who used the road to attend this interregional happening.

Perhaps the primary focal point along the road in Delaware Township was a mill located at the Alexauken Creek just before the road headed south up the hill to Mount Airy (near the present pipeline pumping station). The small dammed lake at that point apparently fed power to the mill as people came from miles around to have grain processed and lumber sawed.

One can conclude that just as transportation facilities greatly affect the culture, commerce, and total way of life of an area/region today (such as regional malls always being built along regional transit lines), it was just so in the past. As Emogene Van Sickle, an early commentator, stated concerning the Old York Road, "Along this historic highway, which crossed New Jersey from Lambertville to Elizabethport, history was in the making, which marked the destiny of America." That larger destiny impacted the culture of early Delaware Township, keeping this small corner of the larger world vitally connected to the greater patterns creating America.

A potentially large volume of trucks and cars very near Delaware Township headed to the Pennsylvania Turnpike was only prevented because citizens in neighboring Bucks County, Pennsylvania, stopped the completion of Route 202 as a four-lane freeway through their county a few years ago. Had that happened, Delaware Township today would be as intensely developed as Bridgewater Township farther north. The importance of these factors for Delaware Township is that any time a transportation line goes in, development always follows. Because transportation of goods and people is one of the most expensive of all human activities, those activities must be as close to transportation as possible to lessen the cost. Consequently, development always comes as a corollary to the emplacement of a transportation facility.

Transportation has been a strong element of life in the township since its very beginning in the 1700s, primarily because the Old York Road passed through Delaware Township; the ancient route was the shortest connecting line between New York City and Philadelphia. The Old York Road ultimately connected with the National Road near Baltimore after the Revolutionary War, and that artery was the main route to the Cumberland Gap and the whole interior of the United States beyond.

The Old York Road began in Elizabeth and passed through Westfield, Scotch Plains, Plainfield, Raritan (Somerville), Three Bridges, Reaville, Larison's Corner, Ringoes, a corner of Delaware Township (about four miles) on its way to Mount Airy, and finally Lambertville. At Lambertville (Coryell's Ferry), the Old York Road crossed the Delaware River on a covered bridge (called a "wooden tunnel") and wound its way to Philadelphia, crossing Broad Street (Route 611) near the present Roosevelt Boulevard (Route 1). It then ran near Broad Street through Philadelphia, ultimately ambling on to Baltimore (Baltimore Pike) and to the western United States.

The Old York Road was a feeder to the National Road (the present U.S. Route 40 and Interstate 70). This meant that a steady stream of carts, covered wagons (including the famous Conestoga wagon), stagecoaches, and assorted mounted riders passed through Delaware Township as they moved back and forth between the two largest cities in America and, more particularly, to the great western frontier. That unending procession along the Old York Road through the township had a social impact on people living there in those early days and influenced development.

Today the township has 455 historic sites located throughout the place with much of the built environment having a patina of use over time but still thriving functionally as dwellings, stores, sheds, and storehouses (barns)—all functional tools for life in the present day as they have been for centuries. The town hall, a former hotel and tavern (seen on the cover at the annual town gathering there in the early 20th century) is a great testament to the preservation of the built environment as it was recycled and preserved in its historical veracity and yet is quite functional as a current town focus and meeting place.

In order to understand the historical dimensions of Delaware Township, this study will focus on its early origins, the farms, the local towns and hamlets, the schools, and finally the people and the physical setting of this historical and current crossroads to all America.

One

THE FARMS

In a memoir of his boyhood on a farm in Georgia, Jimmy Carter, former president of the United States, called attention to the importance of farming and the earth in the affairs of men, as he noted that "times change, and deeds to the various fields will be held in the future by one family and then another . . . but I am confidant that the earth itself will remain basically the same, continuing to shape the lives of its owners, for good or ill, as it has for millennia. After all, the land belonged to the Indians before it was ours." This incisive observation is certainly true of Delaware Township; the land, and the farms that have occupied most of the space, is in many ways the most telling aspect of life in the township. This is particularly so since there are a number of families in the township whose ancestors have lived for generations on the same land that they now occupy.

Delaware Township also occupies one of the most important historic Native American sites in New Jersey. That heritage stretches back to at least 5430 BC, as established by carbon dating obtained in an archaeological dig conducted a few years ago by Seton Hall University in a charcoal pit along the Delaware River not far north of the township. Over the following hundreds of years, the Native Americans in the Delaware Township locale established, evolved, and maintained a very viable culture on the land occupied by the township today.

The dynamic quality of life in Delaware Township over time and the use of the land by the early settlers can in many ways be summed up in a visit to the local Holcombe-Jimison Farmstead Museum. It is a unique slice of farm history maintained by volunteers and is situated on the first farm in Delaware Township, including the oldest house in the township with a date stone of 1711. This is Delaware Township, a vital, connected part of North America in the past and certainly in the changing, dynamic present.

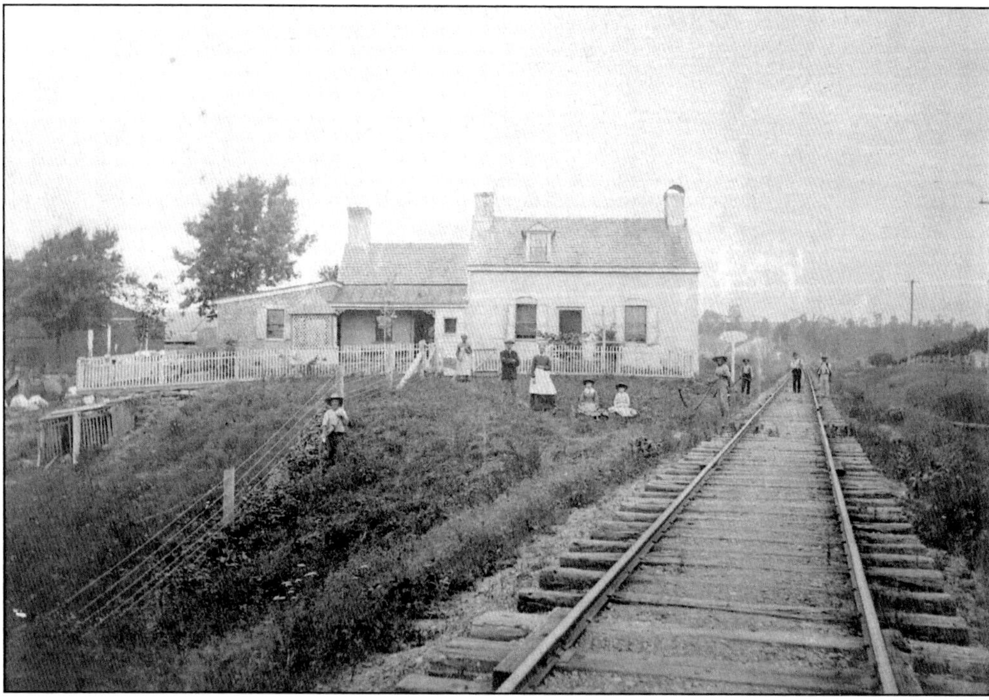

The Jimison farm and family are shown in this photograph. This was the first house and farm in Delaware Township. The house faces the Alexauken Creek, which flows into Lambertville. The creek was originally the main artery of movement since there were no roads. The railroad was constructed between the creek and the house in the 1850s. This is now part of the Holcombe-Jimison Farmstead Museum. (Courtesy of the Holcombe-Jimison Farmstead Museum.)

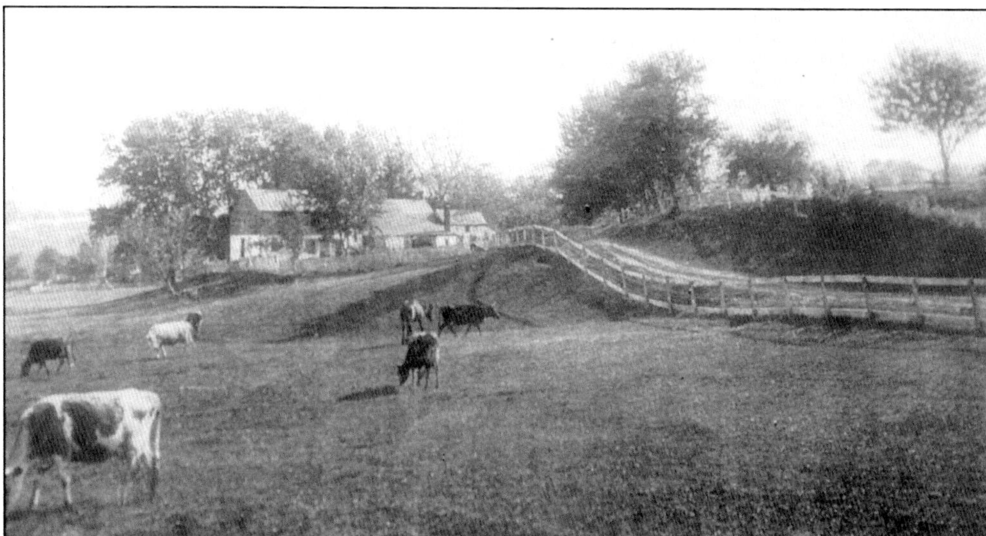

Pictured here in the early 20th century, the Kusant farmhouse on Lambertville-Headquarters Road faces south. This is the original Barber house; John Barber was the first magistrate, or mayor, of Sergeantsville in 1838. The house was built in 1737, and the road curves around it. George Washington watered his horse at a spring in front of this house, and the neighborhood children crowded around asking questions.

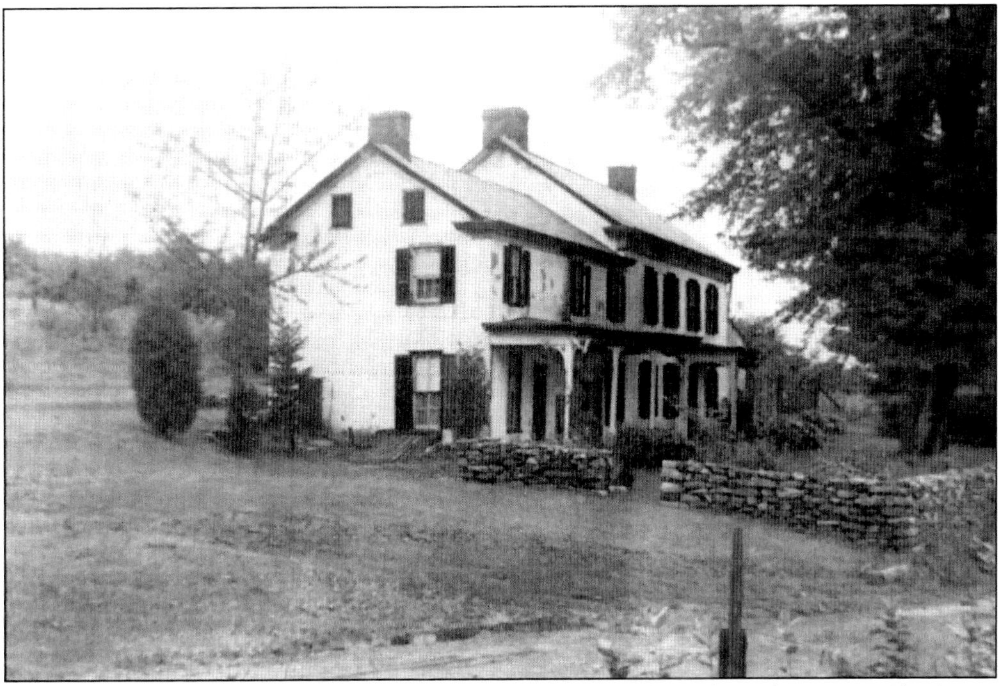

The Cole house on Britton Road in Sand Brook is shown in the early 20th century. This house was near the Sand Brook gristmill.

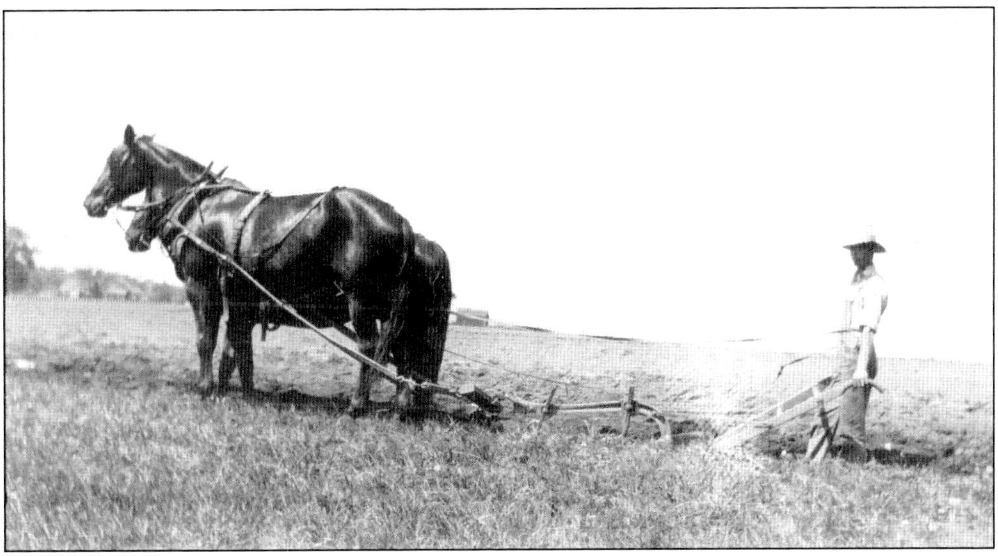

Irvin Shepperd plows with a two-horse team in 1923, just about the time that the first tractor arrived on the Bond farm. (Courtesy of Dave Bond.)

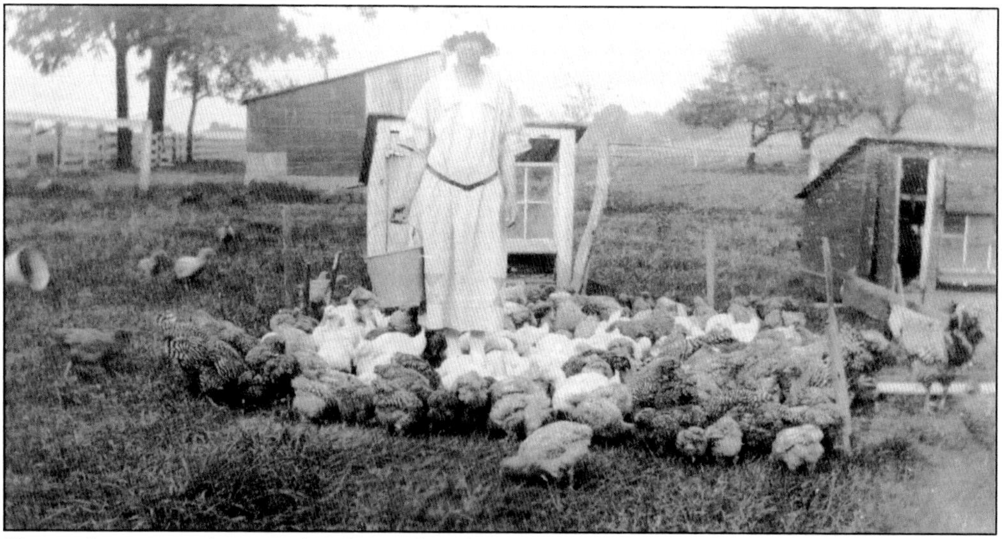

Shown here is a photograph of grandmother Ida Mae Sutphin in 1922 with some of the 2,000 chickens maintained on the Bond farm. (Courtesy of Dave Bond.)

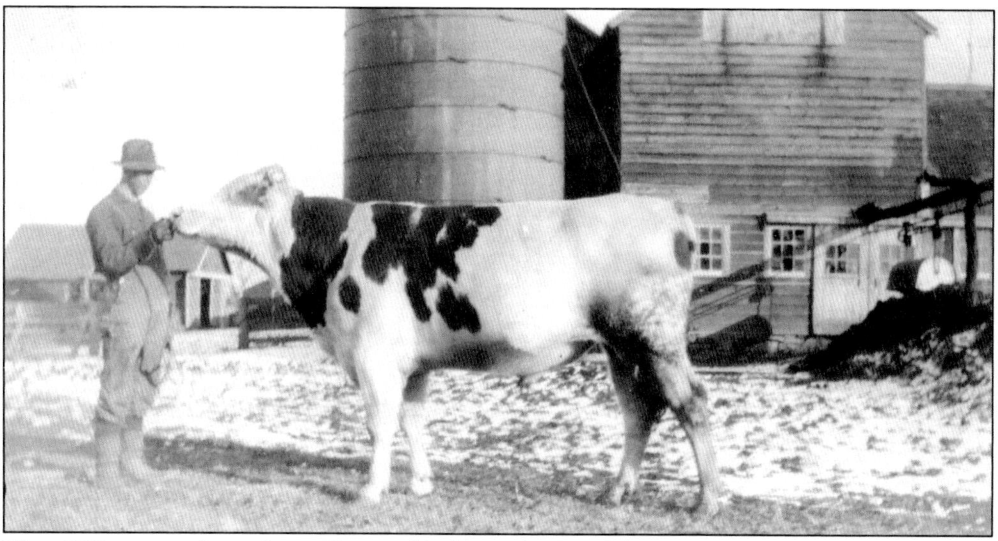

This 1922 picture shows Irvin Shepperd holding the Bond farm's prize Holstein bull. Shepperd lived and worked on the farm for many years. (Courtesy of Dave Bond.)

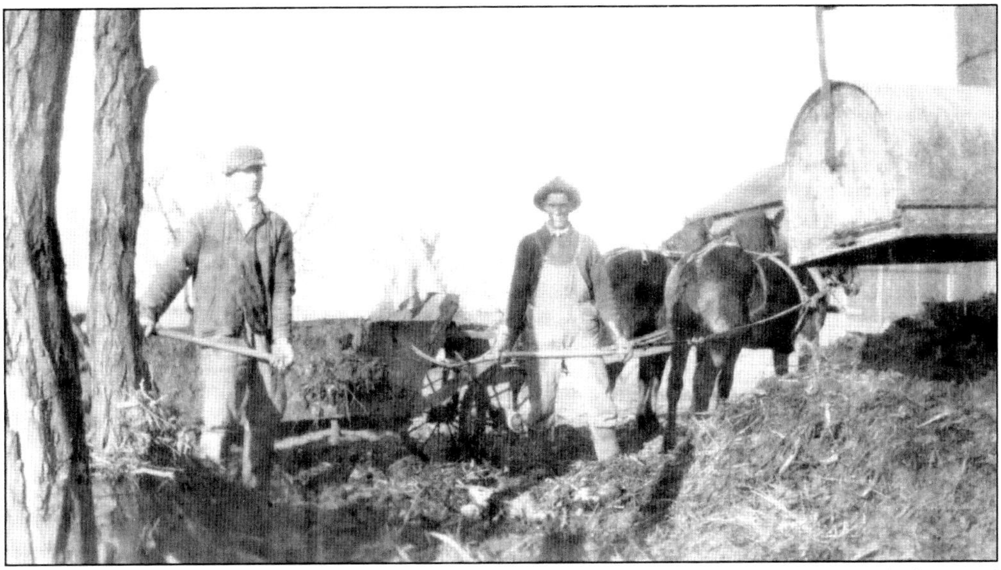

Hard, constant work can be glimpsed in this 1922 photograph of Clarence Bond and Shepperd at work with a team of horses near the barn. This strong work ethic was typical of farmers in Delaware Township, and according to longtime resident Dave Bond, "All the people on the farm worked all the time." (Courtesy of Dave Bond.)

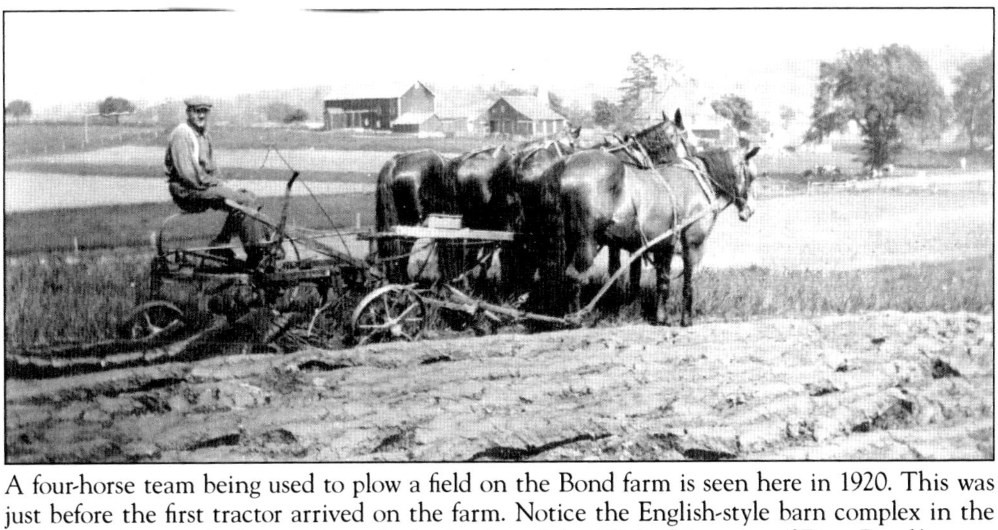

A four-horse team being used to plow a field on the Bond farm is seen here in 1920. This was just before the first tractor arrived on the farm. Notice the English-style barn complex in the background; it was built as early as the beginning of the 1800s. (Courtesy of Dave Bond.)

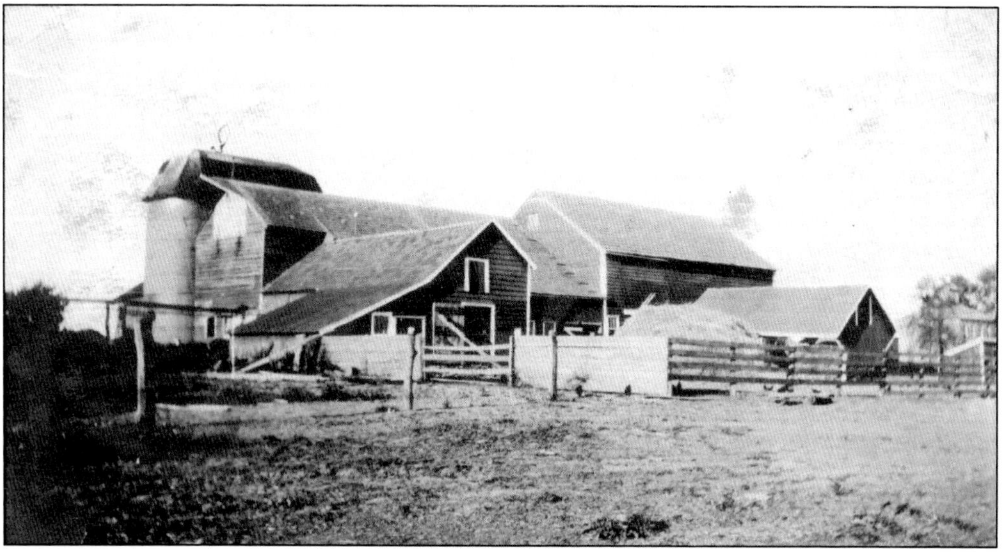

This is a 1921 view of the Bond dairy barn complex that is located along Route 579. These buildings have been in use for over 200 years. (Courtesy of Dave Bond.)

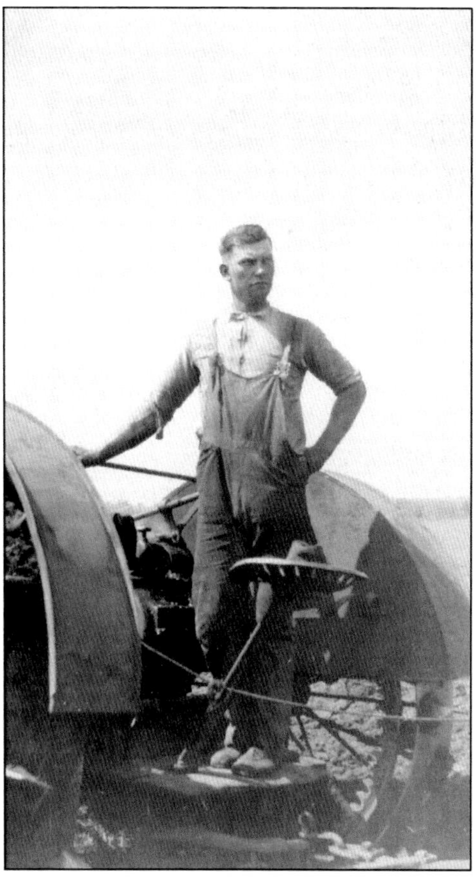

Clarence Bond is shown aboard his new tractor in 1923. Bond was always updating farm equipment and even tended to get a new car just about every year. (Courtesy of Dave Bond.)

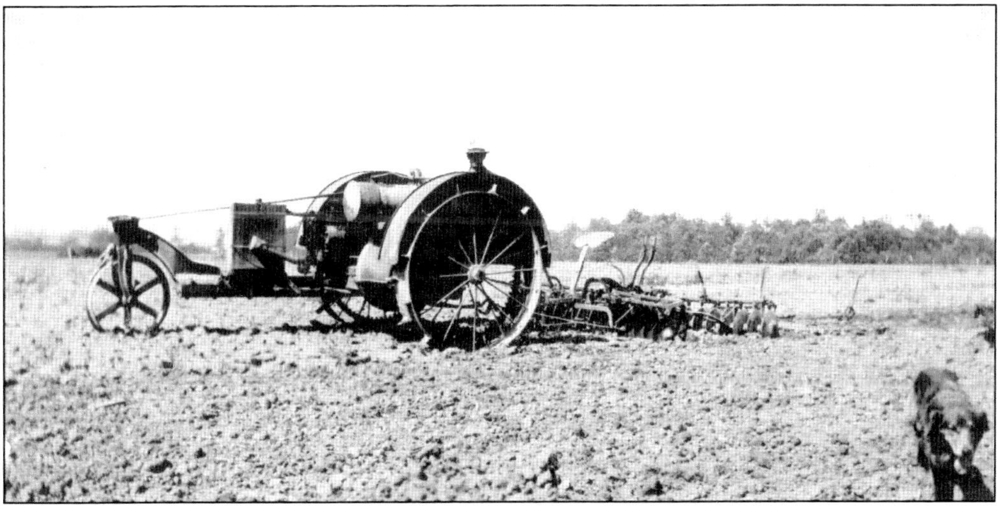

This early tractor was a Happy Farmer brand and was one of the first tractors in the township. It was used on the Bond farm in the 1920s. (Courtesy of Dave Bond.)

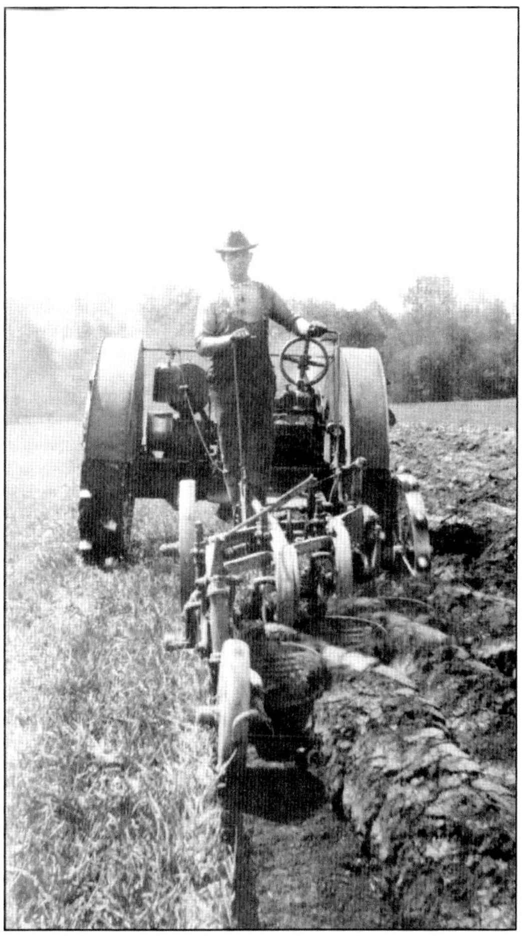

This 1930 photograph shows Clarence Bond using his Happy Farmer tractor to plow. Bond adopted tractors as soon as they were available because he felt they worked much more efficiently than horses. (Courtesy of Dave Bond.)

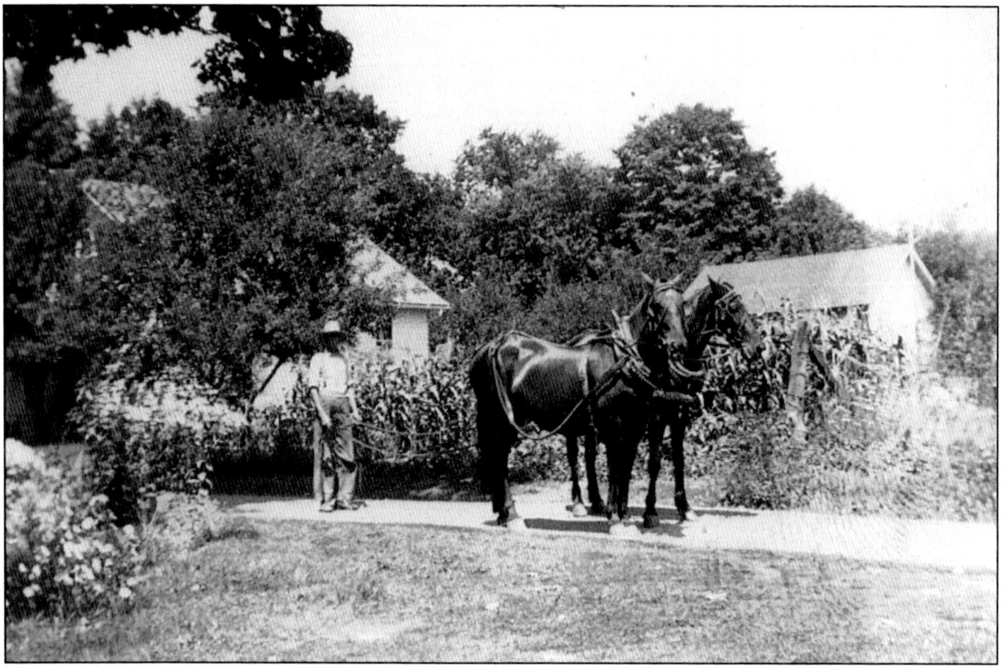

Lew Burd is growing a healthy-looking crop in Sergeantsville in the 1920s. The Burds are an old extended family living throughout Hunterdon County.

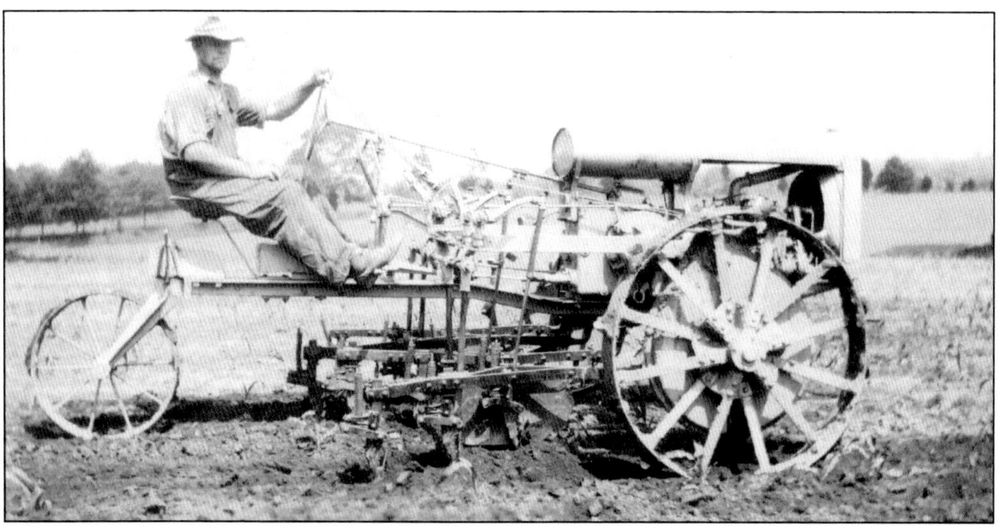

Clarence Bond is sitting on an early mechanical cultivator in 1930. The Bond farm was one of the larger farms in Delaware Township in the early 20th century. (Courtesy of Dave Bond.)

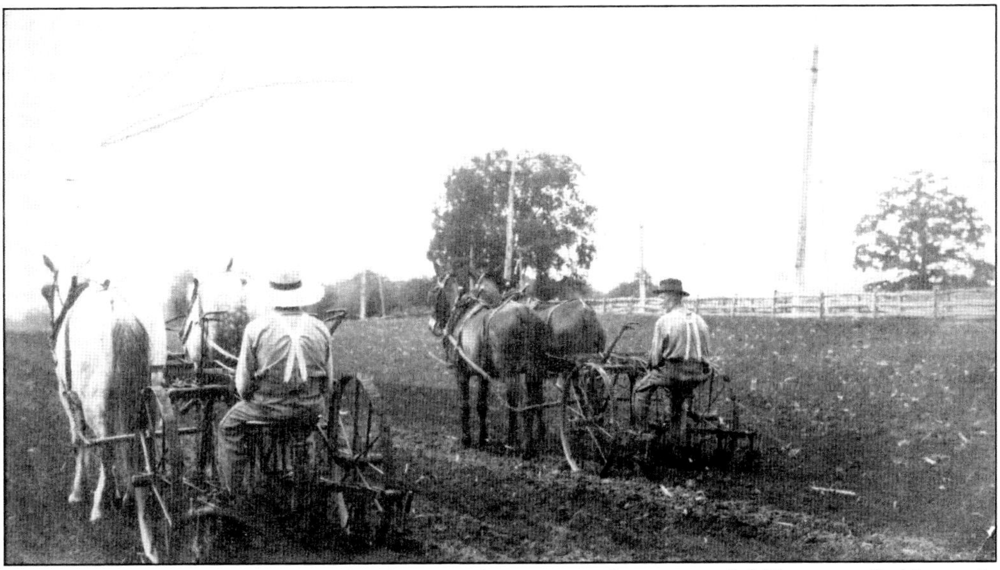

Harry Newcomb (right) and Paul Fisher are shown in a 17-acre cornfield being pulled by mule teams attached to Wiggletail cultivators in the 1920s. Note the high-tension poles on the right along the state road (Route 29 today); they carried 13,200 volts.

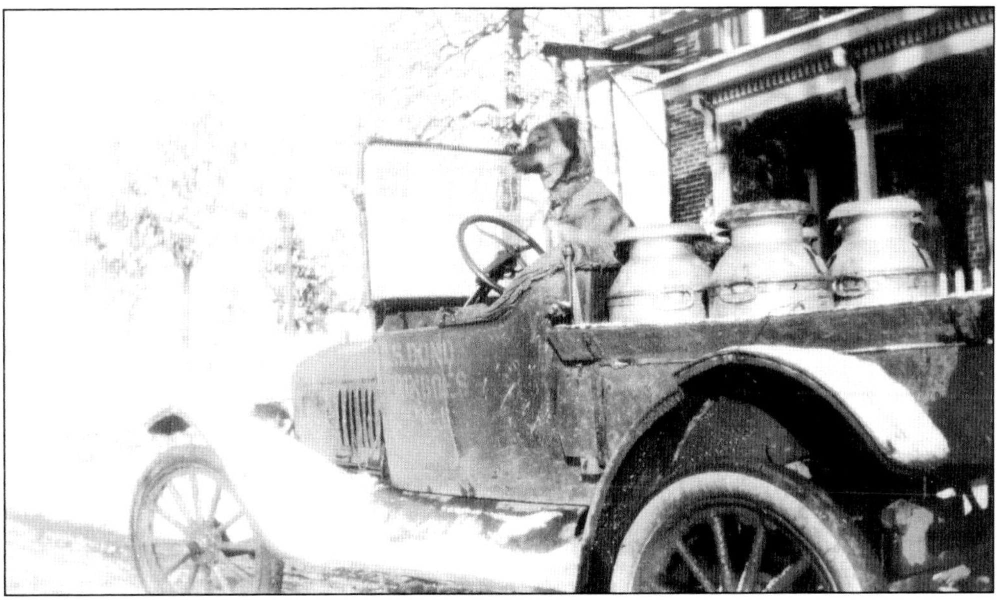

Model T pickups were often converted from a roadster into a truck. This truck was used on the Bond farm in the late 1920s. Milk cans are being delivered to the nearby Harbison's Dairy. Jack the dog is in the driver's seat. (Courtesy of Dave Bond.)

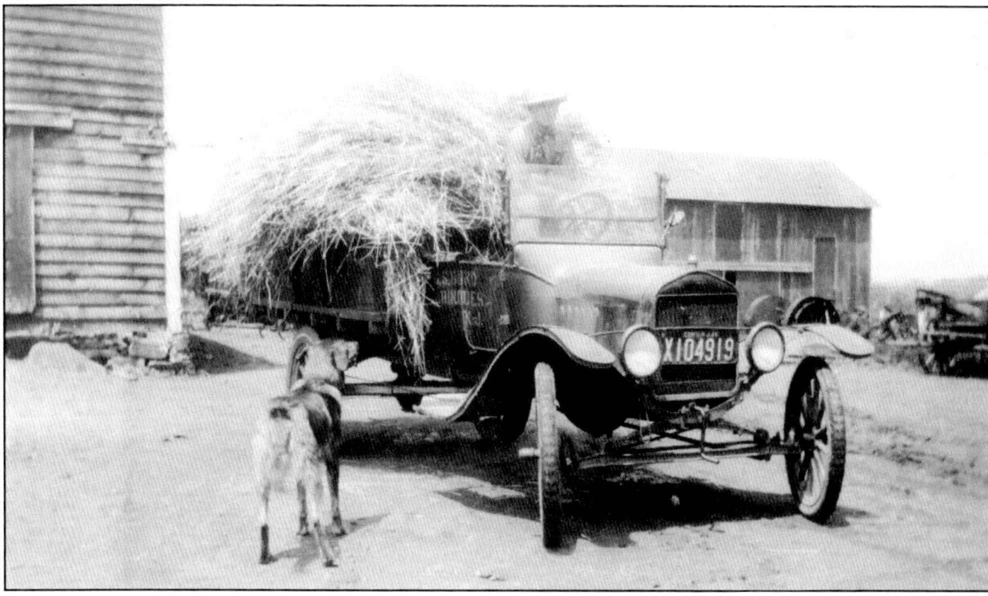

A load of hay is being transported on the Bond farm in the 1920s. Hay was commonly handled in loose piles until the modern baler came into use in the 1930s. (Courtesy of Dave Bond.)

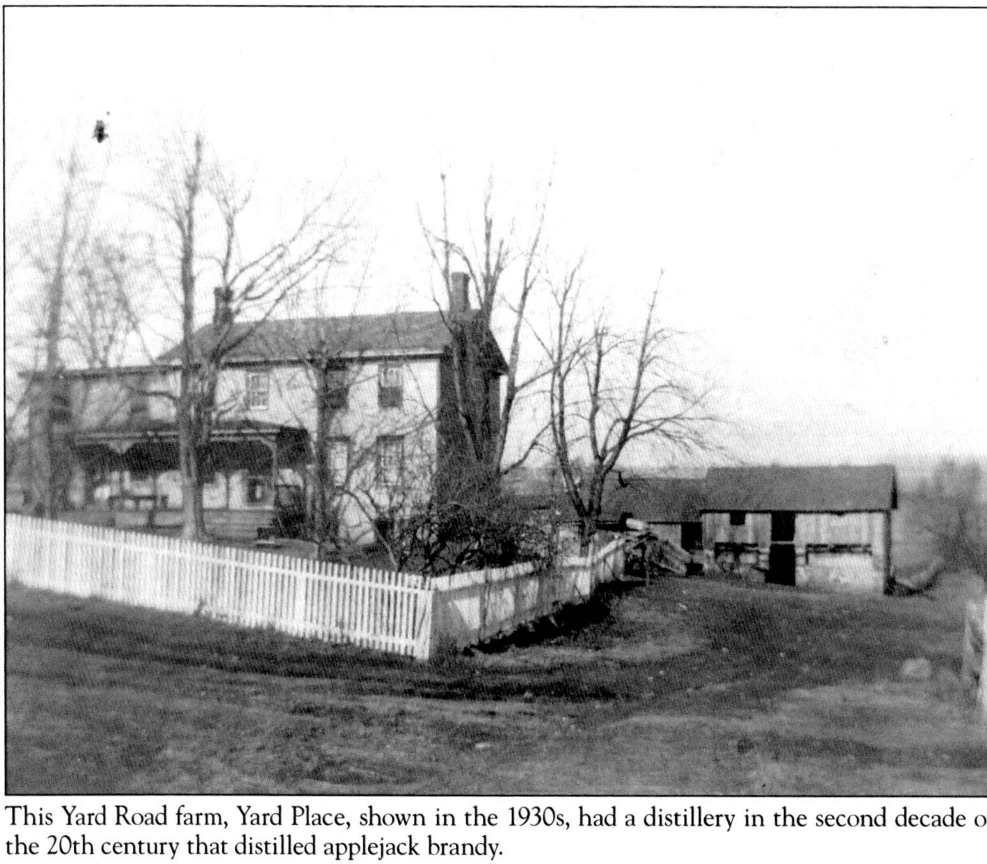

This Yard Road farm, Yard Place, shown in the 1930s, had a distillery in the second decade of the 20th century that distilled applejack brandy.

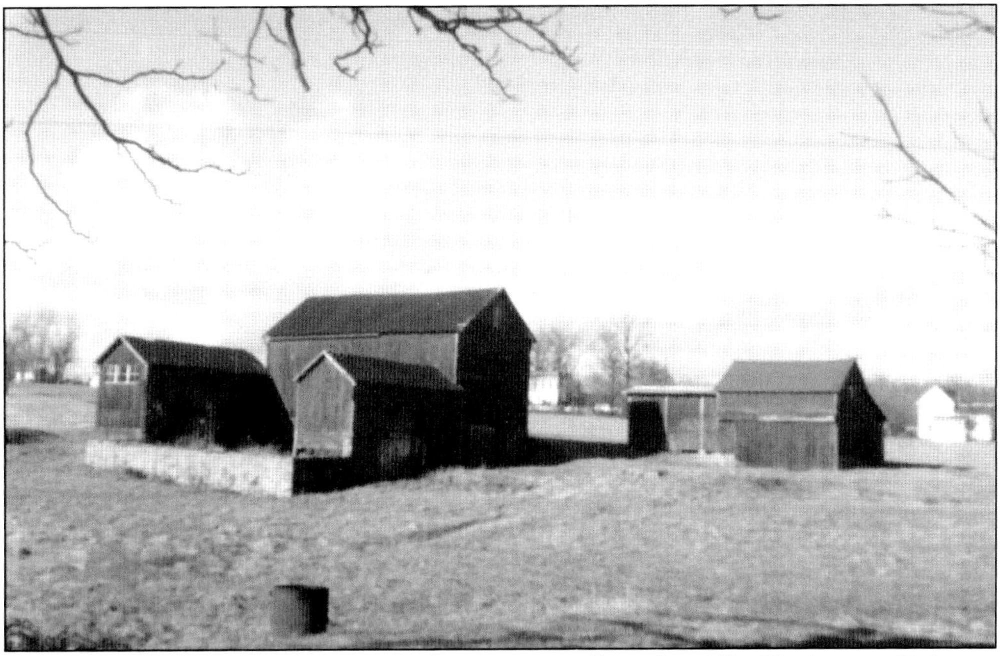

An English-style barn complex is pictured in Sergeantsville in the 1930s. The barns in Delaware Township reflect a number of design styles based on the varied cultures that originally settled in the township. These include the English and the Dutch or German. They can often be spotted by the shape of the roof.

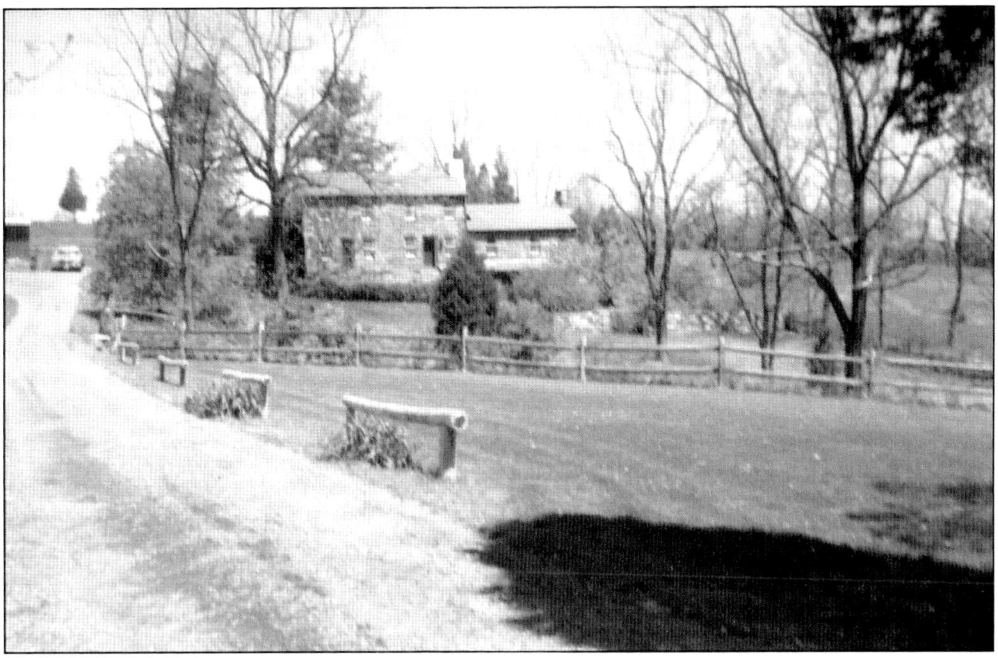

The Kish farm in Delaware Township is shown during an early-1930s spring. This type of classic building was constructed from nearby native stone. It was often built in the 1700s by itinerant German stonemasons who swung through New Jersey from nearby Pennsylvania, contracting the work as they moved about from job to job.

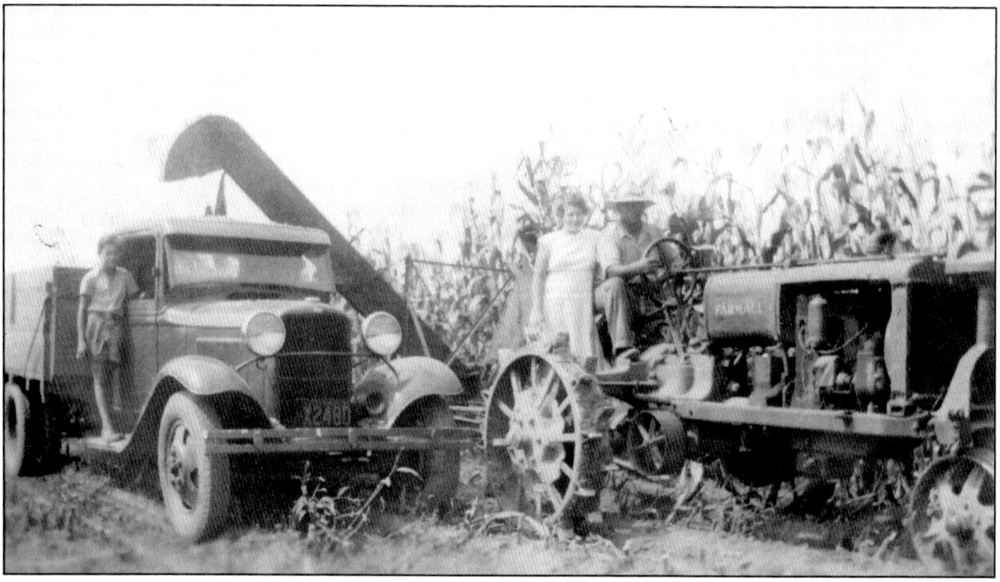

This 1932 picture shows silage being harvested on the Bond farm using an F30 Farmall tractor to chop and load the material onto a 1932 Ford Model B truck. This was one of the first field choppers in New Jersey. (Courtesy of Dave Bond.)

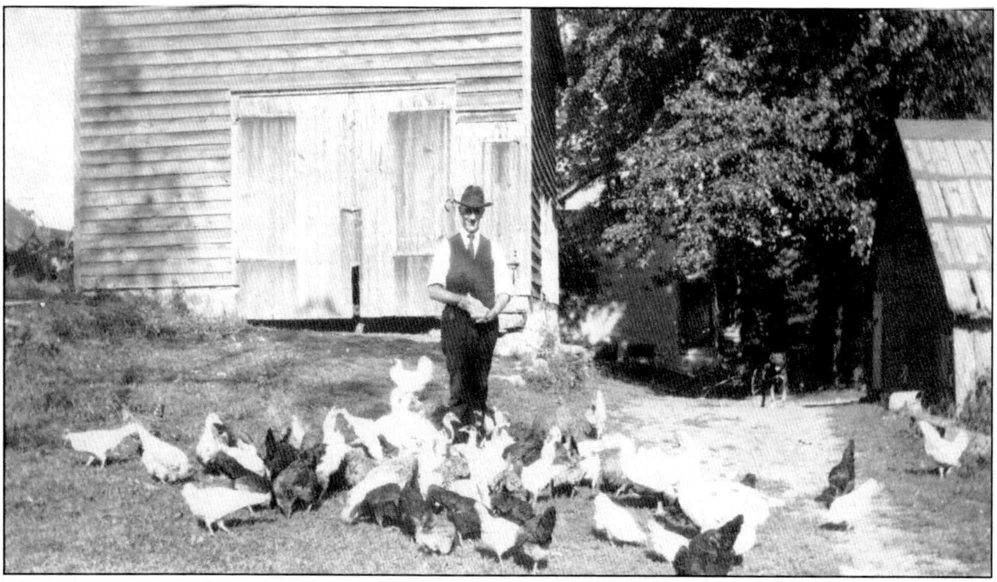

Harry Spain, grandfather of Blanche Carl, is seen feeding the chickens on the family farm near the covered bridge in the 1930s. Notice that he is formally dressed even while actively involved on the farm. This could be a Sunday or a holiday. (Courtesy of Blanche Carl.)

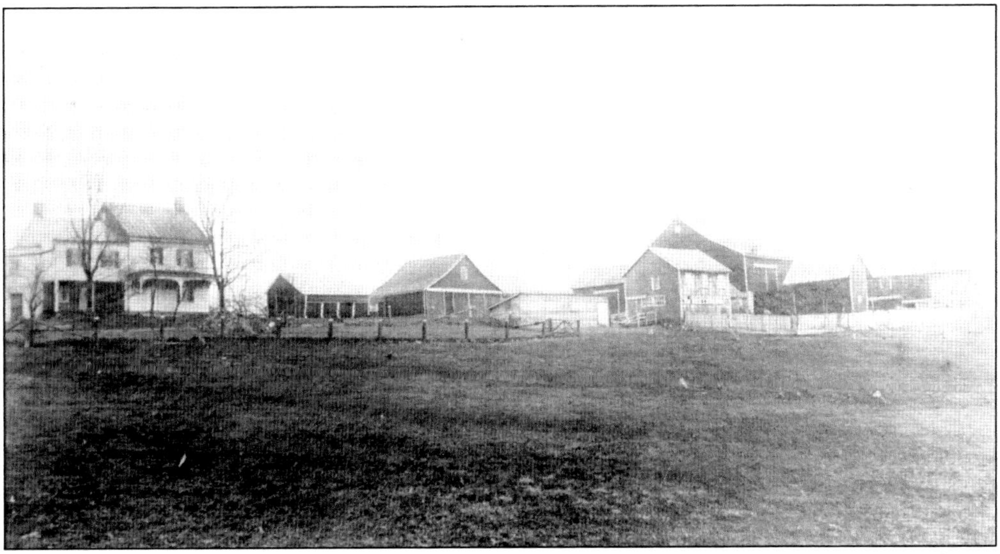

This 1930s photograph shows the Titus-Peters farm on Hamp Road. Notice the substantial barns and outbuildings that were typical of many early farms in Delaware Township.

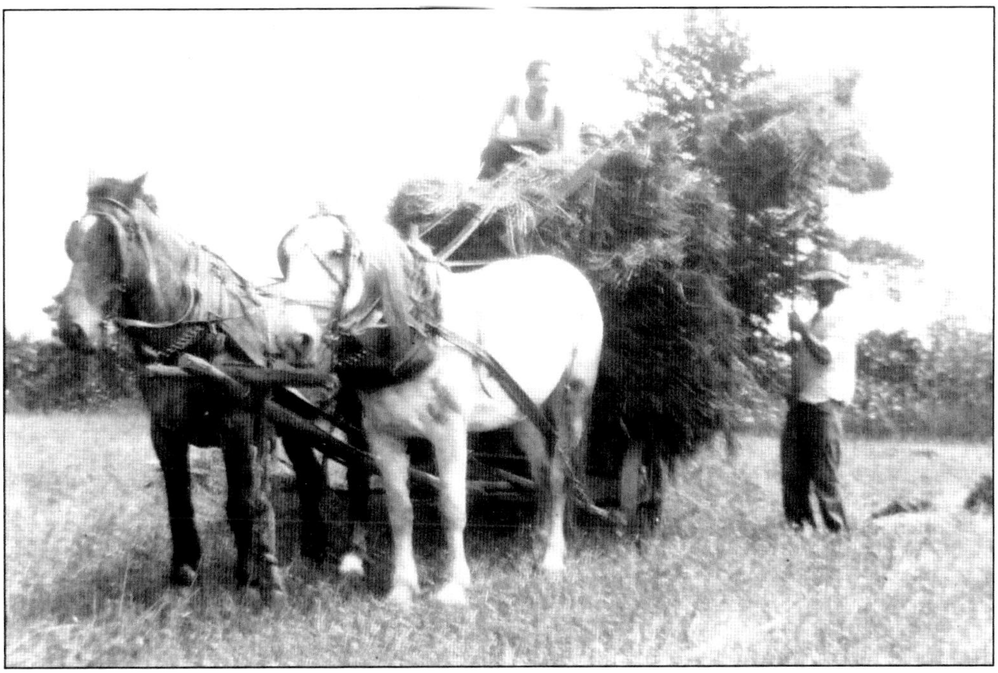

Pitching hay in 1935 with Herb driving was a big summertime activity on the Williamson farm near the Green Sergeant's covered bridge. (Courtesy of Carla Mackey.)

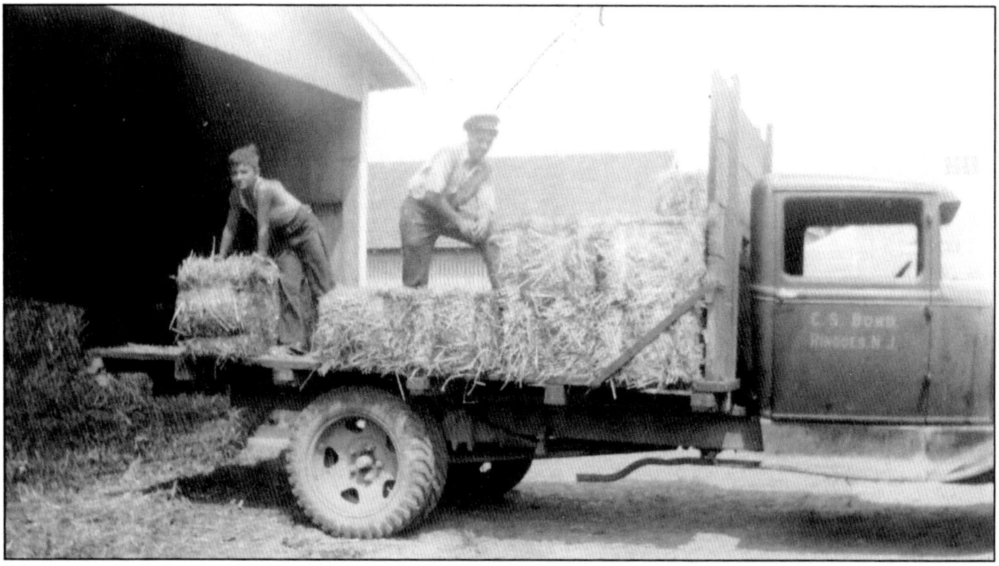

Throwing hay from a truck and hoisting the bales into the barn is backbreaking work. As can be seen from this 1940 photograph, it was still being done by muscle power even at that time. (Courtesy of Dave Bond.)

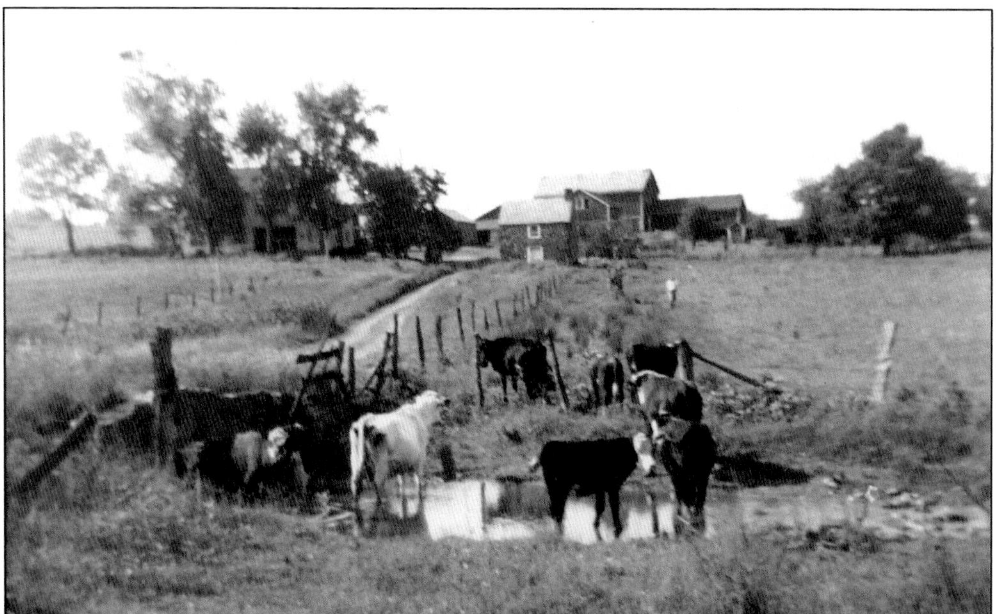

This is a view of the Kurzenberger farm as seen from Lambert Road in 1945. The cows are next to a perfect stone arch bridge that lies in the drive leading to the farm complex built in the early 1800s.

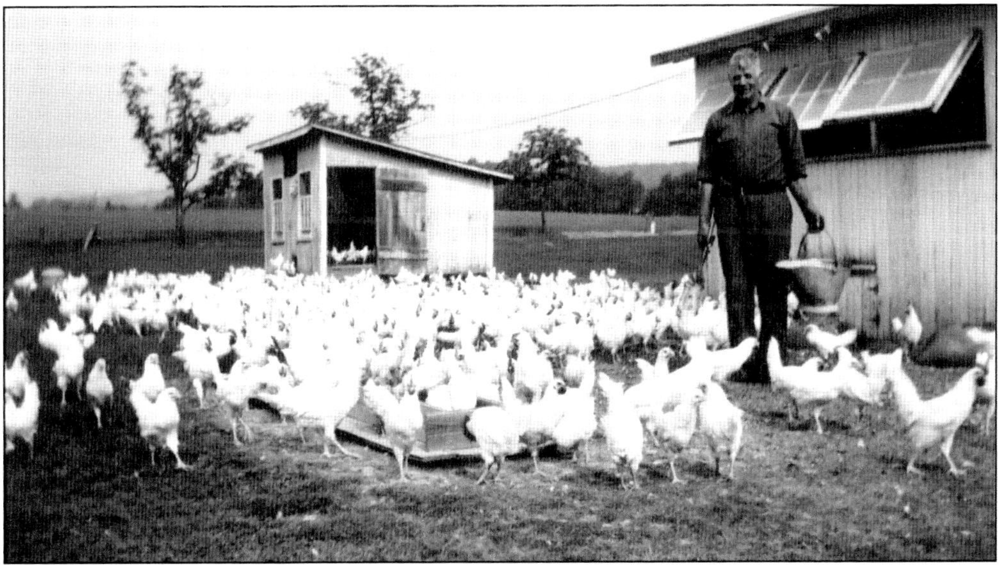

Some of the 2,000 pullets on the Bond farm are shown in 1942. The chickens were only out in the daytime; they were put in the chicken house at night to protect them from predators. The Bonds were very active with the Egg Auction Cooperative in Flemington. Dave Bond, the present operator of the Bond farm, was the last president of the Egg Auction Cooperative in the mid-1970s. (Courtesy of Dave Bond.)

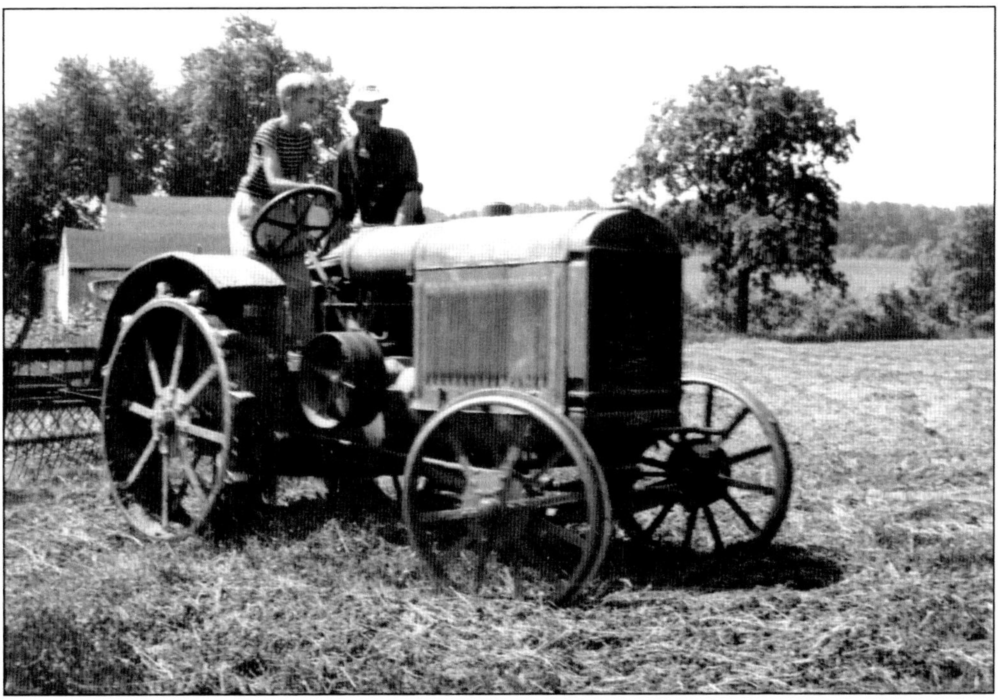

Paul Kurzenberger and his father, Paul Kurzenberger Sr., are shown driving a 1928 International 10-20 tractor, which was used on the farm through the 1940s. It took a real man to drive this behemoth.

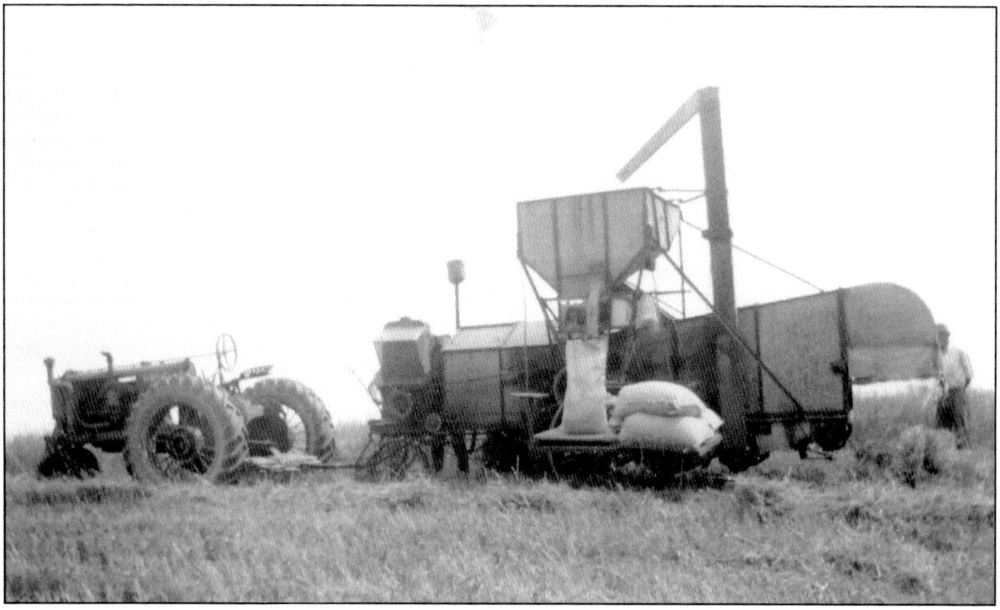

A pull-behind combine is being utilized on the Bond farm in 1940. The pull behind was so named because it was not self-propelled but was pulled behind a tractor. (Courtesy of Dave Bond.)

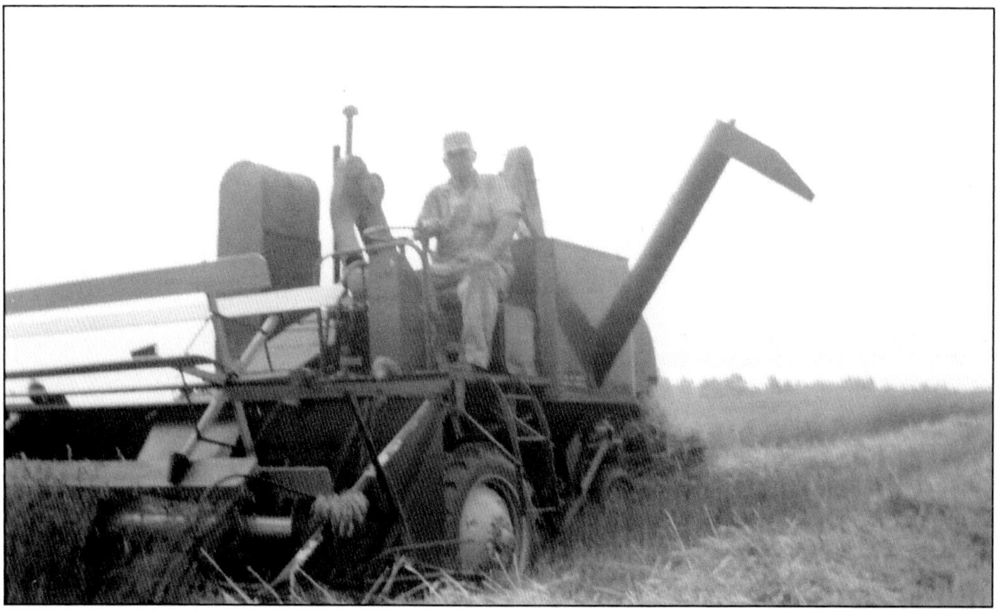

Clarence Bond is driving an advanced combine in 1951. This farm, although a leader in keeping up with modern techniques and equipment, was somewhat typical of farms in Delaware Township in the early 20th century. (Courtesy of Dave Bond.)

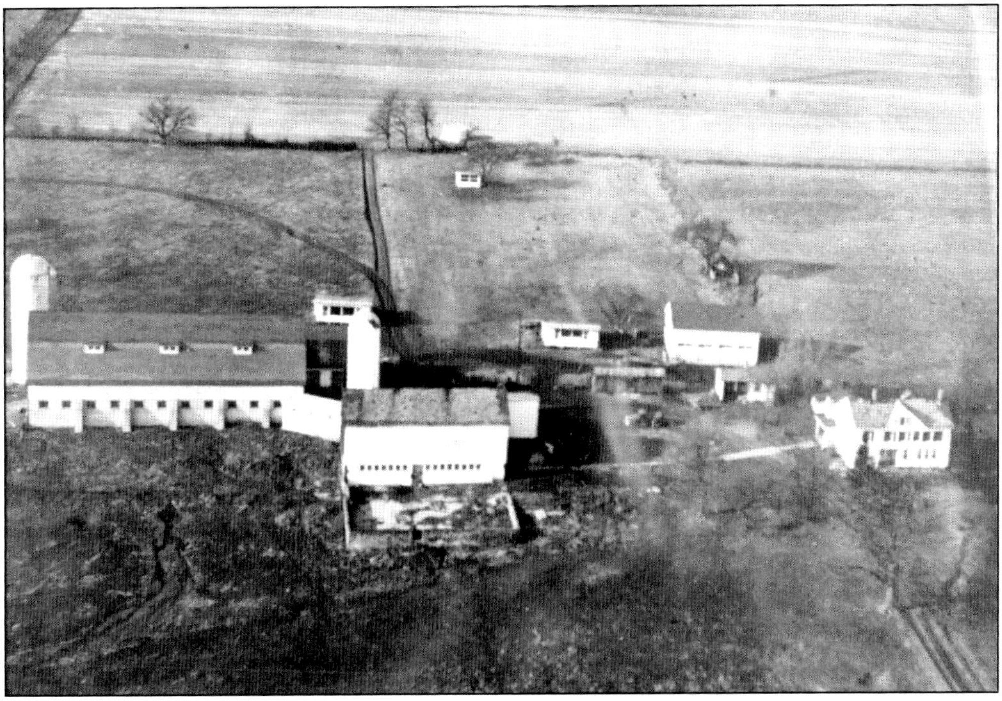

An aerial view shows the Bodine farm complex of Prall and Wesley Bodine. They had 150 registered dairy cattle, and Prall knew each by name. Their father had the large barn on the left built in 1937. It was completely scientific in its operation, with internal piping to carry the milk to refrigerated storage as well as having automated feeding mechanisms. Prall was tragically killed a few years ago when a conveyor belt struck his head. The area around the Bodine farm is some of the best land in the township.

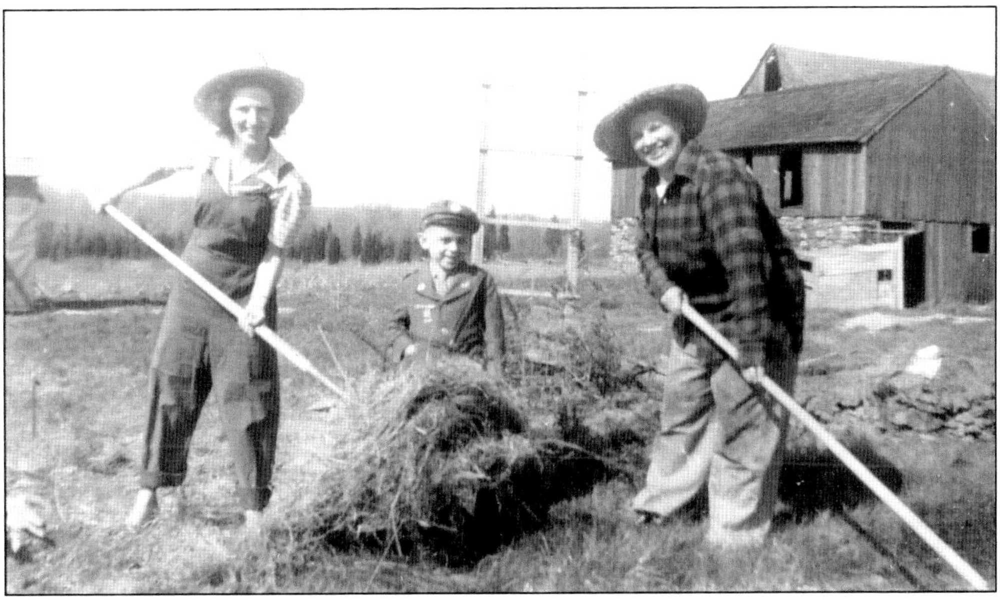

Here all hands turn to haying on the Williamson farm near the covered bridge in the 1940s. (Courtesy of Carla Mackey.)

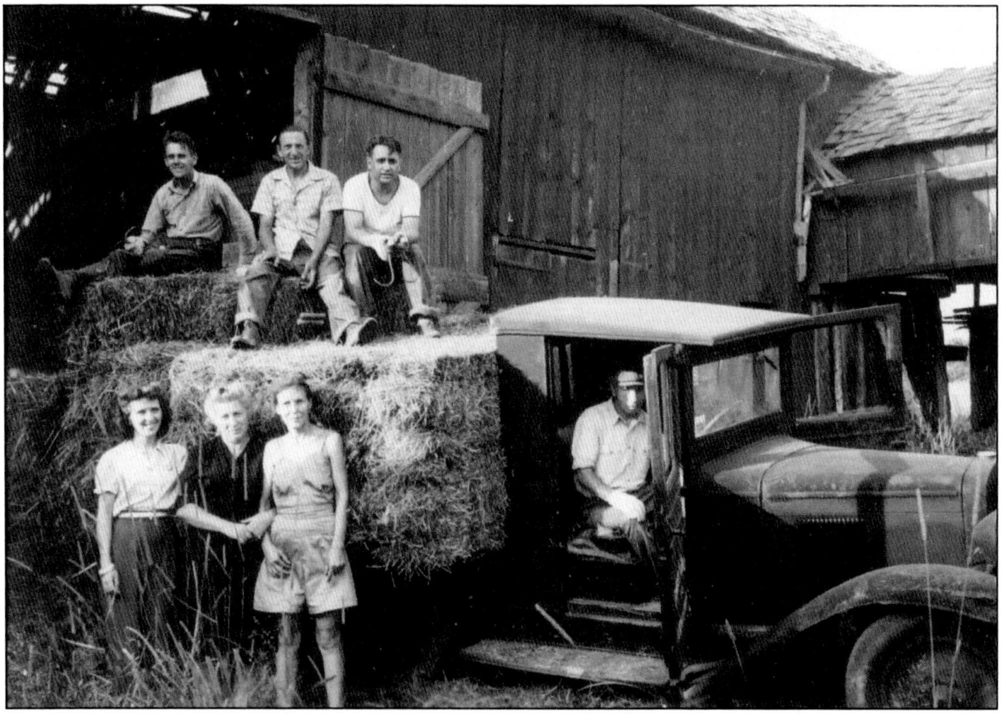

A scrapbook from the Williamson farm states that the "man at the wheel is our Fred" and further indicates that they are "making hay, July 1945." The Williamson farm was near the covered bridge on Sanford Road. (Courtesy of Carla Mackey.)

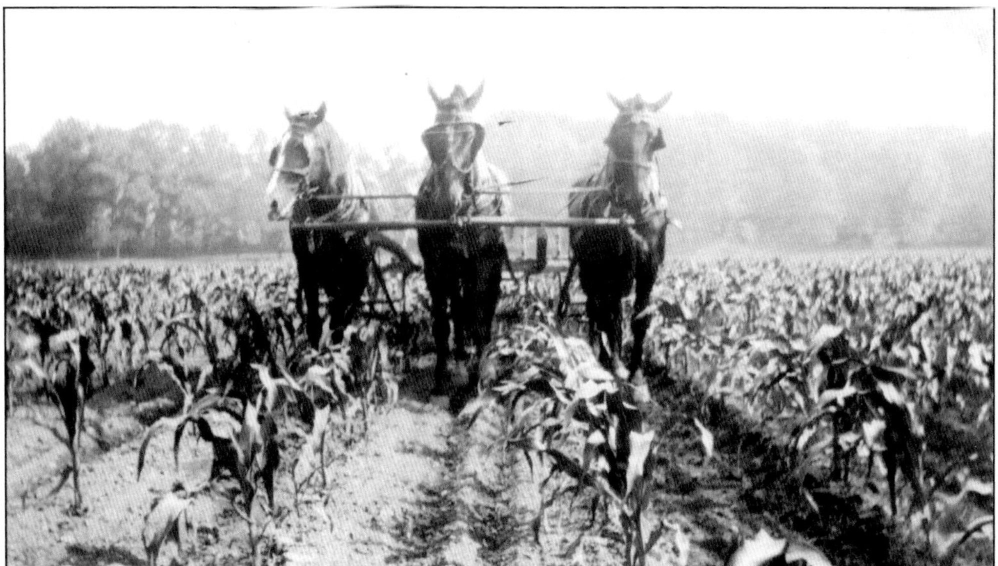

Pictured in 1930 is a three-horse team cultivating two rows at a time on the Bond farm. Horses were still in use at times through the 1930s for performing light chores. (Courtesy of Dave Bond.)

Two

THE TOWNS

Historically life in the township in many ways focused on a number of villages and hamlets located in a regular sequence a few short miles apart. Some of the more notable villages were Sergeantsville, Dilts Corner, Bowne Station, Brookville, Rosemont, Locktown, Croton, Sand Brook, Prallsville, and Headquarters. There were also a variety of other smaller settlements sprinkled through the township, often with a few houses collected in close proximity to one another.

Sergeantsville eventually rose to be the most prominent of the villages since it was near the center of the township and contained the seat of government. It was said to be a "pleasant village" in 1825, with a small grocery, a tavern, and a blacksmith shop. It has been the prime business and government center of the township ever since its organization.

The sense of history evident in preserving old structures and an open agricultural environment has added a historical time dimension to Delaware Township. New structures in the township have tended to key in on the local construction materials and designs preserved in structures from the past.

Delaware Township has always been made up of a rural and agricultural environment; houses and farm buildings have consequently been the most prominent structures, both historically and in the present day.

The village of Rosemont, in particular, has excellent representations of 18th-, 19th-, and early-20th-century structures and complexes. As the Cultural Resources Survey of 1999 stated, "The area [around Rosemont] has great significance in terms of architecture, agriculture, settlement patterns, transportation, industry, and commerce." These factors are also applicable to virtually all the towns in the township, as they represent a slice of life as it has been lived over the centuries.

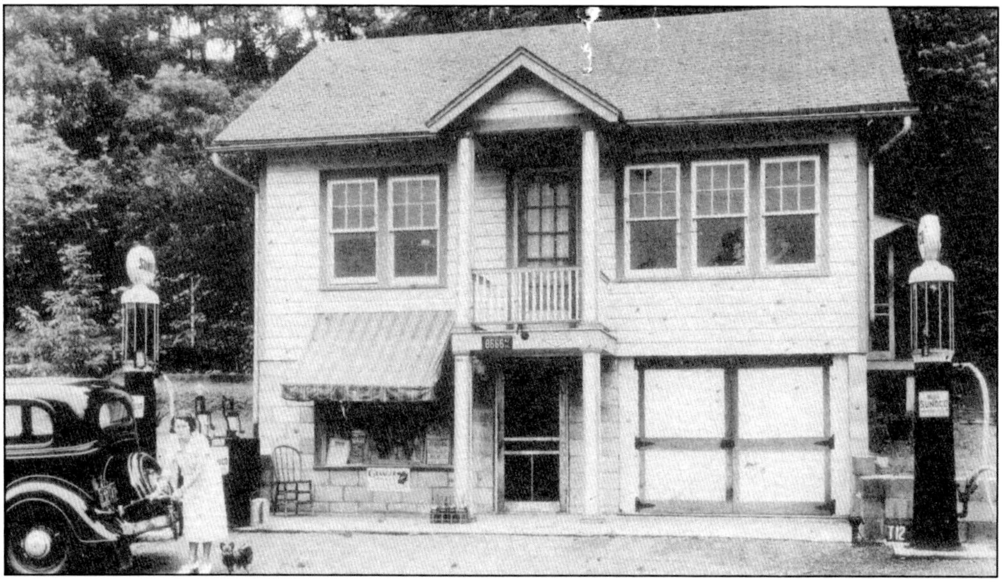

The Luk-en-Nuf gasoline station in Brookville Hollow Village (along Route 29) sold gasoline in 1932 for 17.8¢ a gallon. (Courtesy of Blanche Carl.)

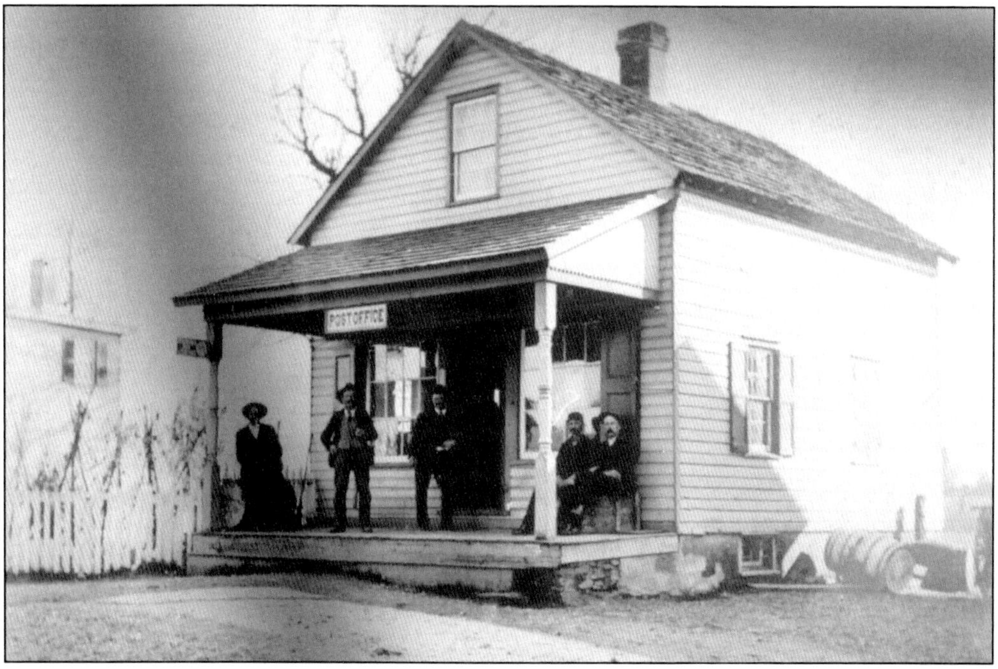

The Croton Village post office is pictured in the 1920s. Notice the local guys observing the passing scene and socializing on the porch. Croton was on the main turnpike that went from Trenton to Easton in Pennsylvania (Route 579). This building was a stagecoach stop along the road in the early 1800s.

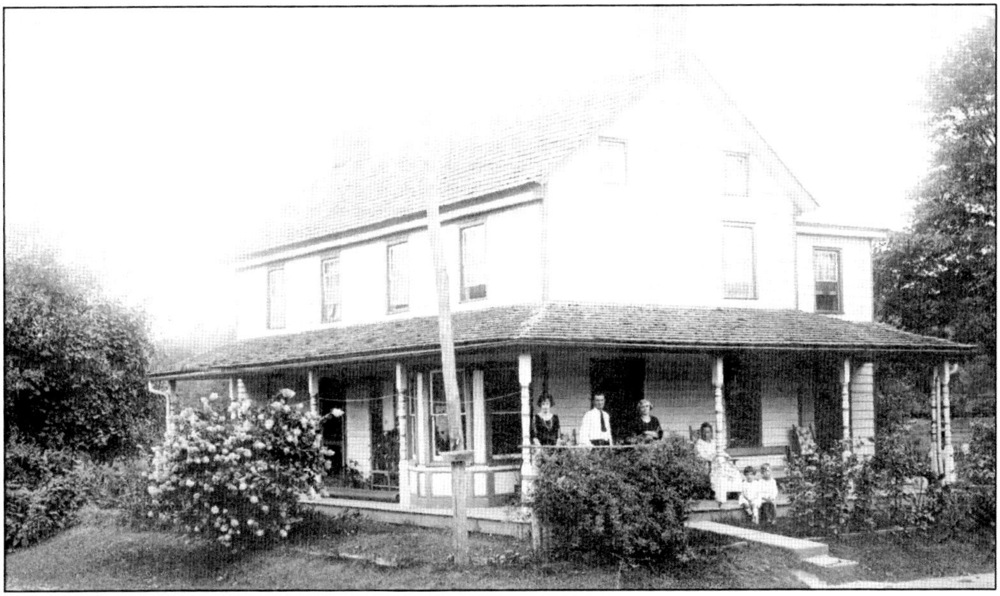

The Ellen B. Walker house in Locktown Village, shown in the early 20th century, is where William Rockafellows lived in an earlier time. The Rockafellows were one of the early Delaware Township families and also the family from which John D. Rockefeller of Standard Oil fame originally descended. Note the use of the porch for socializing and the rocking chair for relaxing. This was typical of small-town life with people out and about.

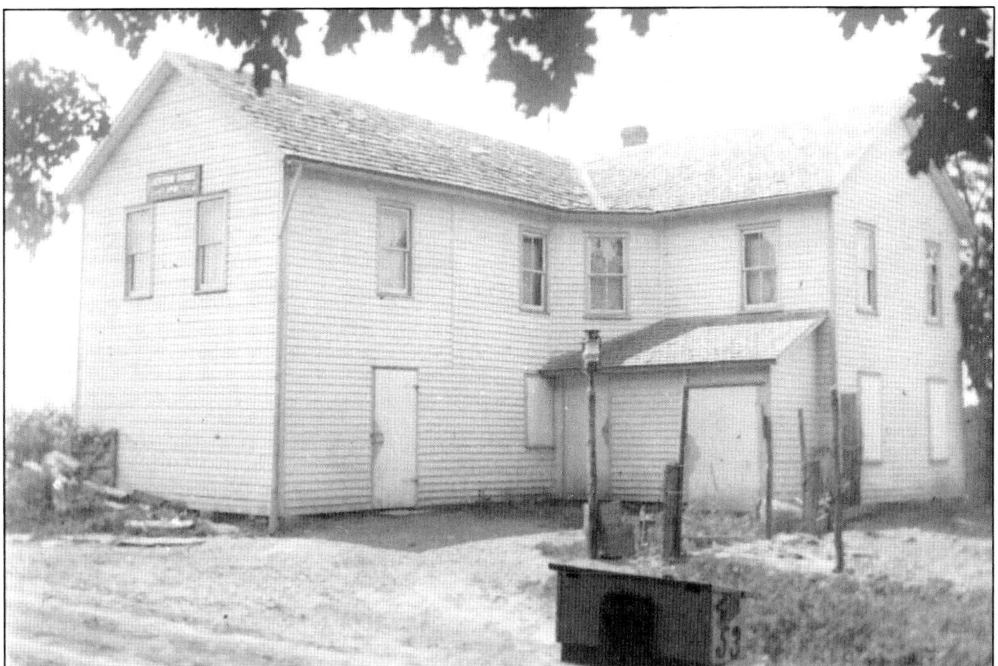

The Grange hall in Locktown Village is shown in the early 20th century. This hall is still in operation today, but it has recently scaled back its program, with the chicken barbecue only being held every other year.

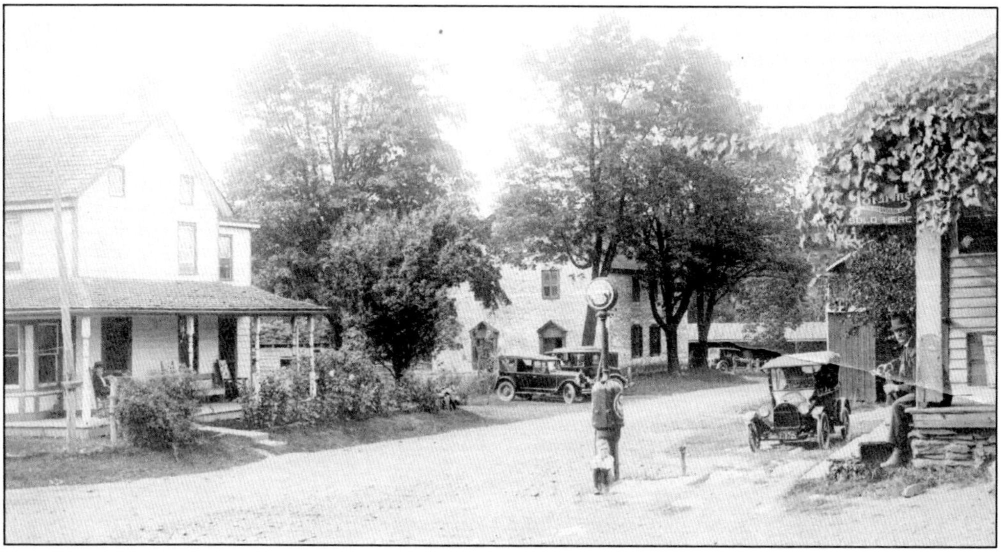

Milton Smith (who later became mayor of the township) is shown next to the gasoline pump as a boy in Locktown during the 1920s. This streetscape view clearly indicates the physical evidence of a town structure, which has been lost in many rural communities today. These towns today have been restructured to the extent that they are only place-names and even that has been lost in many cases. The businesses have gone, the trees have been cut down, and they are often just passing stretches along the highway.

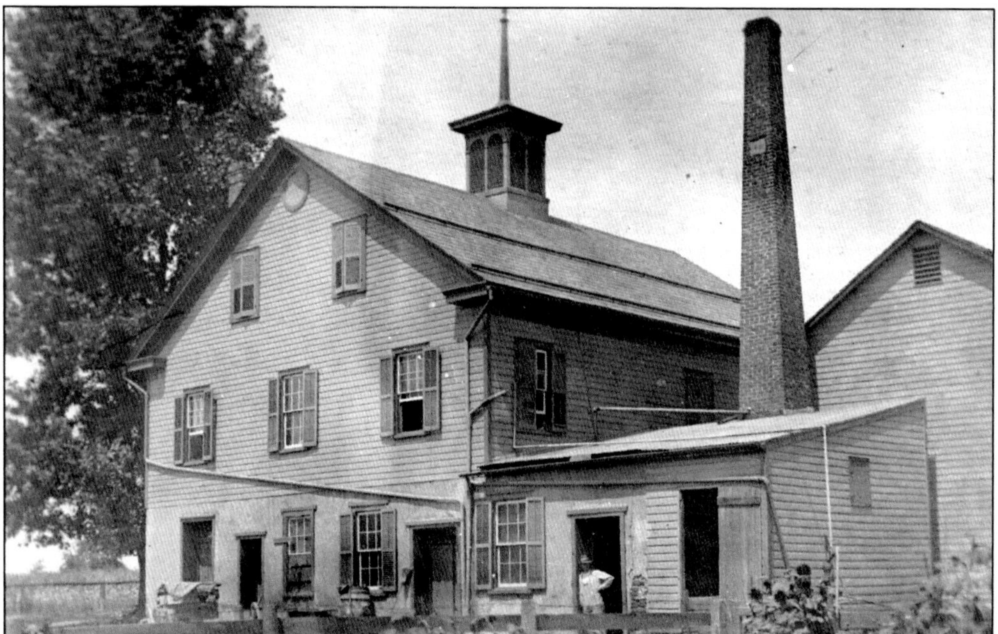

This is the creamery as it looked in the village of Locktown in the early 20th century. It has since become a residence, and the chimney has been removed.

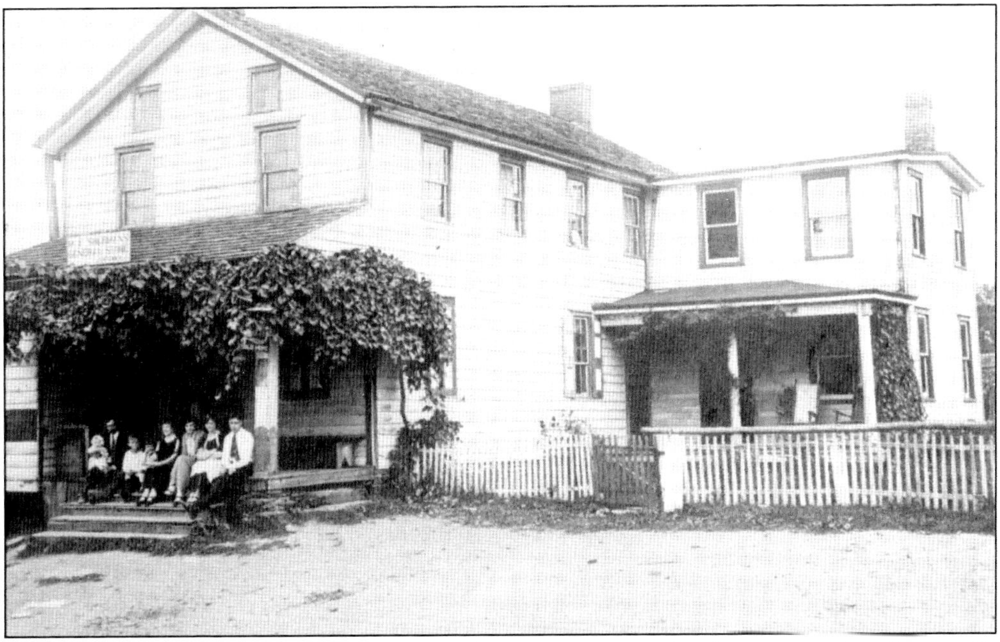

The 1920s scene pictured here shows the Locktown house that Smith lives in today. Smith tells of a story that, he says, "needs to be told": When he was mayor and electric streetlights first came in, he was in a position to buy the privately owned lights for the township. There was a political battle over such a purchase (that New York and Philadelphia papers covered), and he opted to buy the streetlights. Ironically they now keep him awake at times since they shine directly into his bedroom these many years later.

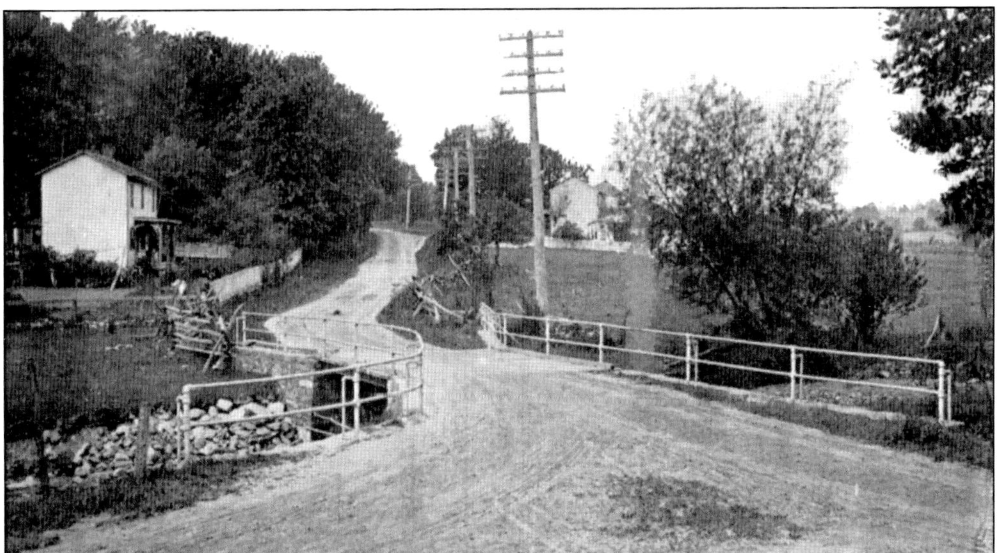

A view of the road from Sergeantsville to Flemington (Route 523 today) at Sand Brook Village is shown in the early 20th century. The county highway engineer has recently surveyed this very spot and has heavily marked the asphalt for rebuilding the bridge. This has been a point of contention with some local residents.

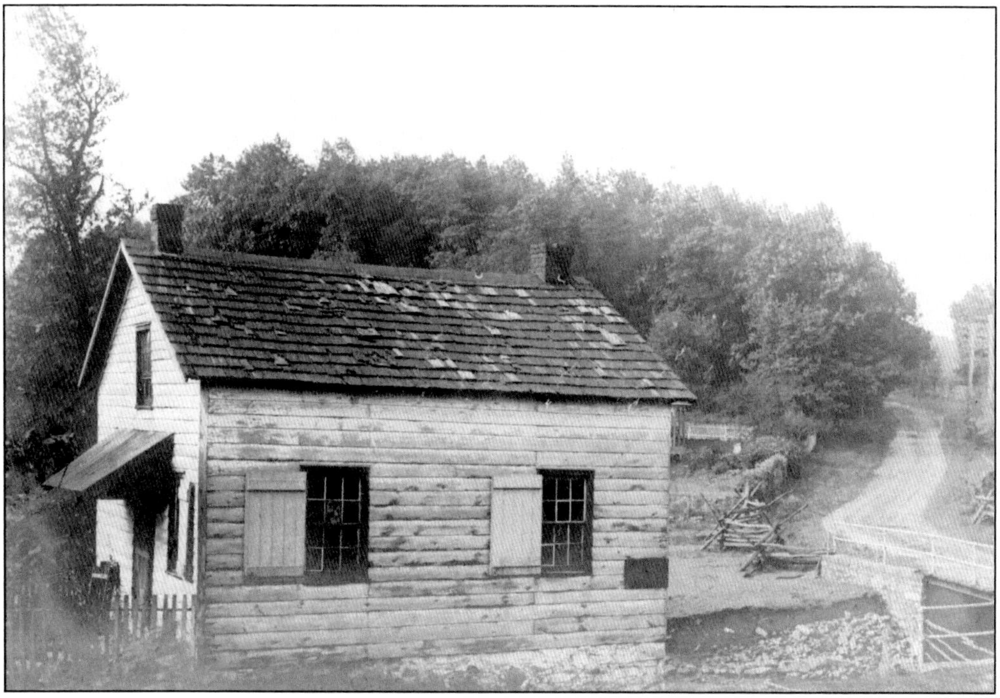

The Sand Brook Village building pictured here was originally a tollhouse for the adjacent Flemington-Sergeantsville Road. It is the office of a local resident today.

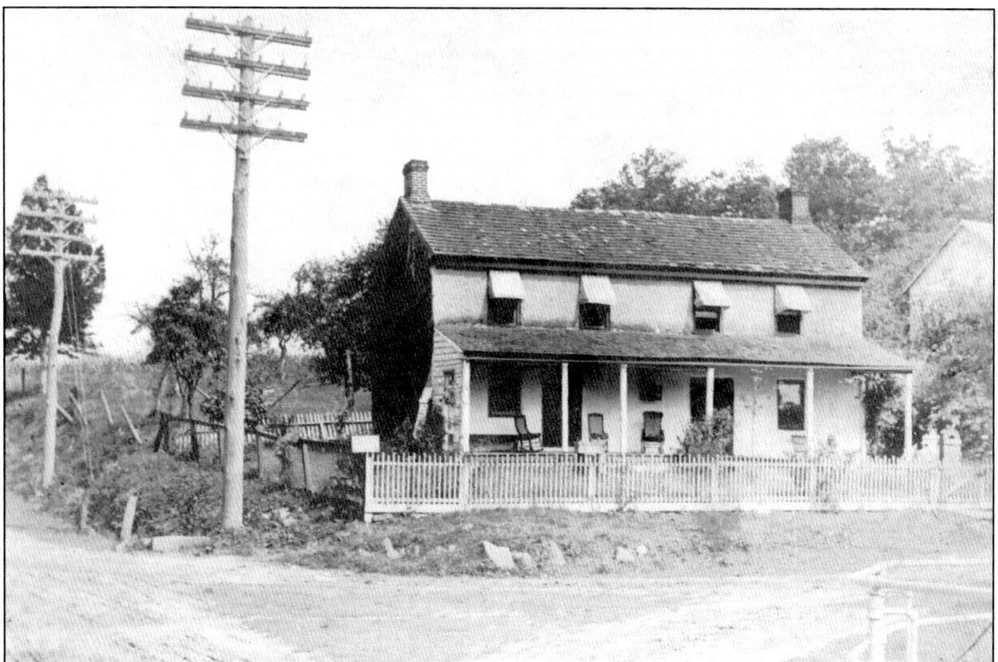

A Sand Brook Village house is shown in the early 1920s. Note the heavy electric wires and somewhat tumbledown fencing. This house is at the corner of Route 523 and Sand Brook Road today and is extremely well kept.

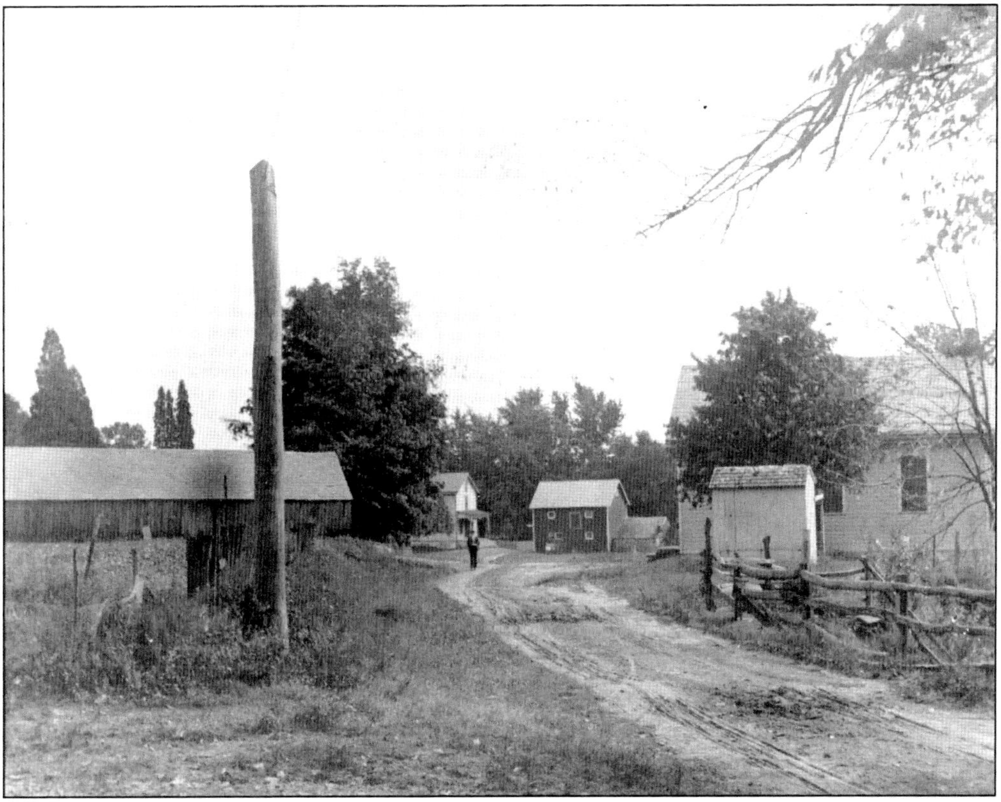

An early-20th-century view of the village of Sand Brook shows the Sand Brook Brethren Church just beyond the horse barn on the left, with the Sand Brook Village School on the right. The long horse barn was used for hitching horses during church services.

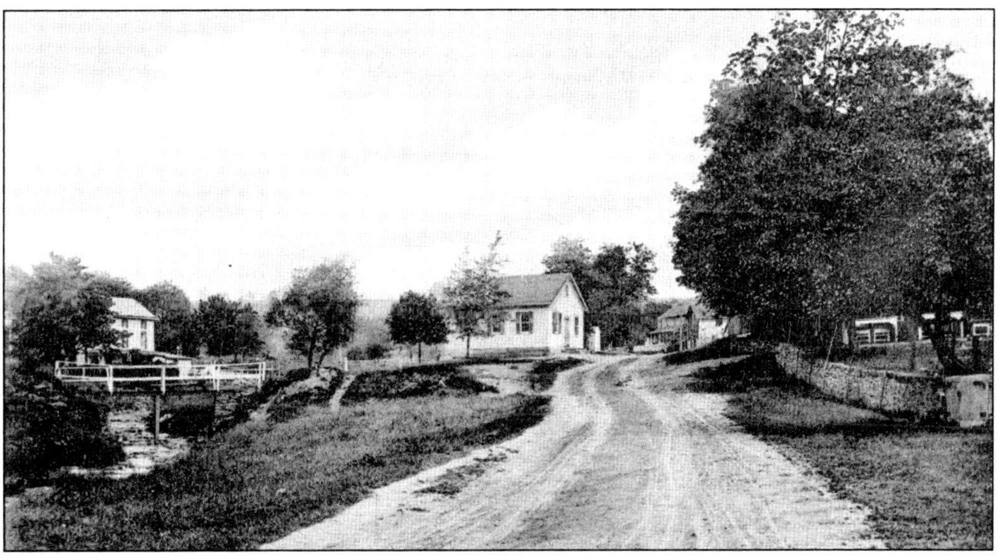

This view from the second decade of the 20th century shows the center of the village of Sand Brook. The schoolhouse is on the left. Notice the typical old dirt road.

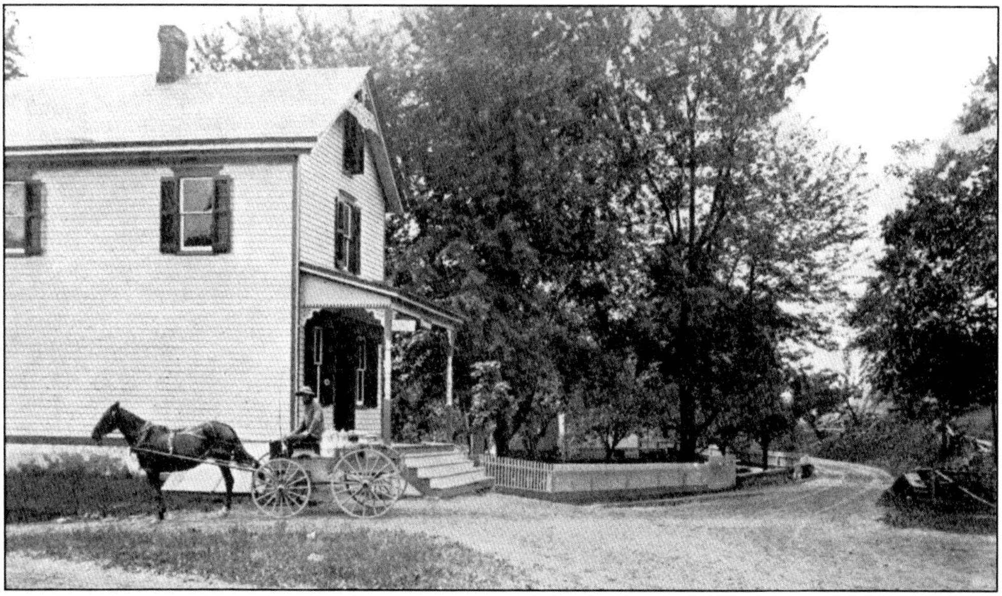

This photograph of the center of Sand Brook in the early 20th century shows Frank Yasunas's store and post office. Earlier it was Johnson's store.

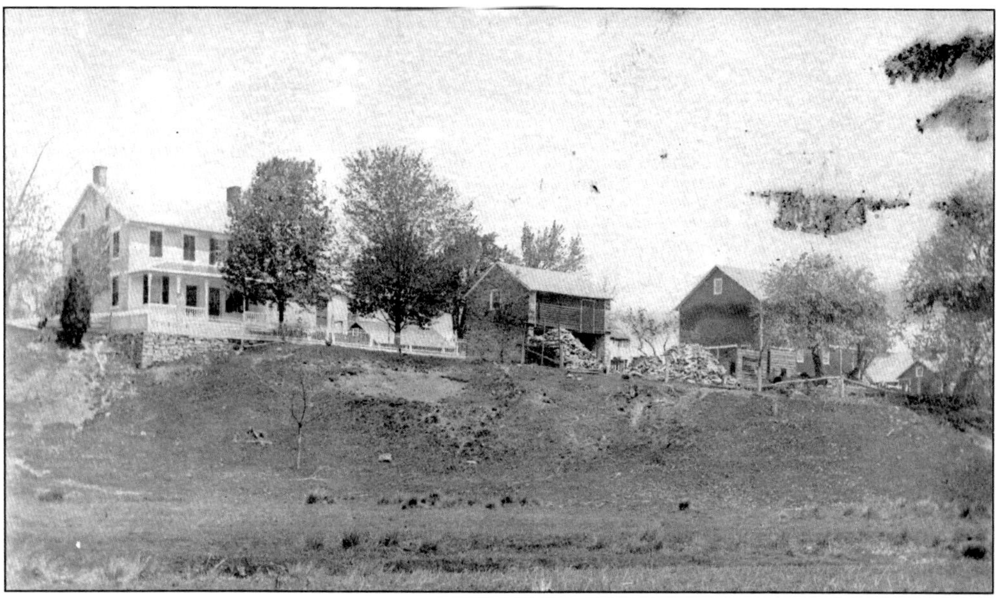

The Sand Brook home shown here had an unlicensed tavern in back during Prohibition in the 1920s. It is near the corner of Sand Brook and Britton Roads.

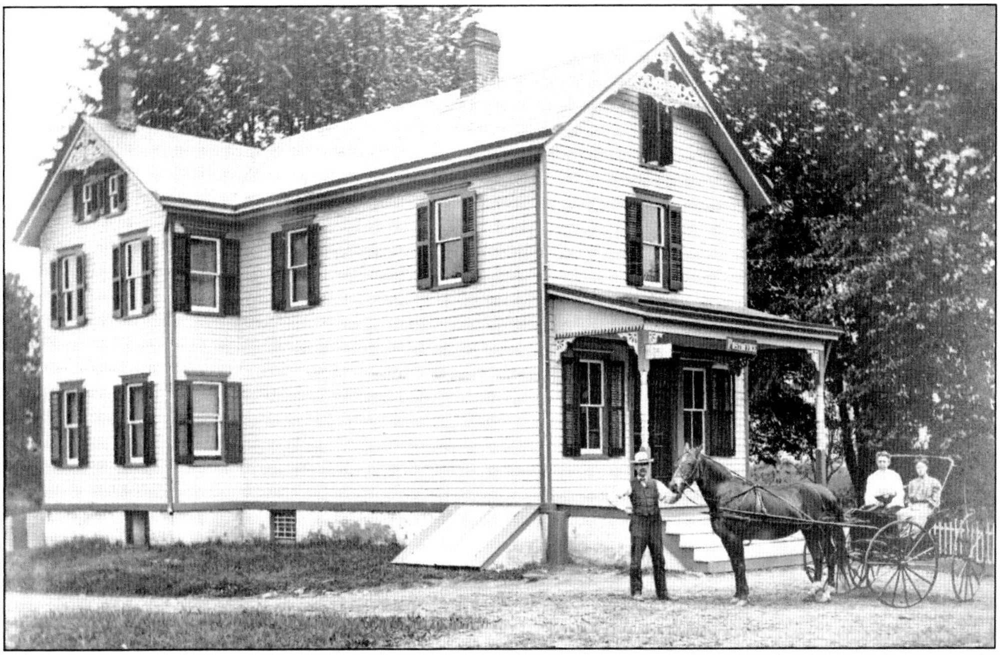

A local family is shown picking up mail at the Sand Brook Post Office in this 1907 photograph. Rural post offices have always been about more than mail delivery; they are also places where local people meet and socialize. Even today, for example, the Sergeantsville Post Office is a place where people catch up on all the local news.

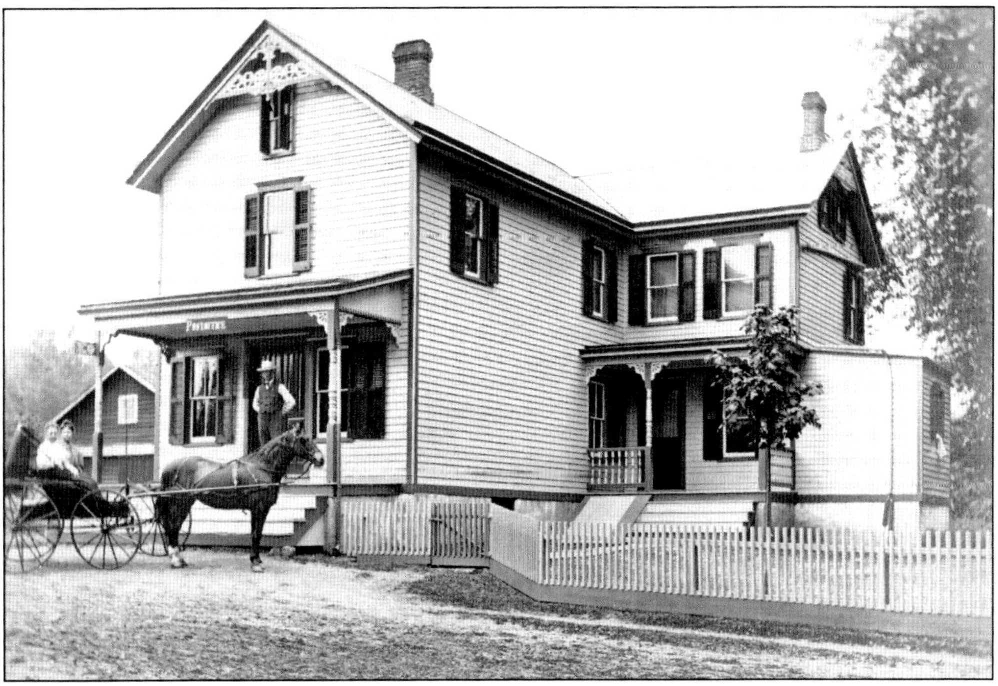

The store in the village of Sand Brook is shown in the early 20th century. Yasunas was the storekeeper and had the local post office there. This building still stands at the corner of Sand Brook and Britton Roads.

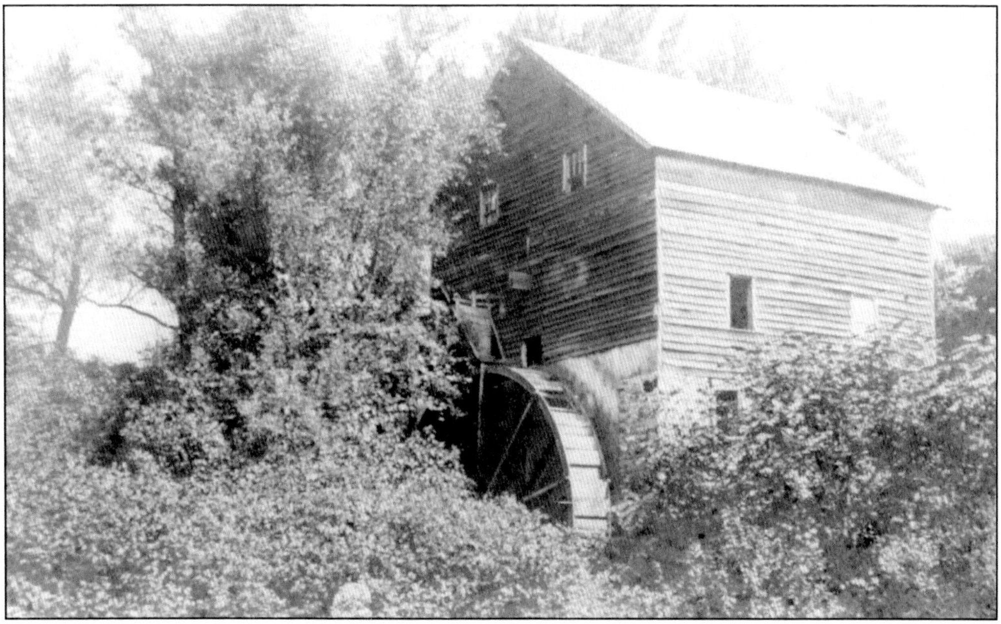

The gristmill shown here in Sand Brook was photographed in the early 20th century. This mill was just off Britton Road at Sand Brook Road. Notice the intact and operative waterwheel.

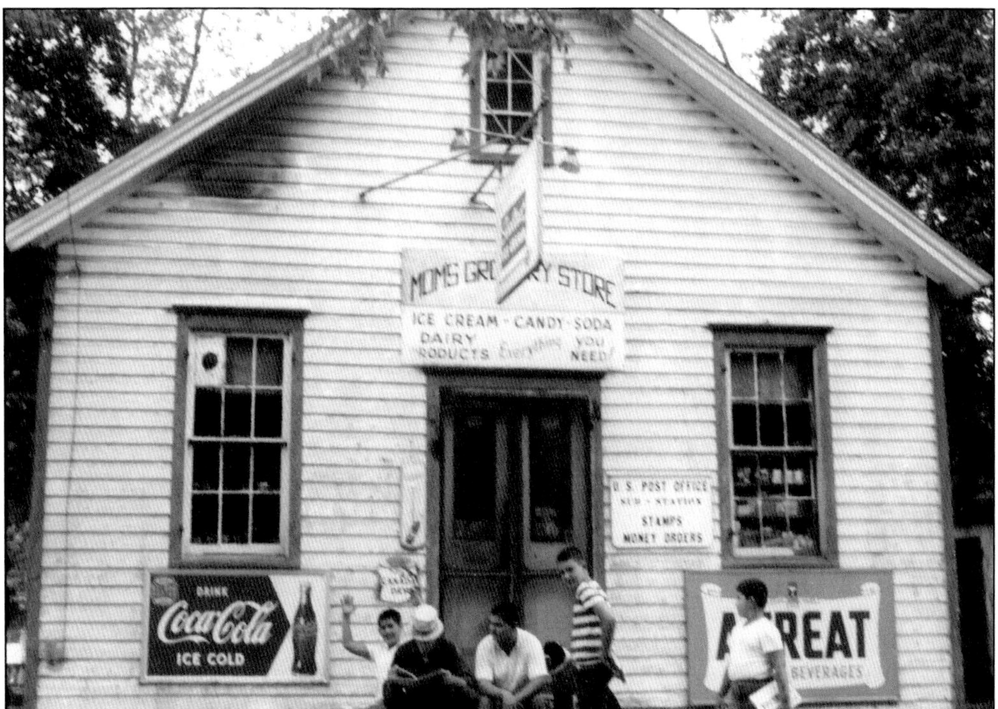

This photograph from the 1930s shows the store and post office in Sand Brook. This place was a point of village gathering and socializing. It was previously the village schoolhouse. Clint Wilson taught here for two years.

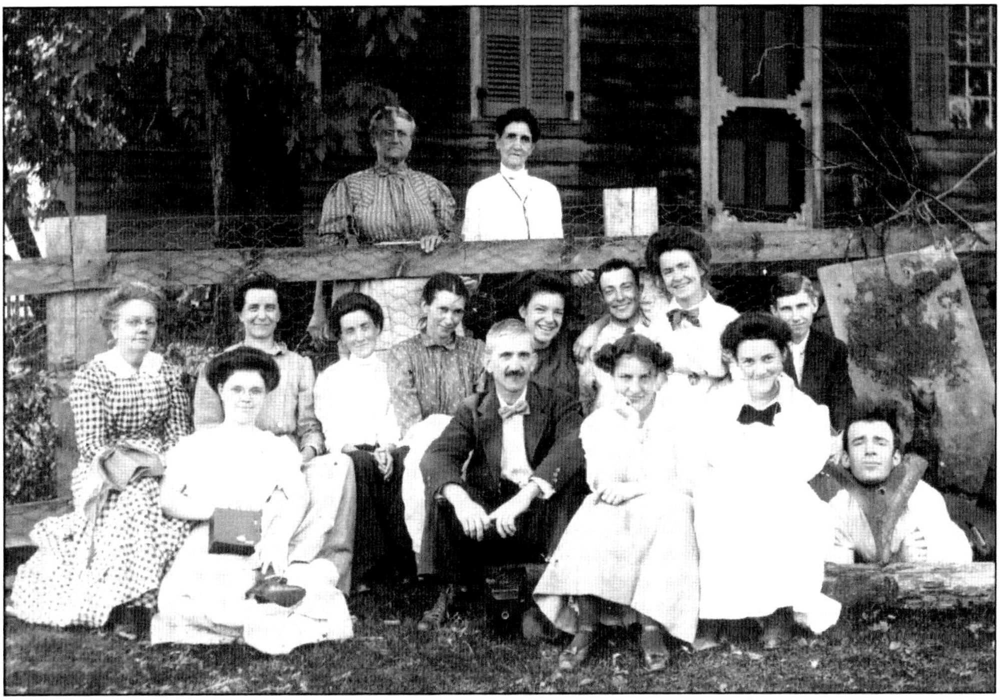

Shown here is an art class held in Sand Brook during the early 20th century. People came from other places and boarded locally to attend class. Notice the hairstyles and the somewhat avant-garde clothing on several of the students.

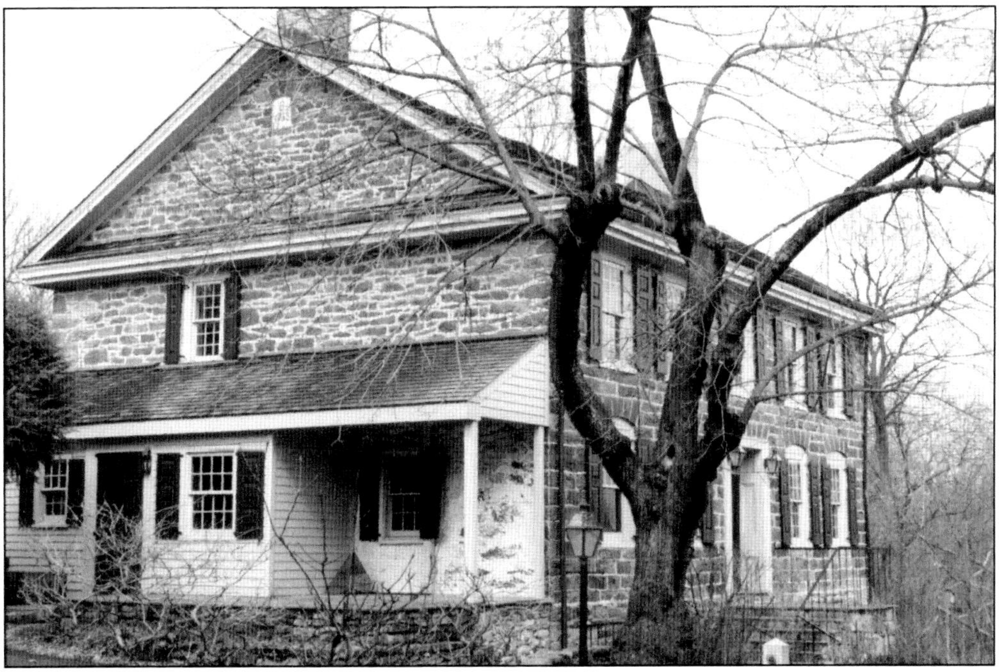

This is the main building of the Headquarters farm and gristmill in which George Washington was reported to have lived during his short stay in the area. These buildings are still in prime condition. The old mill has all the machinery intact.

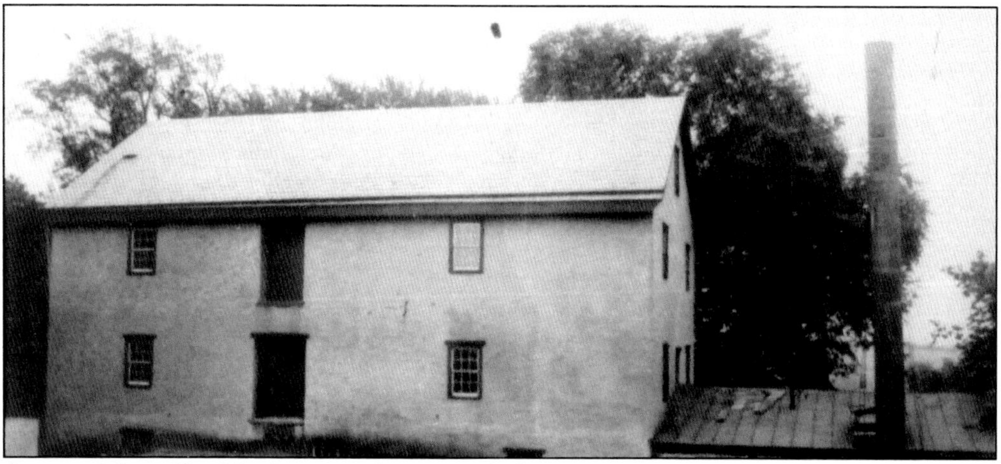

A view of the mill at Headquarters shows it with the stucco coating still covering the stone. The stucco has since been removed, exposing the striking stone underneath. The small building in the lower right was a steam-powered sawmill.

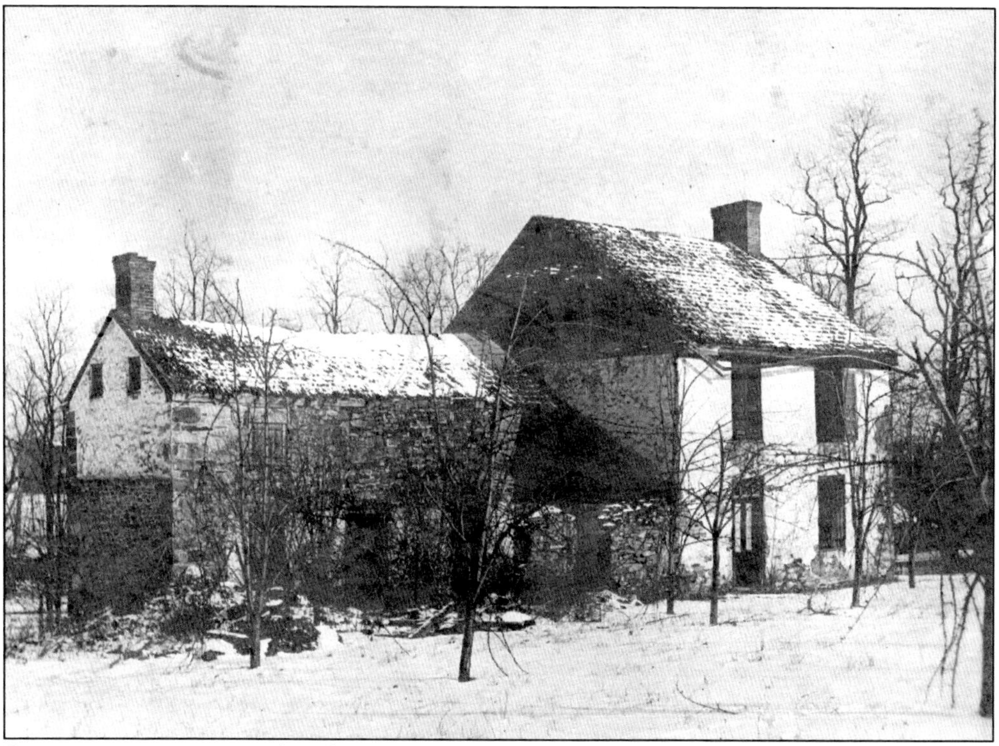

Some accounts maintain that this stone structure, the Whitehall Tavern, in Headquarters was one of the buildings used by George Washington during his stay in the area. It was situated on the corner of Lambertville-Headquarters Road and Sergeantsville-Ringoes Road (Route 604) and was torn down in the early 20th century. The structure was built in 1775 by John Opdyke, who built and operated a number of gristmills in the area.

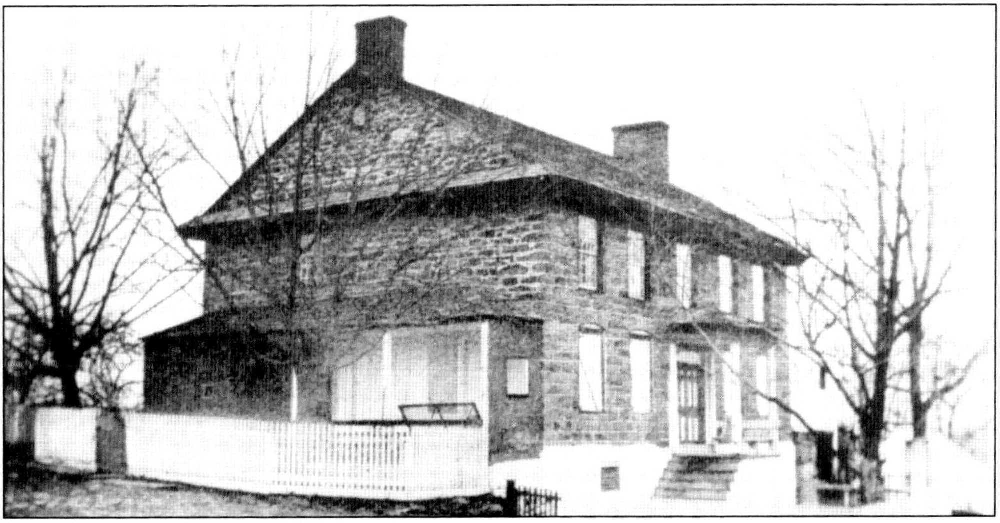

The Opdyke house (Headquarters Farm today) is shown in the early 20th century.

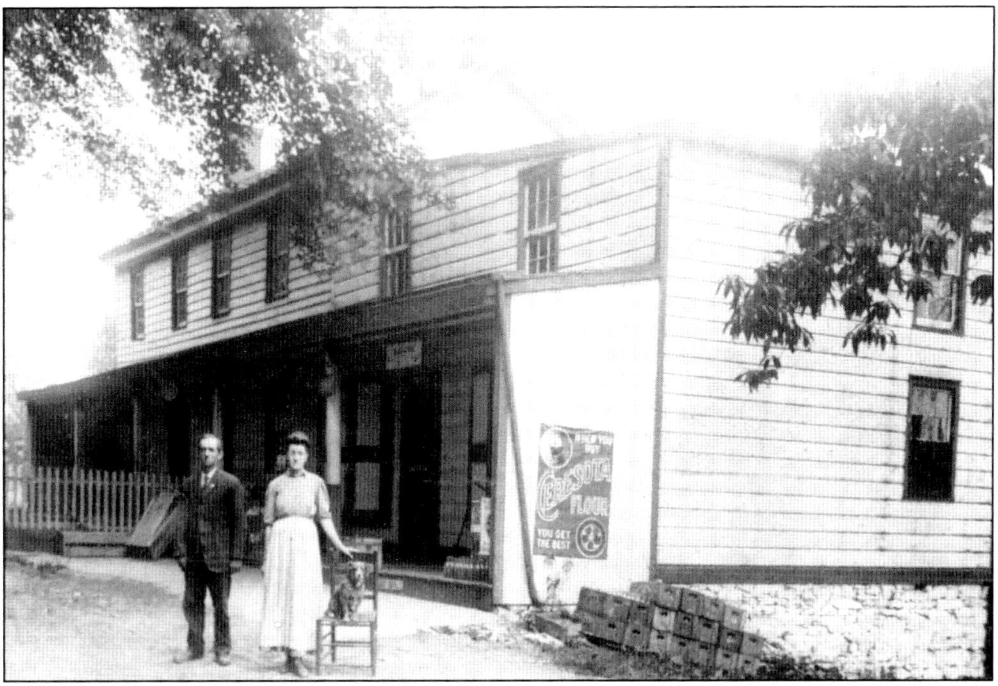

This store in Headquarters in the early 20th century was the center of village life. Today it is very difficult to imagine that Headquarters was a town with a center locus of activity; it is now just a part of the passing scene along the highway.

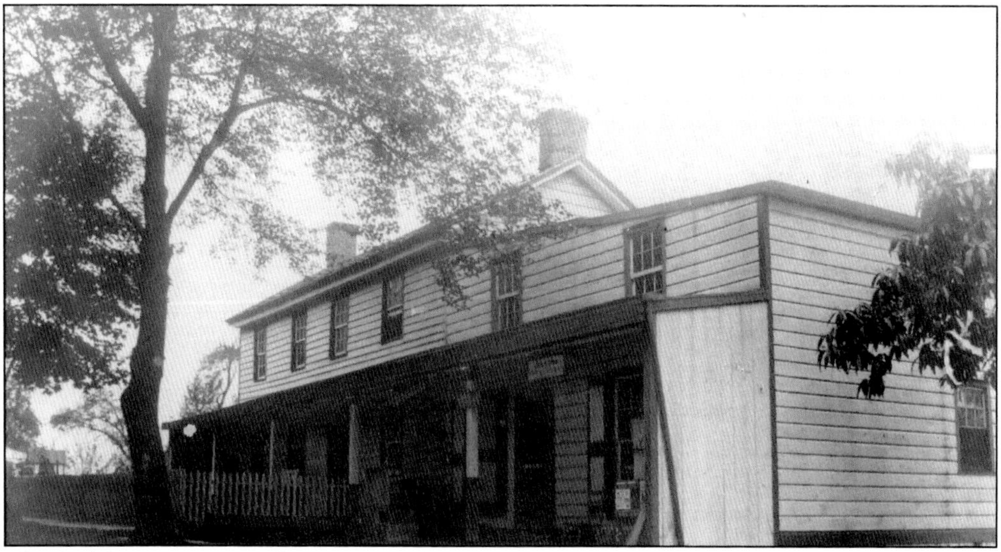

This building was a general store in Headquarters during the 19th century and operated into the 1950s. The proprietors from the 1930s through the 1950s were Bert German and his wife. Today this building is a private residence that has been restored. It is located at the corner of Route 604 and Zentek Road.

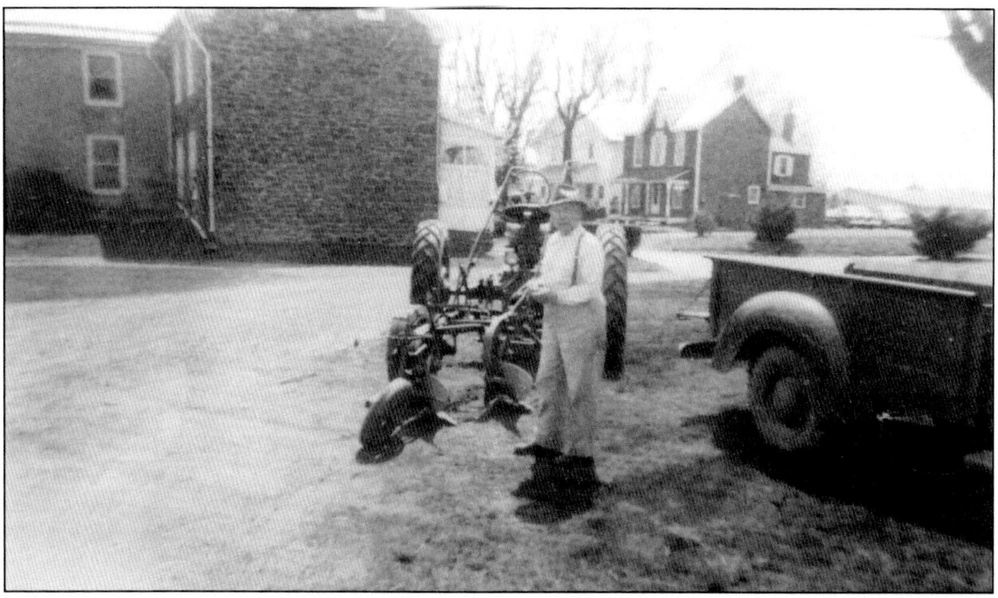

Bill Reading of Rosemont is shown with some of his farm equipment in the 1940s. The farm and town had quite permeable boundaries where one melded almost seamlessly into the other.

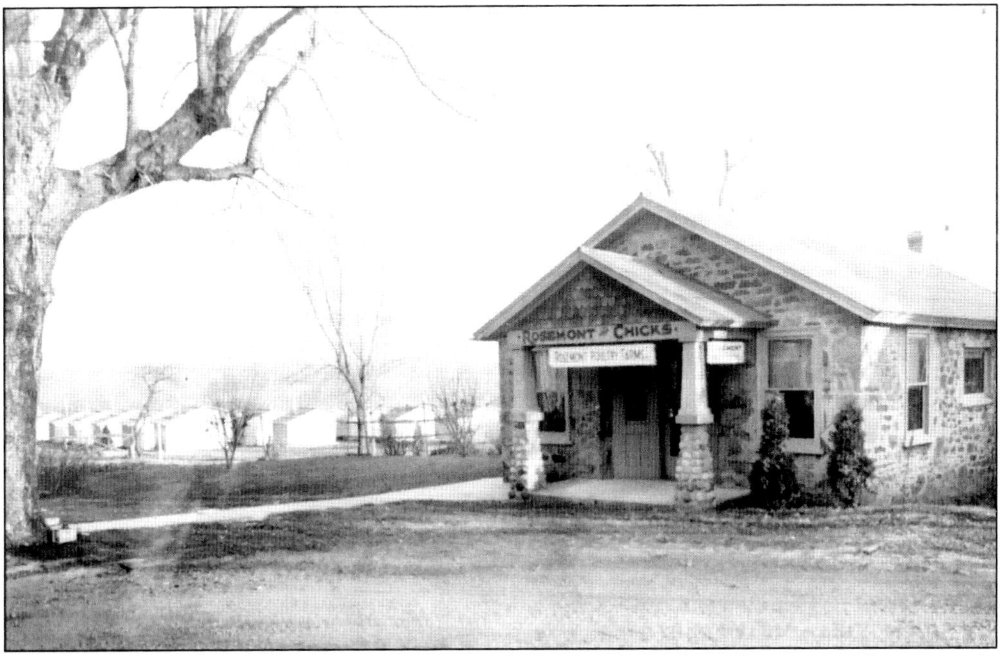

This building in Rosemont was once a blacksmith shop in the early 20th century. More recently it was used as a clock shop. In the background are brooder coops for raising chickens; these could be seen throughout the township in the 1940s because of the very intensive chicken production that existed in Hunterdon County at that time.

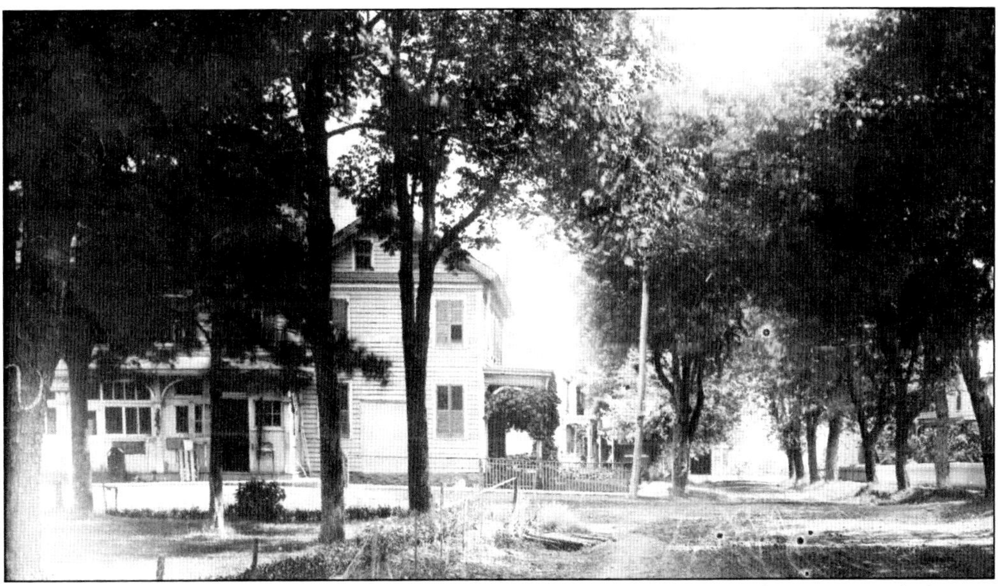

This Rosemont building, seen in 1914 on the corner of Routes 604 and 519, currently houses a restaurant.

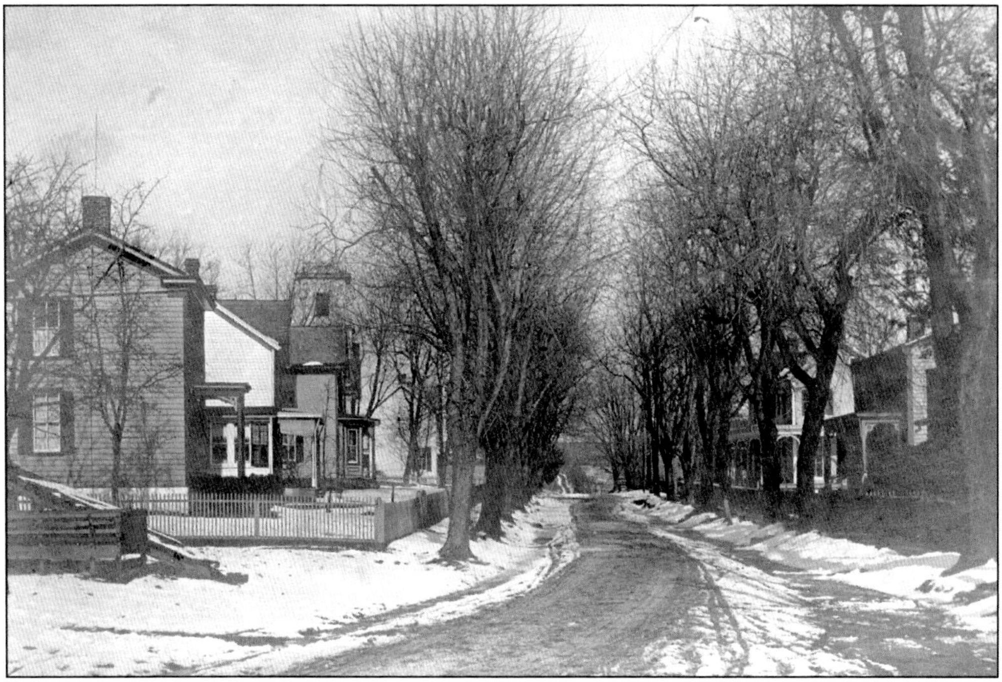

The main street through Rosemont is shown in a winter scene during the second decade of the 20th century. The town aspect of physical structure can be seen in the tree-lined street, the closely built housing, and the neighborly string of houses facing one another.

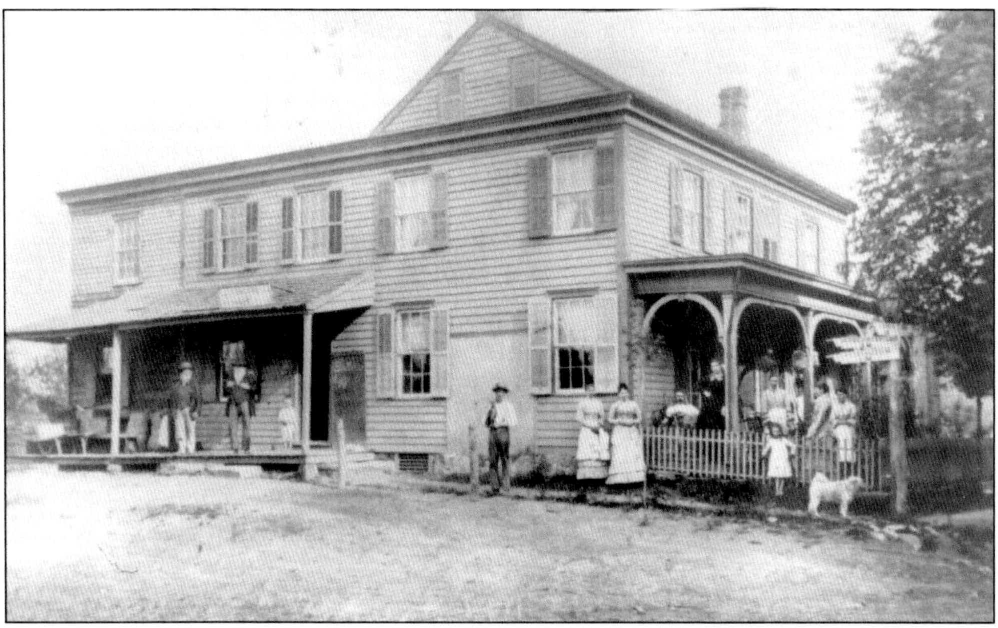

A typical village gathering location was Place's Store in Rosemont during the early 20th century. This building is on the corner of Routes 519 and 604.

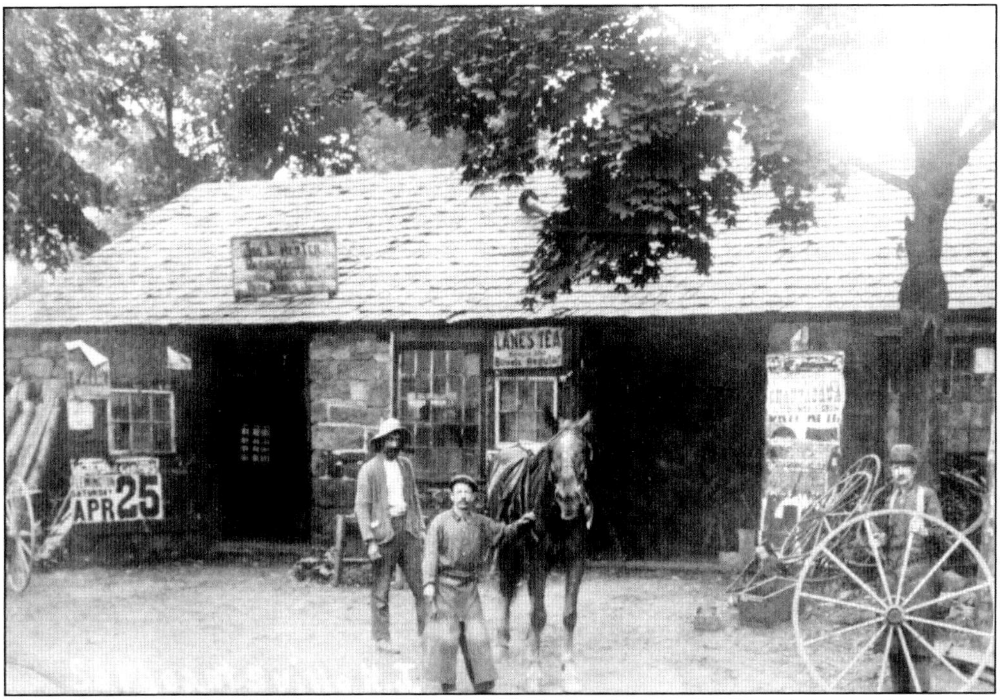

The Sergeantsville blacksmith shop is captured in this 1913 photograph and shows wheelwright Theodore (Dory) Green holding a wheel with Herbert Smith on the left and blacksmith James "Gussie" Harned holding a horse. Gussie Harned was a blacksmith here into the 1930s. Notice the sign advertising Lane's Tea over the middle door. This enterprise was thriving at the time just before the onslaught of the automobile changed everything.

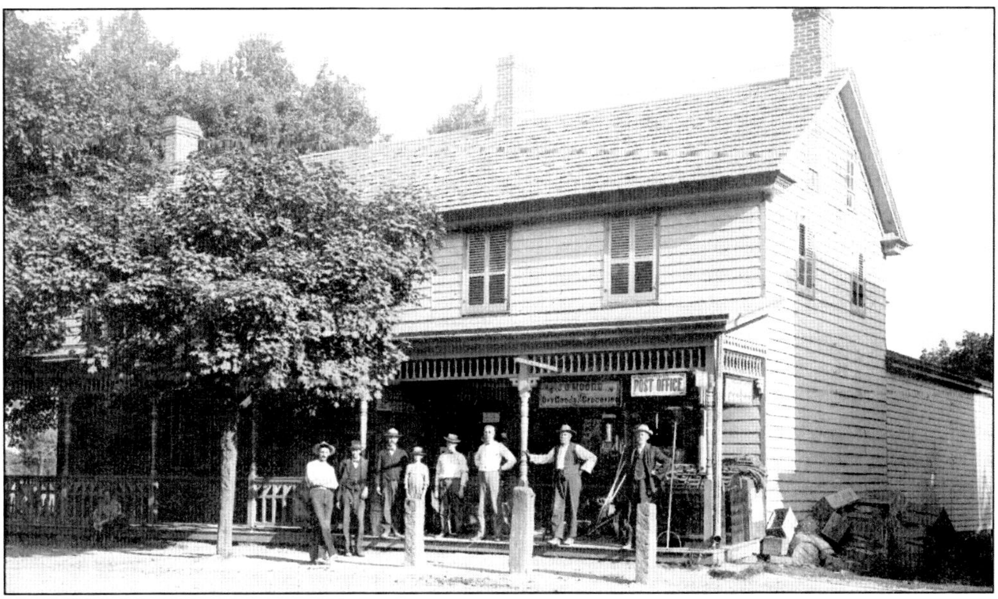

Clint Wilson's store and post office in Sergeantsville is shown in the 1920s. Wilson helped his father and mother run the store, which he eventually took over. He resided in the living quarters in the back of the store.

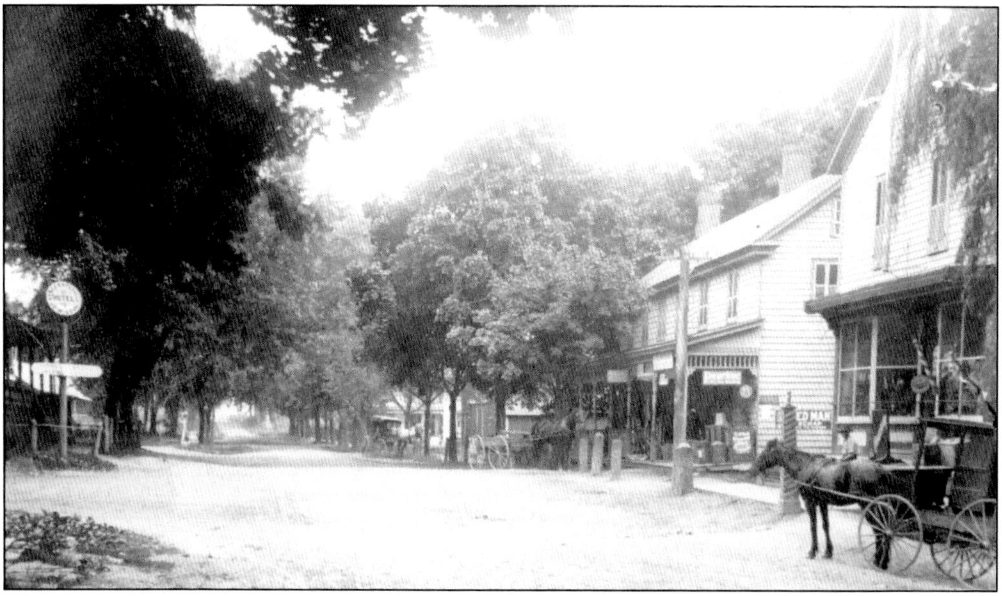

This is Maple Avenue (Route 604 today) in Sergeantsville during the early 20th century. Lew Higgins, the barber, was in the building on the right, and the village store was next door. Notice the Redman Chewing Tobacco sign on the store and the horse with carriage waiting on the corner. The tree canopy provides an embowered streetscape that clearly marks a townlike structure.

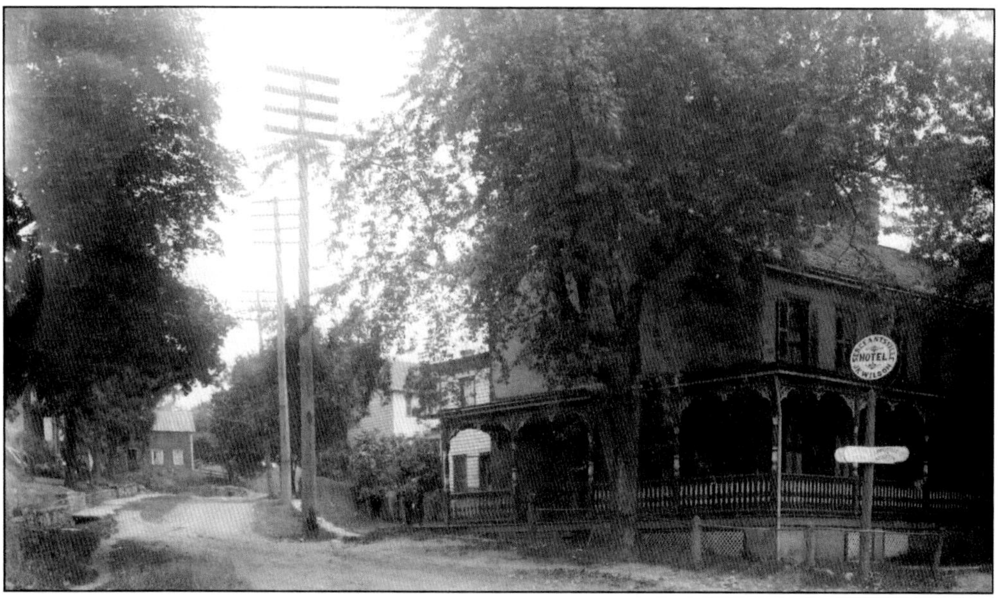

A view of Sergeantsville looking north up the hill toward Flemington (Route 523 today) shows Wilson's Hotel on the right. Notice the sign and large electric wires. This photograph was taken between 1915 and 1919, and the road was still unpaved. The hotel is today's municipal building, minus the porch. At various times, the building housed the hotel, a tavern, a barbershop, a school in the 20th century, and the library. The Wilsons closed the tavern mainly because of Prohibition.

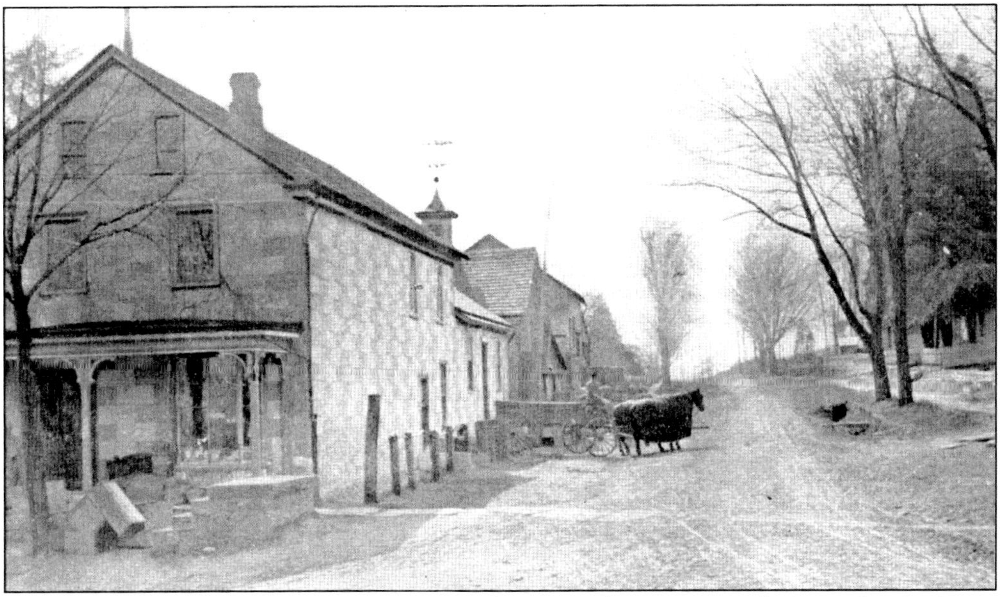

The first building on the left is Shepherd's store, known as the Sergeantsville Inn today. As shown in this 1910 photograph, the building still had the end porch and the unique checkerboard stucco facade covering the stone. This winter scene looks west toward Rosemont as a blanket-covered horse team and wagon waits at a loading door on the far end. The road was unpaved and the view is looking west toward Rosemont. At that time the road was called Maple Avenue; it is the present Route 604.

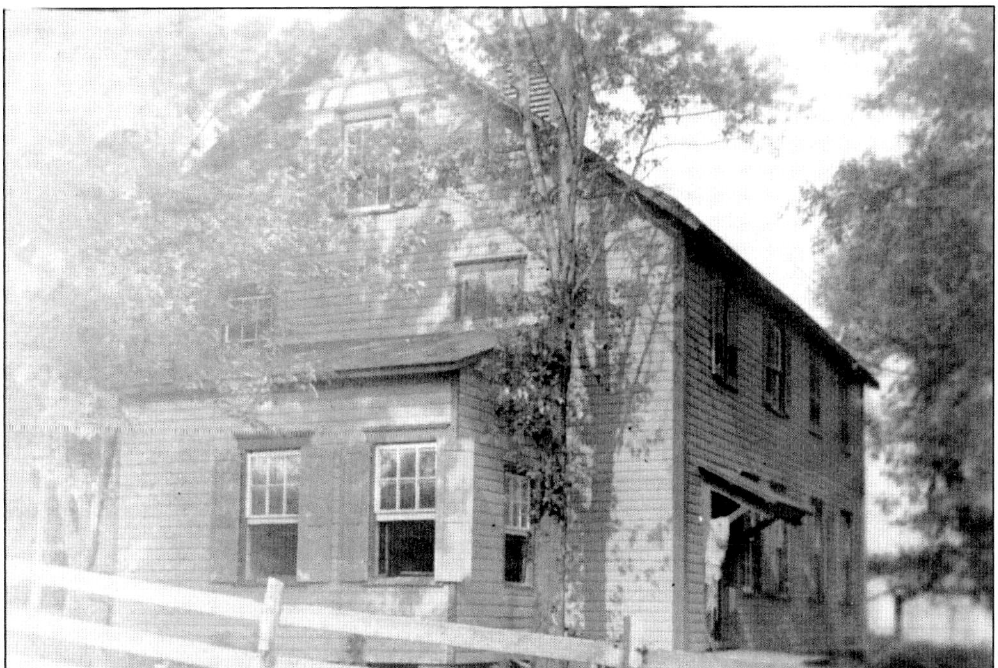

The creamery within Sergeantsville is shown in 1907. This facility had been in operation as early as the 1880s and sold dairy products beyond Sergeantsville.

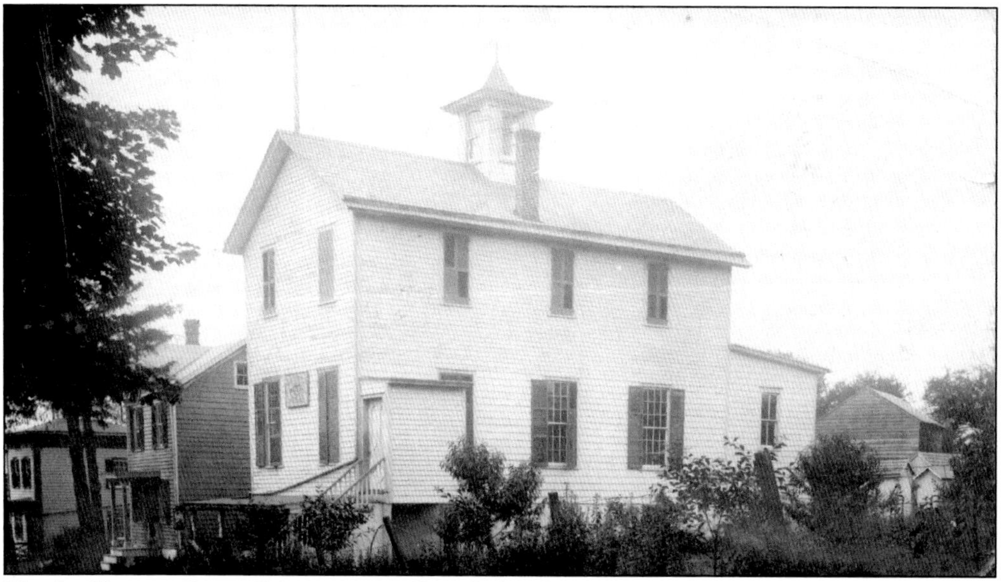

This building on Route 523 was originally called Military Hall and was used in the Civil War as a center for military training. It was later called Mechanics Hall and was used as a lodge. Notice the witch's watch (the cupola) on the roof peak for observing the area. The structure is a few houses up from today's general store on Route 523.

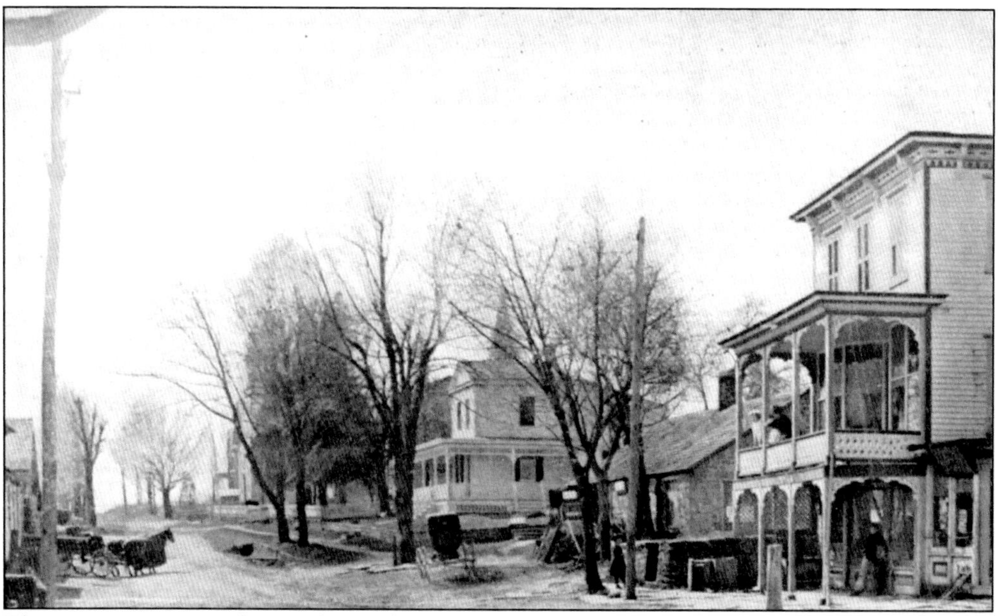

The winter scene shown here from about 1907 looks west along Maple Avenue (Sergeantsville-Rosemont Road). The current Sergeantsville General Store is the first building on the right with the blacksmith shop next door (the present radio station WDVR). Note the blanket-covered horse team with attached buggy on the left as well as the buggy waiting in front of the blacksmith shop.

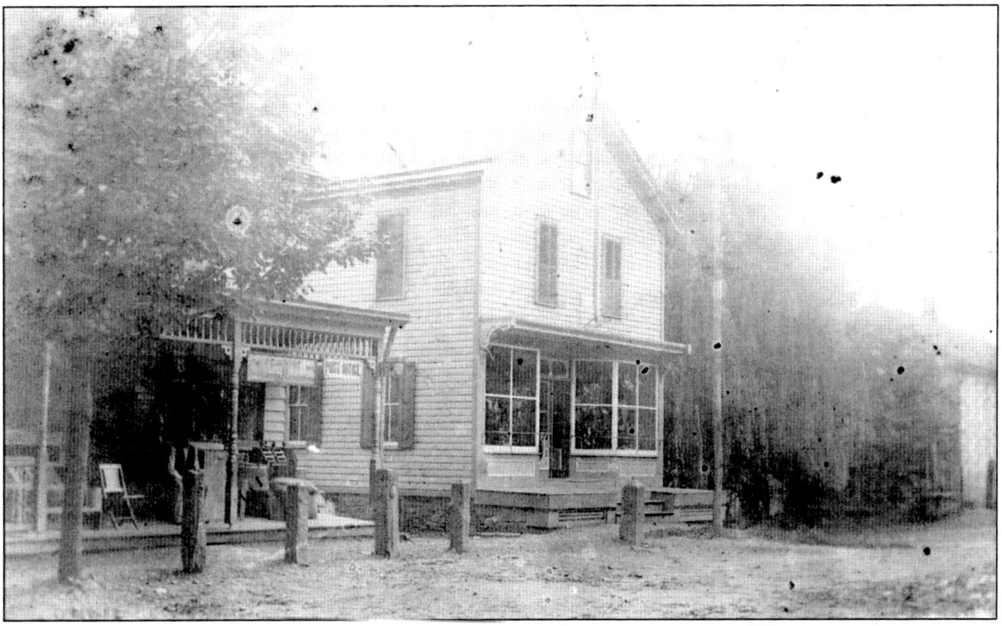

The center of the Sergeantsville business section is shown about 1910. These are the stores on the south side of Maple Avenue (today Route 604). The building in the center was the Fisher Harness Shop. Note the horse hitching posts lining the front of the stores. The building on the far right is the Sergeantsville Inn today. Lew Higgins's barbershop was in the middle building after the 1920s and operated through the 1950s. "Lew chewed tobacco while he cut hair and was a mild, mellow, slow-going person," according to a former client.

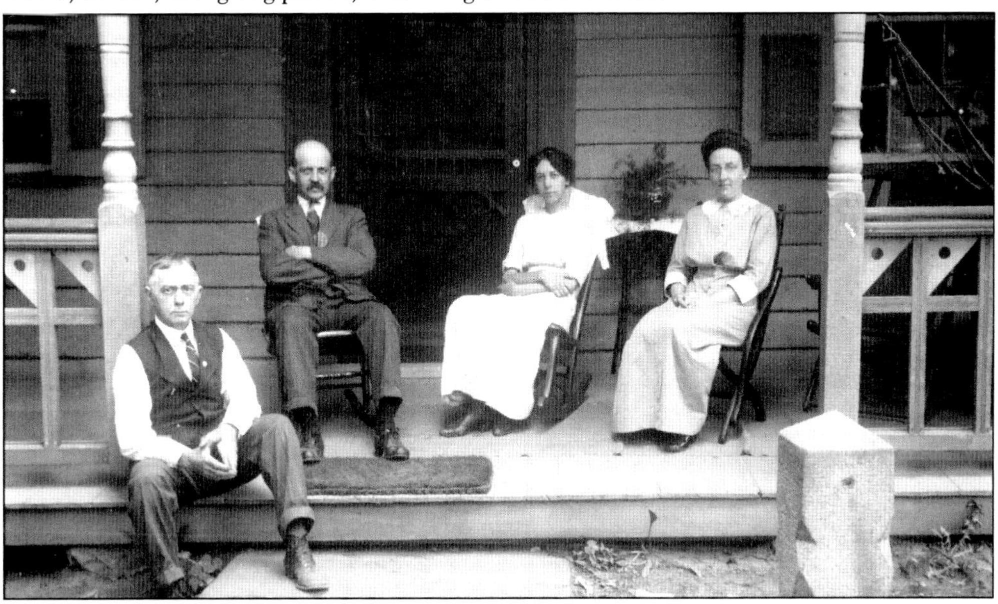

This 1915 porch scene in Sergeantsville shows friends relaxing at the building that today is a delicatessen called Bobbi's Place. A note attached to the photograph says the writer "will be down if the roads are good." Note the dress, particularly the men's shoes. Delaware Township people of these early days dressed to the nines; they often looked like fashion plates outfitted by Ralph Lauren.

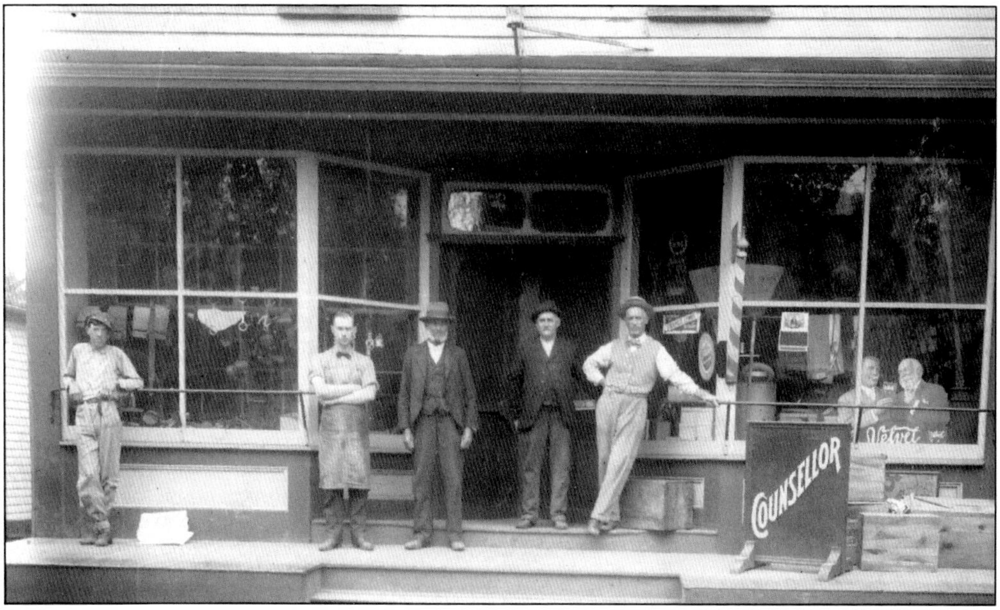

This scene at the southeast corner of Routes 604 and 523 around 1910 shows the barber and the harness maker (note the leather apron) with a local lawyer or counselor. The store building was chock-full of enterprises, including the oyster bar on the side lower floor. A slim barber's pole is attached to the right of the door. Lew Higgins later became the barber in this shop.

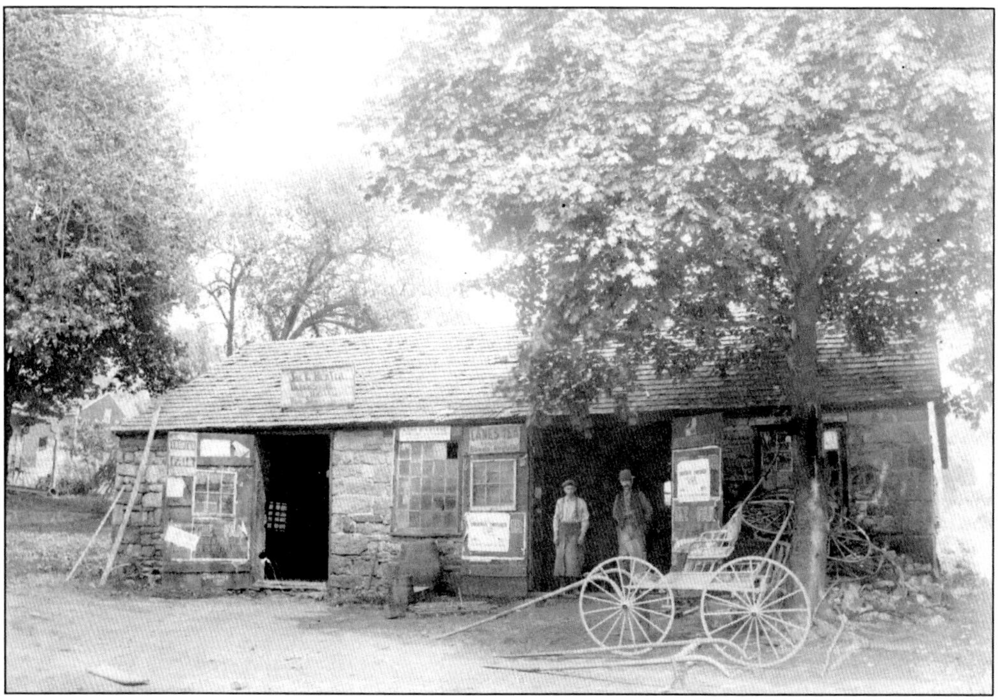

Taken about 1910, this photograph shows the blacksmith shop (presently housing the radio station WDVR) with blacksmith Gussie Harned (left) and Theodore (Dory) Green. Harned continued operating the shop through the 1930s. Note the buggy waiting for service.

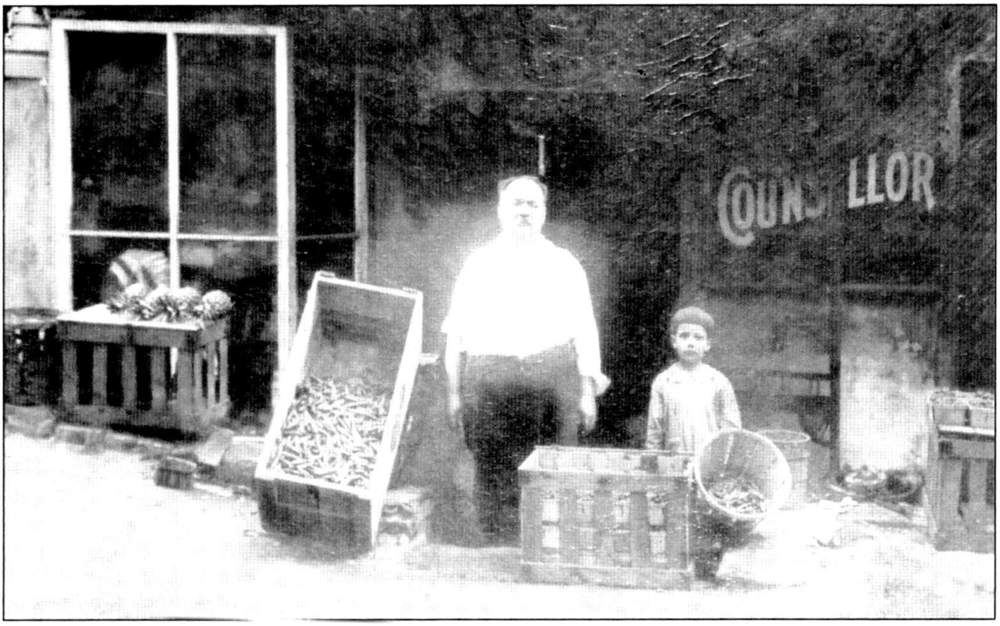

A view of the lower part of Dobbin's store around 1910 shows the oyster bar. This store was across Route 523 from today's Sergeantsville Inn. The counselor or lawyer and barbershop were on the floor above this basement store.

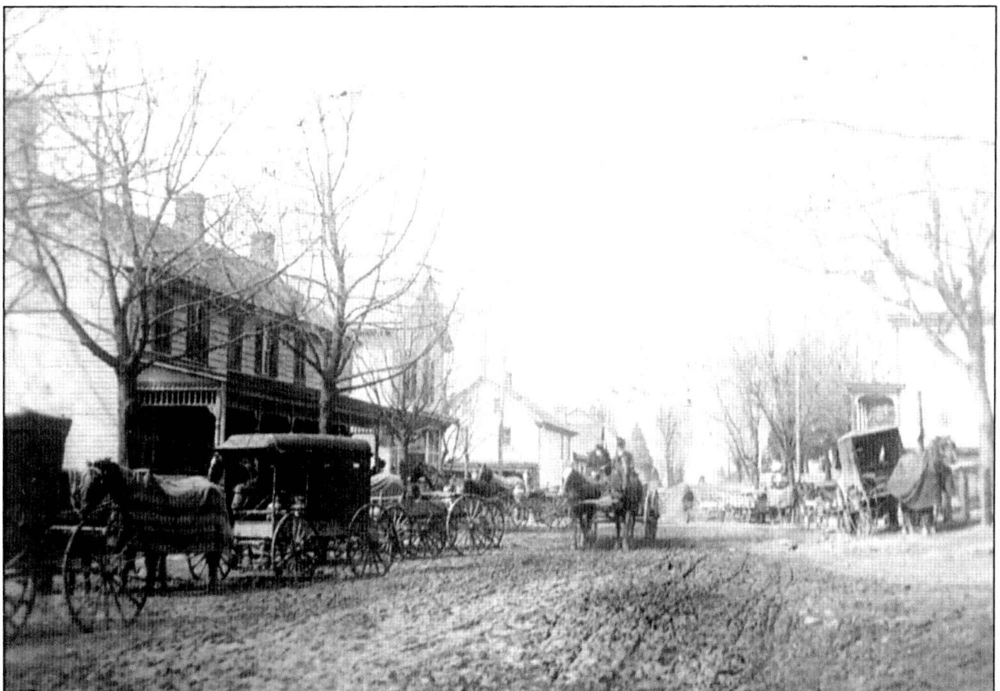

This 1908 view shows the main street (Maple Avenue) of Sergeantsville looking west. The first building on the left is today's Bobbi's Place, a delicatessen; in 1908, it was Amos Wilson's store. Note the buggies, wagons, and variety of horse teams. The road is quite muddy as well in this late-winter photograph.

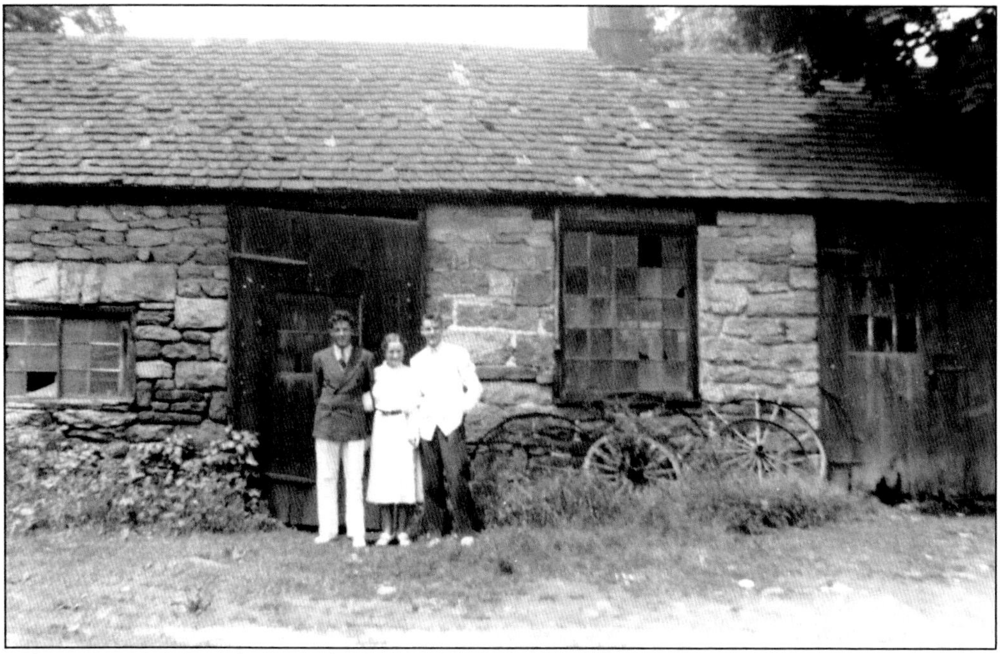

Taken in 1937, this photograph shows the front of the blacksmith shop, which was still in operation; note the wheels against the wall. The people, including Bob Perry on the left, Walter Kurzenberger on the right, and his sister Elizabeth Kurzenberger, are quite striking in their dress. As their nephew Paul said, "This is the way we dressed when we dressed up."

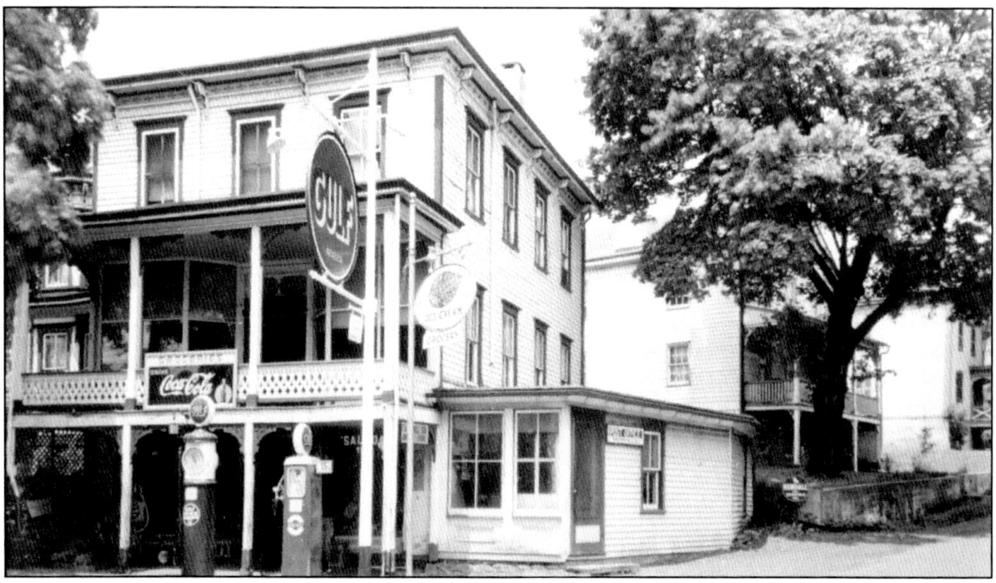

A 1920s view of Venable's store on the northwest corner of Routes 523 and 604 indicates the brands on sale, including Gulf gasoline, Breyer's ice cream, Coca- Cola, and Kendall oil. This is today's general store, serving Chinese as well as a variety of other foods. The small attached building on the right side was built to house the post office.

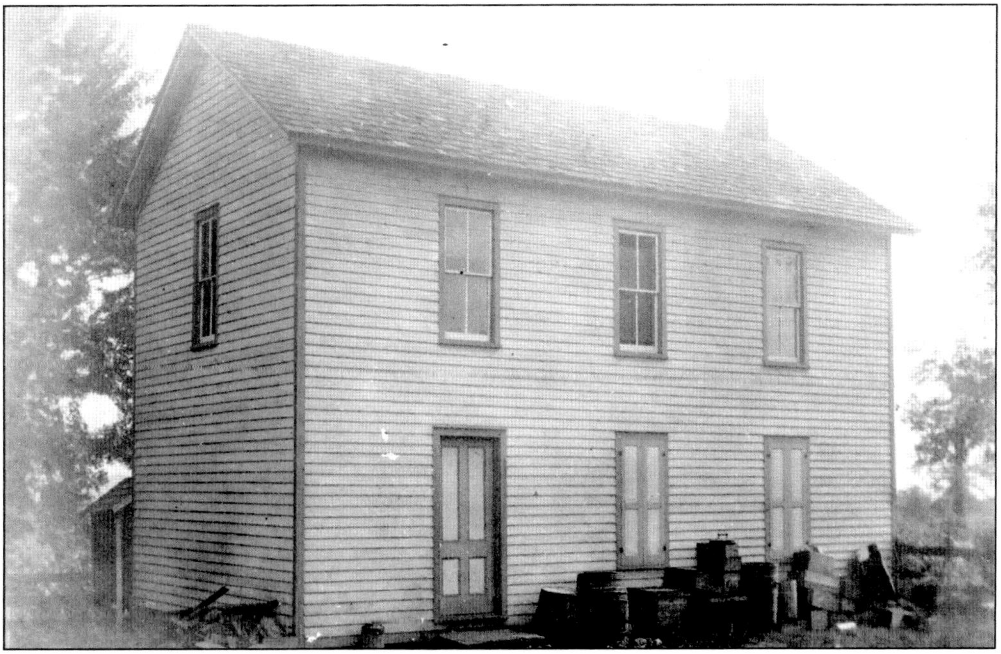

The Grange hall in Sergeantsville is shown around 1907. Notice the barrels in front. This building has been remodeled and is situated along the Rosemont-Ringoes Road (Route 604) on the outskirts of Sergeantsville.

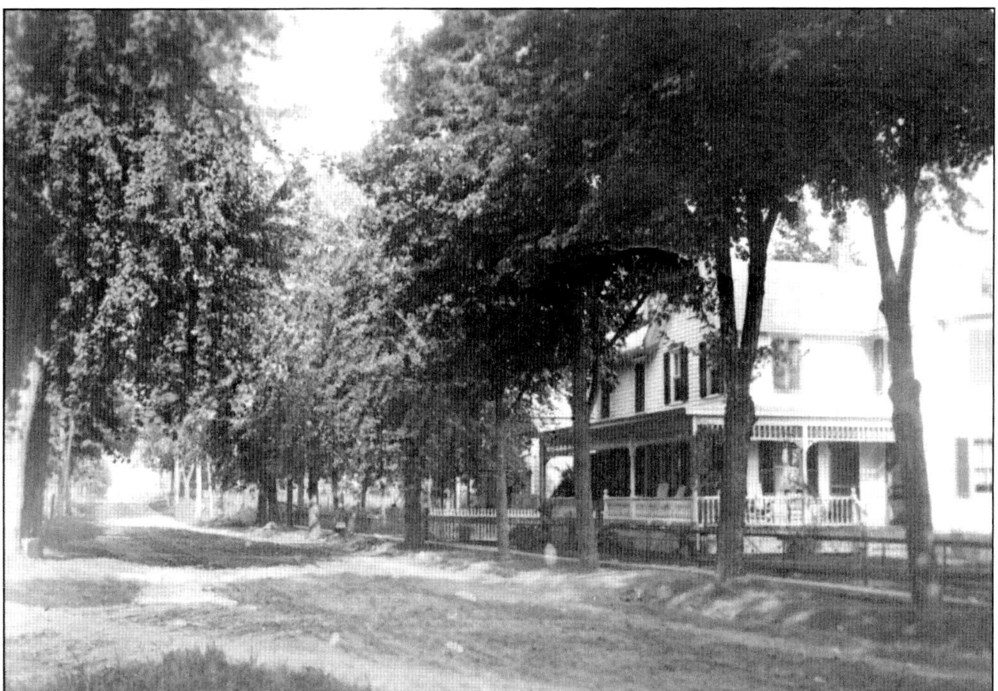

This view looks east on Maple Avenue (today's Route 604) in Sergeantsville about 1910. The present post office is the next building down from the residence pictured. This view vividly illustrates the streetscape nature that defines the physical layout of a small village.

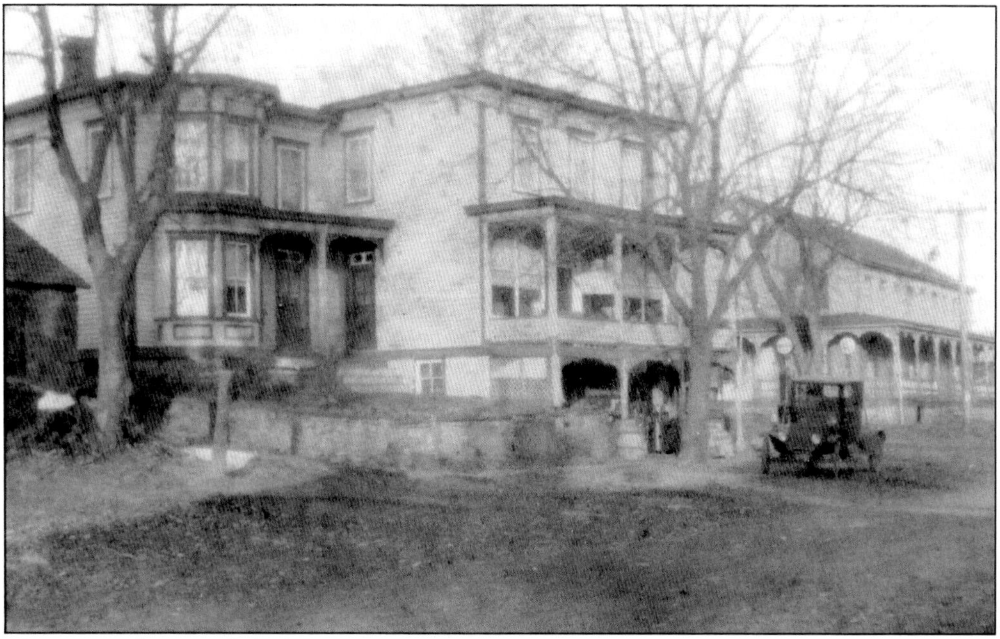

This 1920s photograph looks east on Route 604 and shows the general store with the hotel on the right across Route 523. The road was still unpaved. Notice the Ford Model T parked in front of the store.

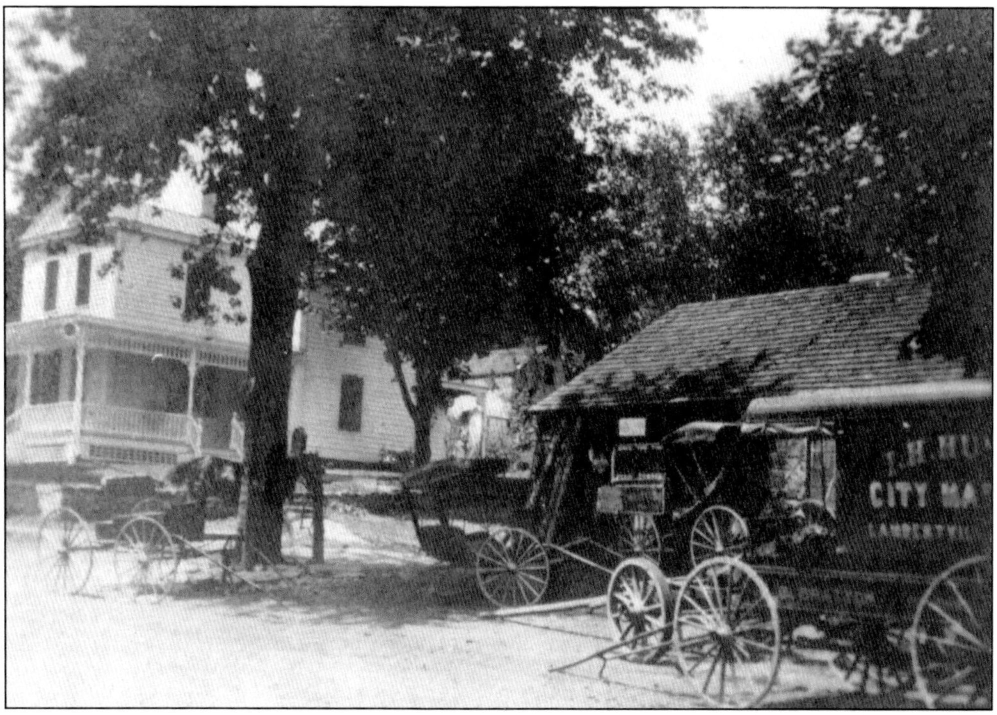

A photograph taken during the summer in the 1920s shows the Sergeantsville blacksmith shop with wagons and horse vans awaiting repair. The Lambertville City Market van is clearly visible.

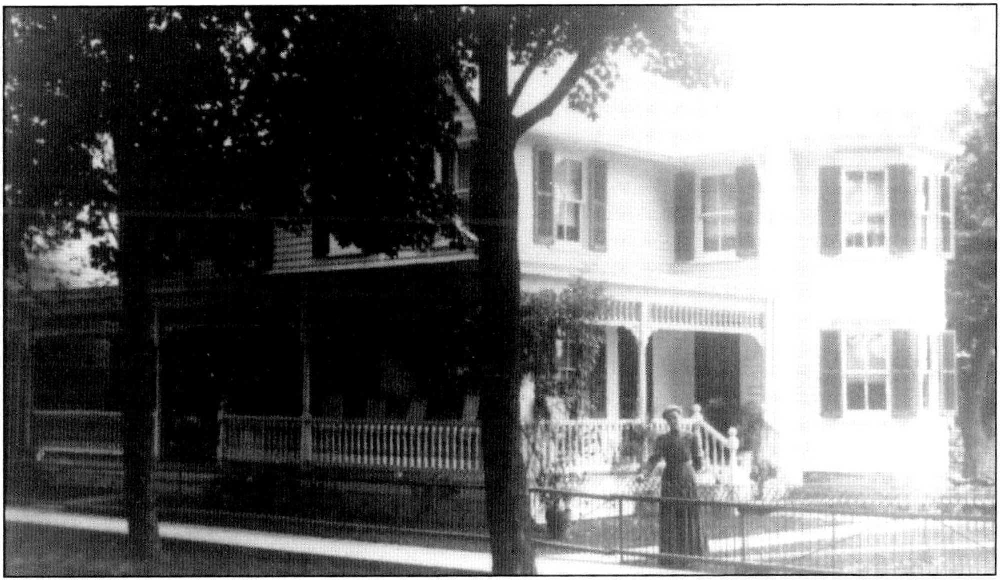

Maple Avenue (Route 604 today) in Sergeantsville is shown in the early 20th century. Note the long dress and the iron fence. This is the residence just adjacent to today's post office.

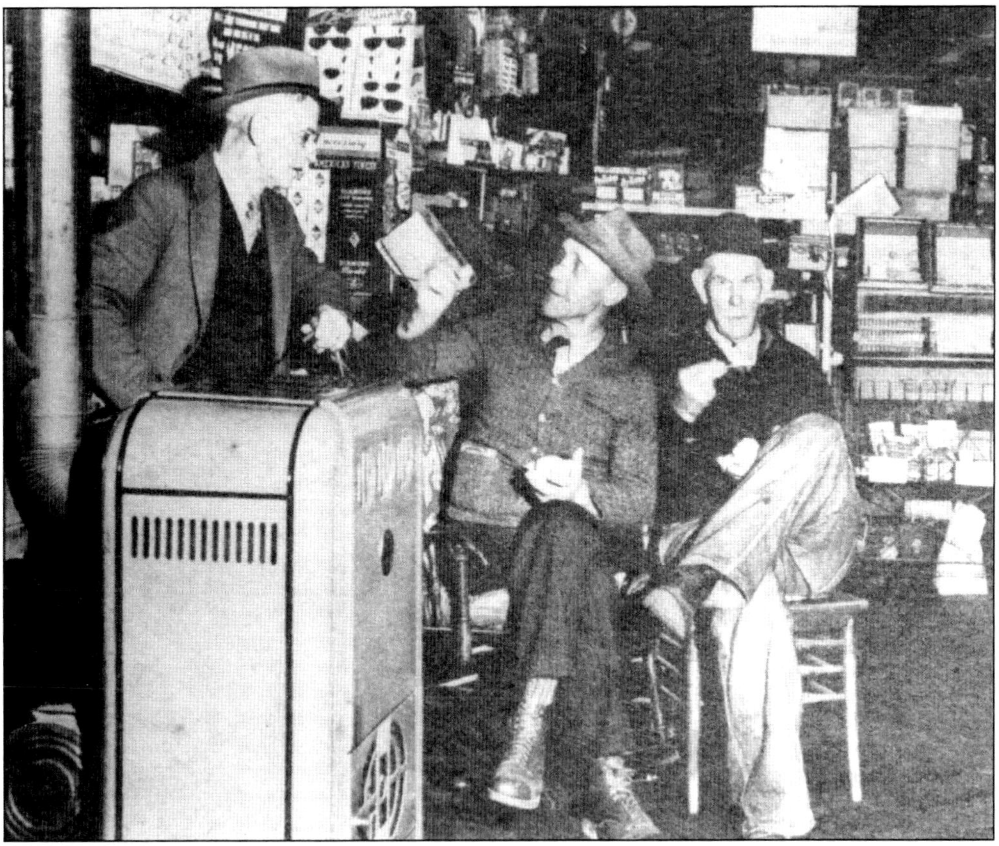

A 1930s photograph taken in Clint Wilson's general store shows Ed Brown (center) and Gabriel Lee (right) in hot discussion around the warm stove with an involved bystander.

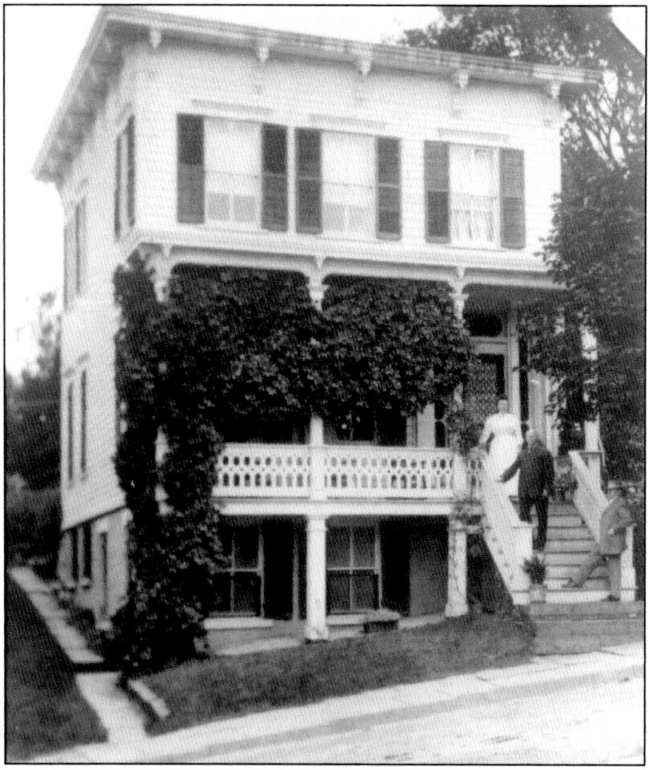

A Federal-style house in Sergeantsville is shown in 1915. The house on Route 523 is directly behind the general store up the hill going to Flemington. There was a barbershop on the ground floor in the 1950s and 1960s. Note the early-20th-century-style dress.

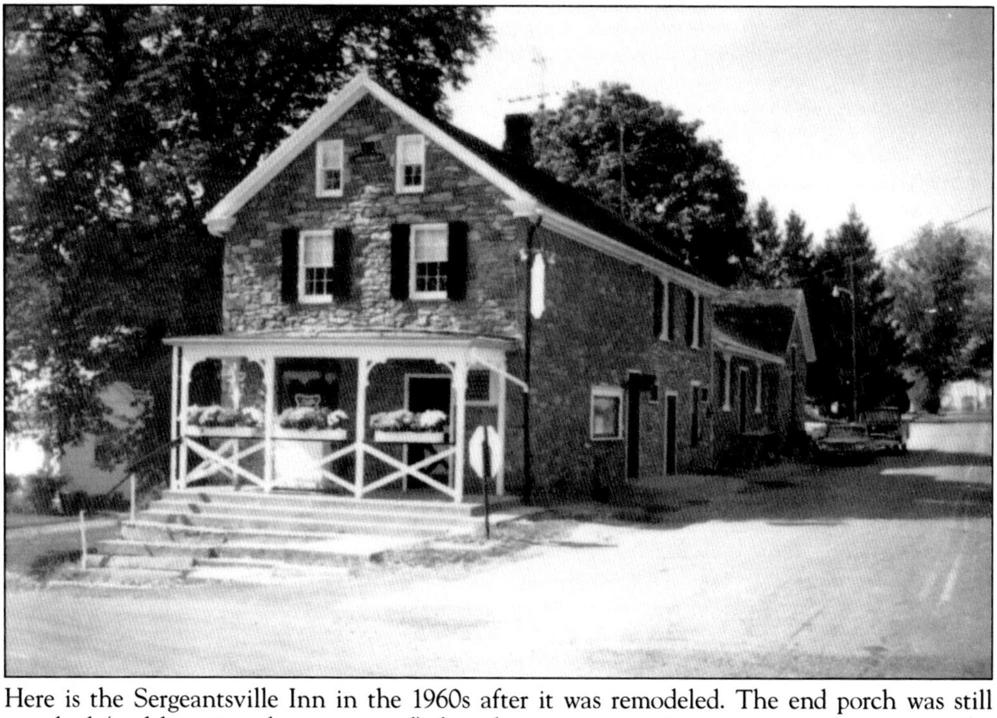

Here is the Sergeantsville Inn in the 1960s after it was remodeled. The end porch was still attached (and has since been removed), but the stucco covering was stripped, exposing the beautiful stone underneath. (Courtesy of Blanche Carl.)

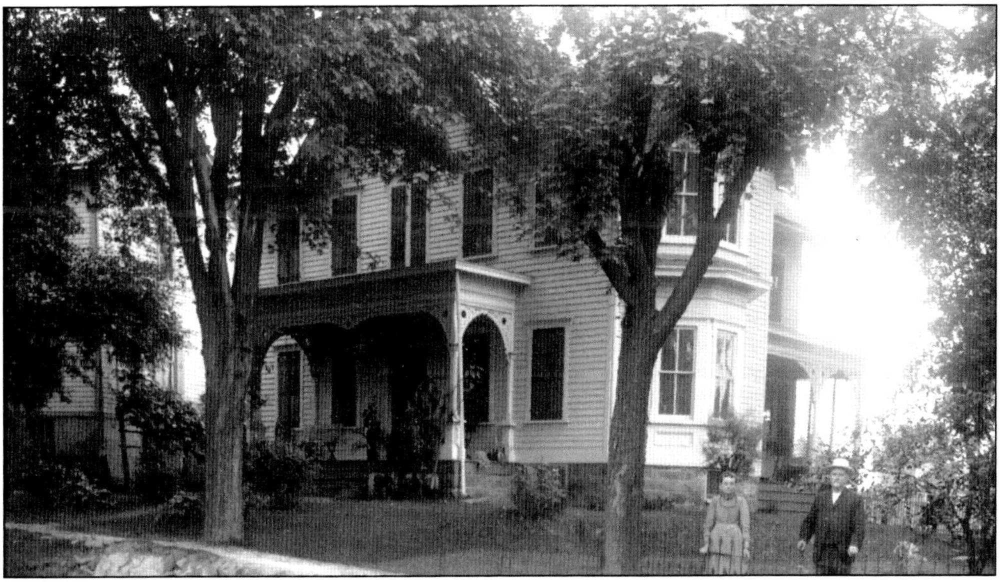

The Sergeantsville house shown here in 1910 originally stood behind the corner store at Routes 604 and 523. It was moved in the mid-20th century and is now the PNC Bank building a few hundred feet south toward Stockton. The lot on which it originally stood is now the parking lot for Sergeantsville Inn.

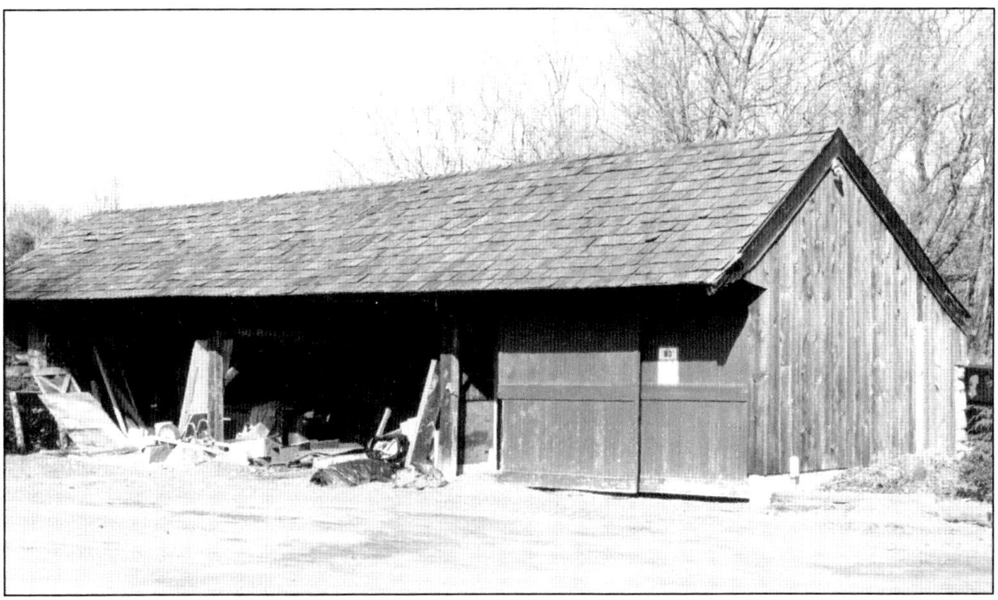

Shown in this photograph is the classic horse shed for the hotel that was demolished in the 1990s to provide parking for the municipal building. The shed was bought and possibly reassembled in another town.

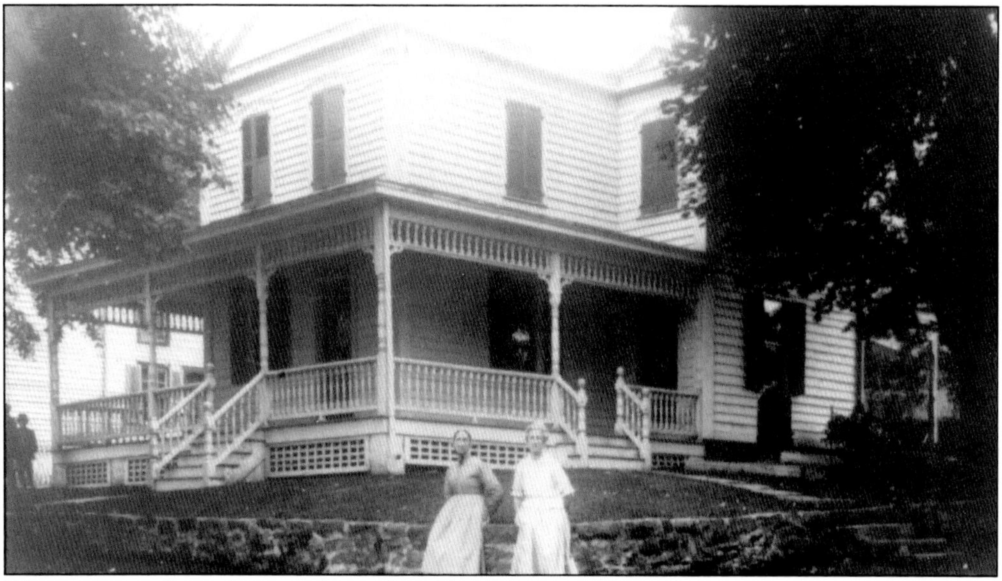

The residence shown here in the early 20th century is next to the blacksmith shop and is now the home of former fire chief Charles Higgins. Earlier it was the home of Jinny Green, widow of Theodore (Dory) Green, a blacksmith in the 1920s and 1930s.

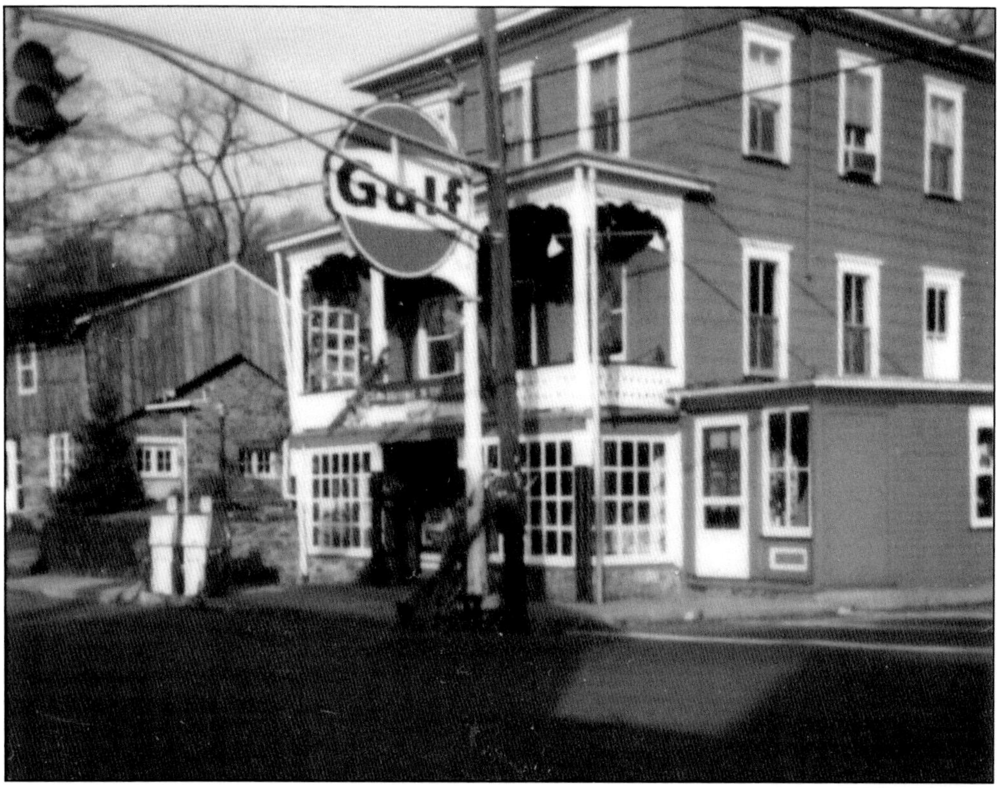

Today's general store on the corner of Routes 604 and 523 is shown during the 1960s. Notice that the blacksmith shop next door has been remodeled, and today it houses the radio station. (Courtesy of Blanche Carl.)

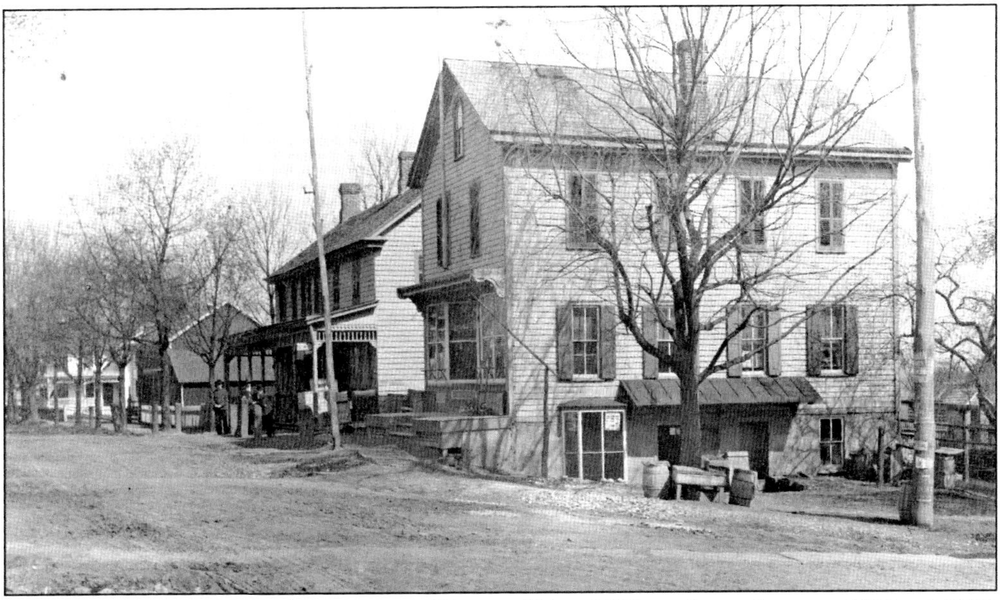

These buildings on the southeast corner of Routes 604 and 523 are shown between 1910 and 1920. Lew Higgins's barbershop was on the middle floor of the corner building. Dobbin's ice-cream and oyster bar was on the ground floor. This is directly across Route 523 from today's Sergeantsville Inn. Clint Wilson's store is the second building from the right. Notice the third building, a barn, which since has been torn down. The local farmers' market now utilizes that empty lot during the summer.

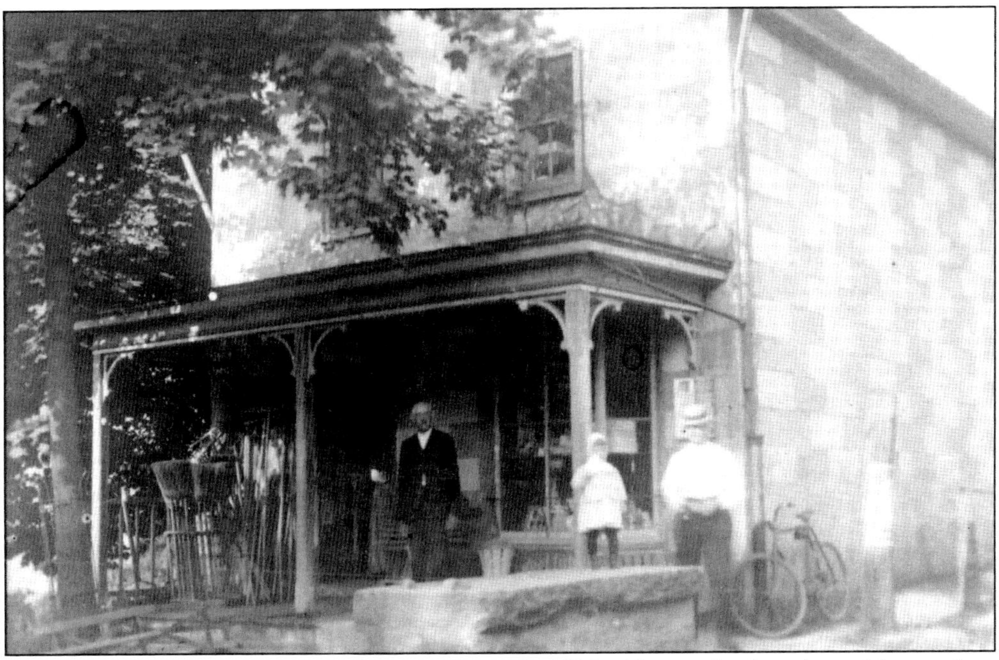

Edward Shepherd's store is seen here in the early 1920s. Notice the bicycle and boater hat. Brooms are on prominent display for sale on the left side of the porch. A stepping-stone for exiting a carriage is shown in the foreground. The building is now the Sergeantsville Inn, but the porch on the end and the checkerboard stucco are long gone.

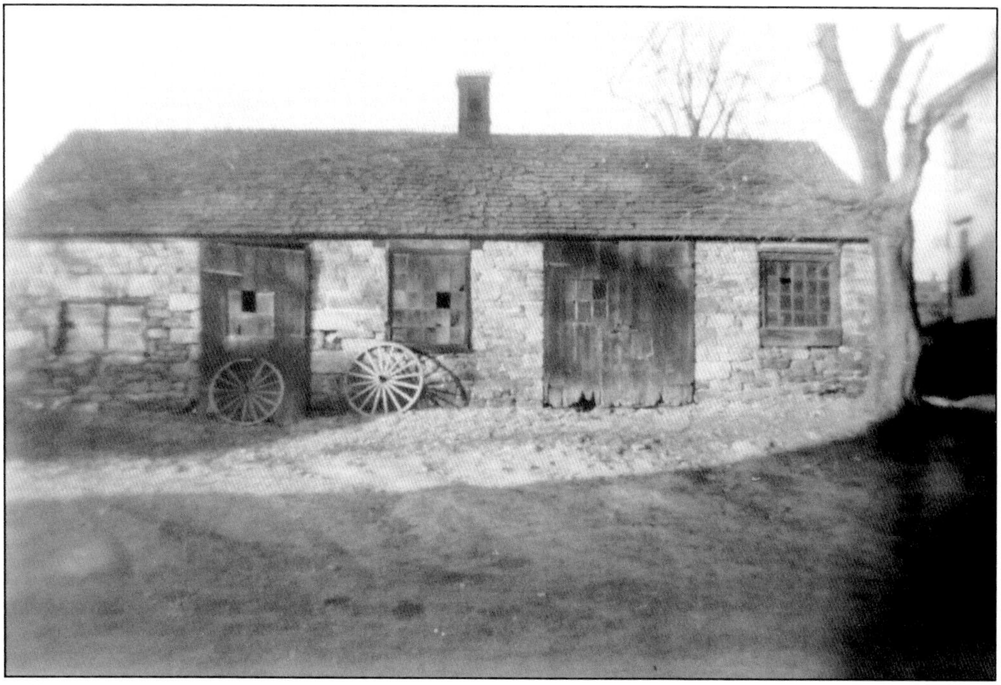

Although wagon wheels are still evident, business has obviously lessened at the Sergeantsville blacksmith shop in the 1930s. This building has been remodeled and is used to house the radio station WDVR today.

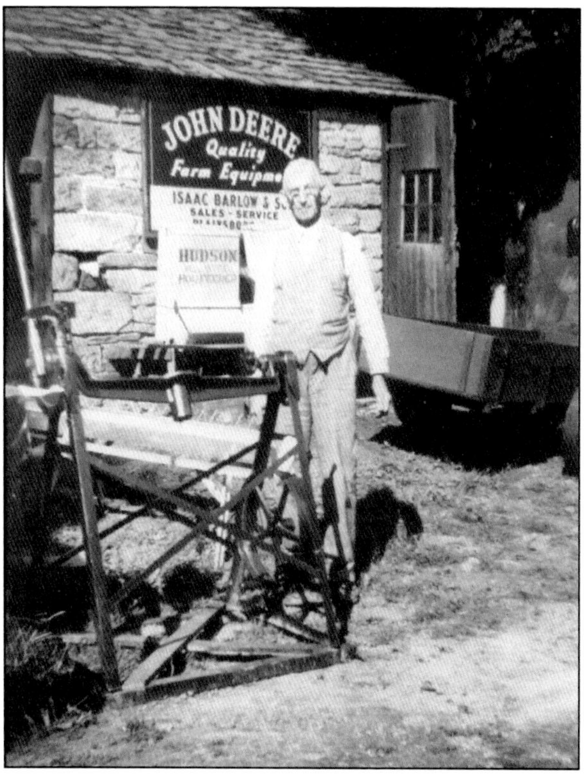

Ike Crum, a salesman for Isaac Barlow, the local John Deere dealer, is shown in front of the Sergeantsville blacksmith shop as he demonstrates a farm implement in the 1920s.

Three

THE SCHOOLS

One cannot talk to longtime residents about life in the township without the local schools becoming a prime point of discussion. Schools and the teachers had a major influence on overall life in the township and in many ways set the tone of the local culture. In the 1880s, there were 11 school districts and 12 teachers. The schools were guided by a local board of trustees and were open 10 months a year.

One account of the very earliest schools noted that they "often stood empty . . . for a long time, as schools were made up by subscriptions; at such times the children attended the adjoining districts." An early schoolhouse was built in 1796 and was located in the west corner of the township. It was 20 feet square and constructed of stone. However, there was also apparently a schoolhouse on the east side of the township as early as 1776.

Some of the school buildings were moved to various nearby sites around the township. Moore's School, for example, located between Ringoes and Sergeantsville, was moved twice over a distance of a mile. The Higgins District school on the east side of the township was also moved about a mile north as the trustees "put the house on wheels, and, with several yoke of oxen removed it" to another site. This removal in 1831 was done because the trustees all lived in another part of the district.

Perhaps the most unique school building was the Van Dolah's School located near the center of District 96 a half mile down the hill from the Sandy Ridge Church. This building was classically octagonal in shape and made of stone.

Some of these old school buildings are still in use around the township but have been primarily converted to dwellings. Several local district schools were phased out when the present school was built in Sergeantsville in 1950 and consolidated the education in the township. Many older residents look at the loss of those local schools with great and understandable nostalgia.

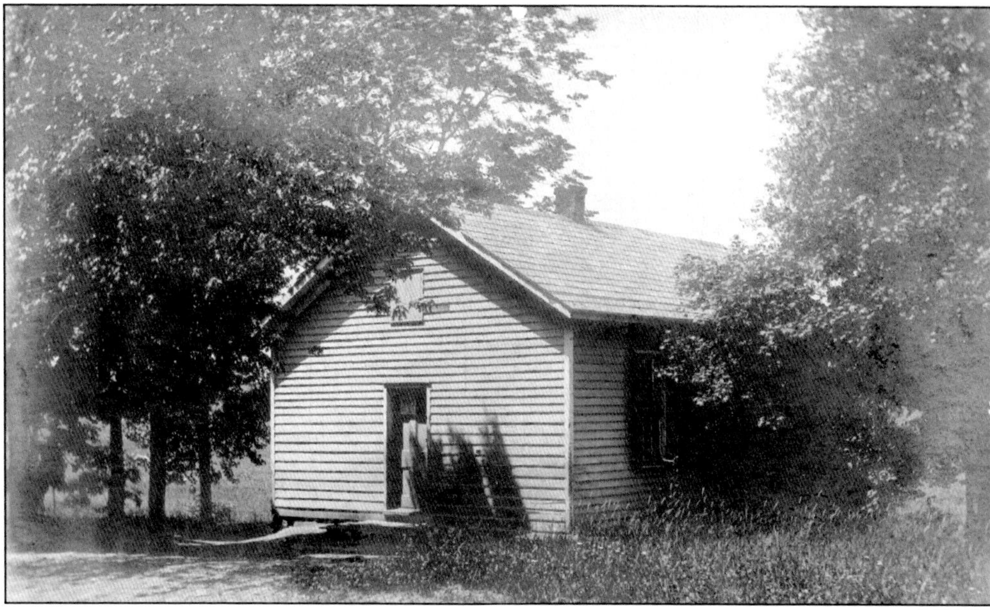

The Moore School, shown on August 1, 1908, was moved twice and rebuilt in 1866. Daniel Moore was the school founder and was born on the Wagner farm in 1729. A Moore School reunion was held on the day this photograph was taken, indicating the importance of these schools to the community in general and to those having attended them in particular.

MOORE'S SCHOOL RE-UNION,

August 1, 1908.

Daniel Moore, the founder, was born on the farm now occupied by Frank and Emma Wagner in 1729.

COMMITTEE.

Miss Emma Wagner,
Mrs. Frank Whitlock,
Rev. Amos Harris,
J. G. Moore,
Theo. S. Moore,
Reading D. Hoppock,
Charles Case,
Willis Myers,
Miss Rachel Bissey,
Mrs. I. P. Shepherd,
Cyrus Van Dolah,
Geo. R. Hann,
Wm. J. Fisher,
Amos H. Wilson,
Lemuel White,
Lewis Case.

The Moore School reunion announcement of August 1, 1908, gives a list of the people on the committee, including Wagner, Moore, Hoppock, Myers, Shepherd, Van Dolah, and Fisher. Interestingly, these names, among others, have all been important through the years in the township.

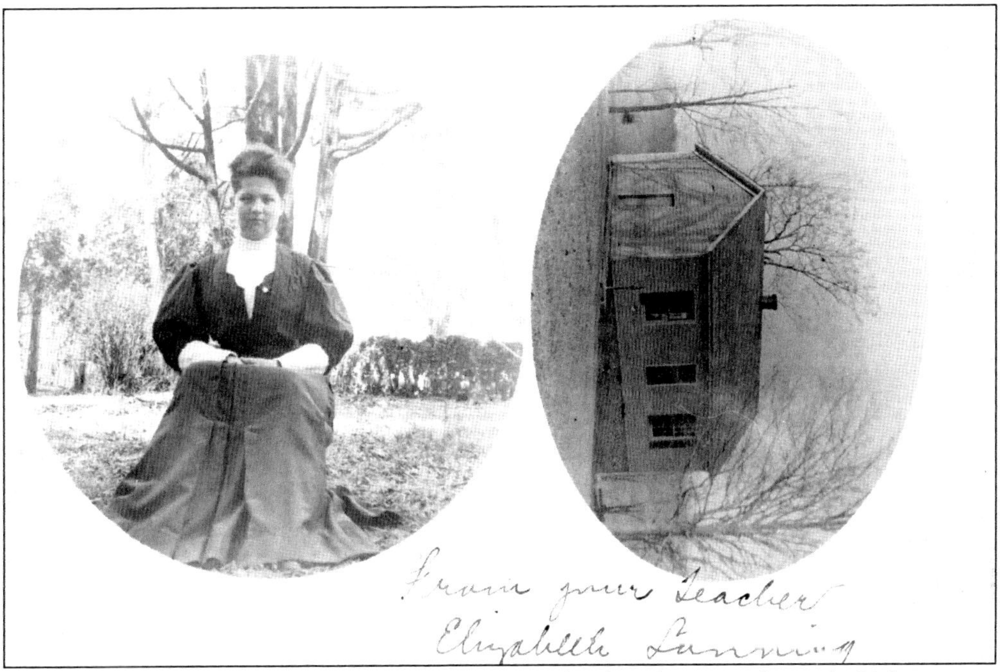

Elizabeth Lanning, a teacher in the fabled Moore School is shown in the early 20th century. Notice the classic pre–World War I dress worn by Lanning.

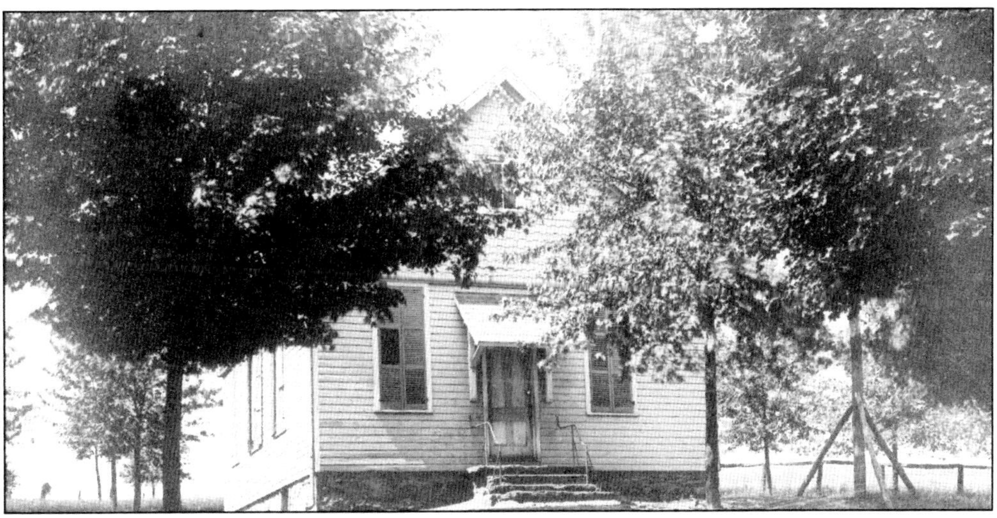

The Kendall School in Sergeantsville is shown in 1914. Additions were later made to this building. Notice the old stone foundation.

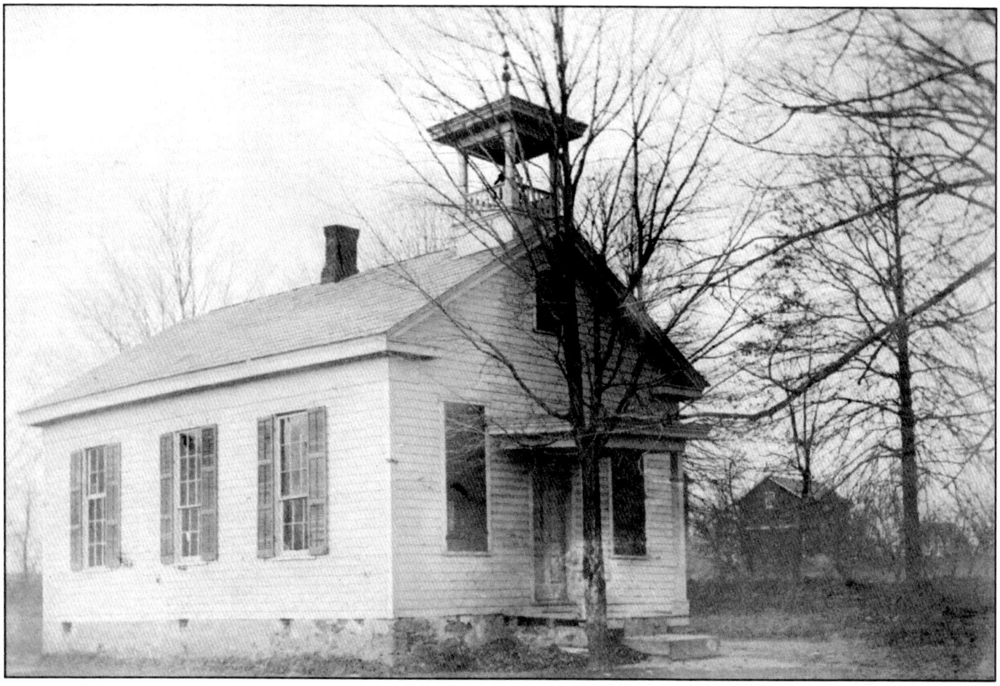

The public school building in Croton is shown during the winter in the early 20th century. Notice the striking bell tower and shutters. The building is still in use as a residence in Croton.

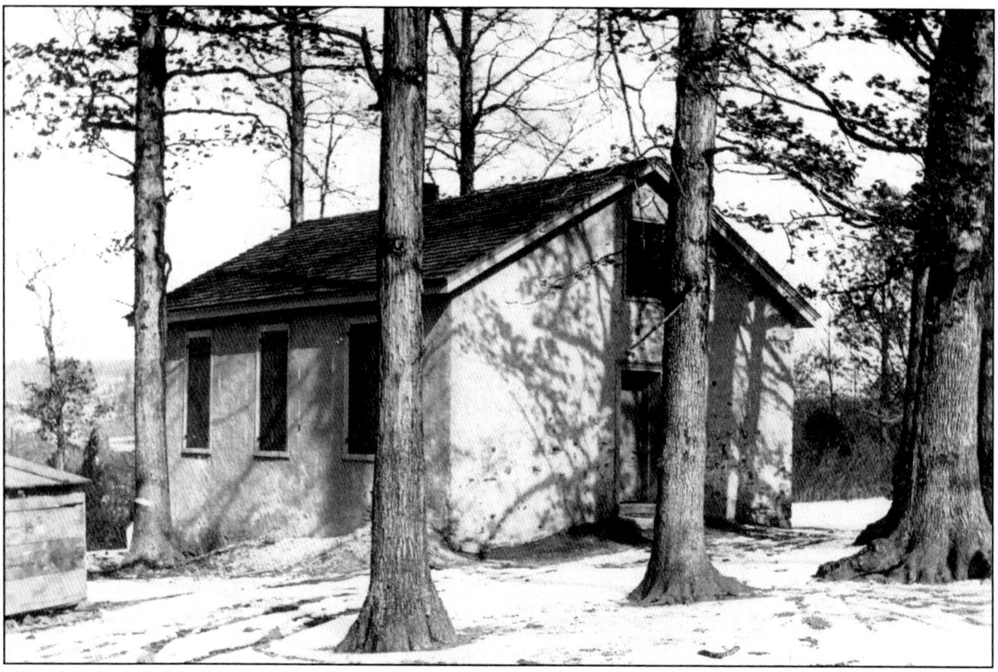

The Reading School, located in Rosemont, is shown in its wooded locale on the Rosemont-Raven Rock Road in the early 20th century.

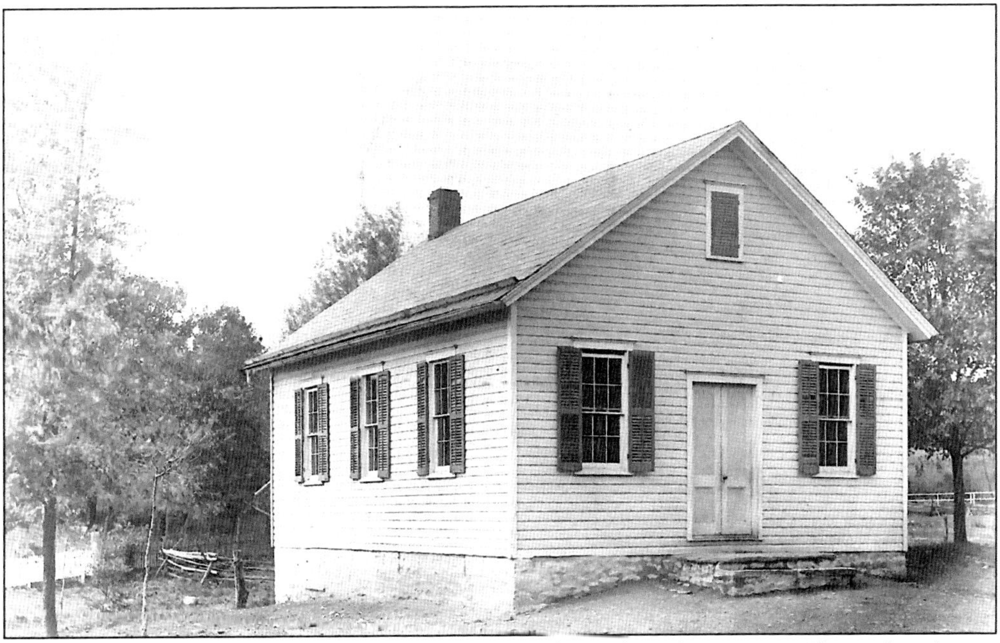

The Sand Brook School, seen here as it appeared in the early 20th century, still stands today on the left of Sand Brook Road near Route 523. It served at one time as the post office and a store.

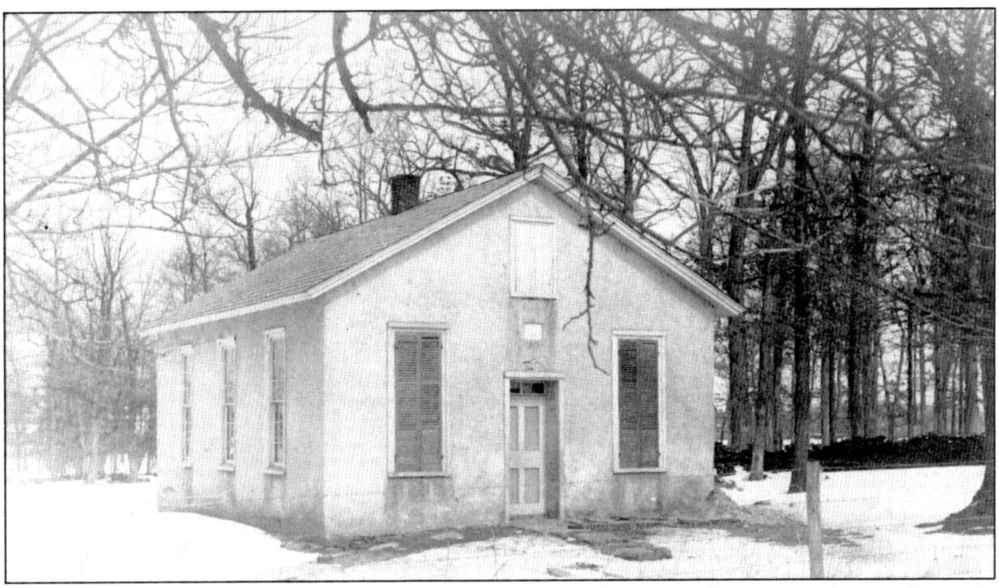

The Locktown School, which is a residence today, is shown in the winter during the early 20th century.

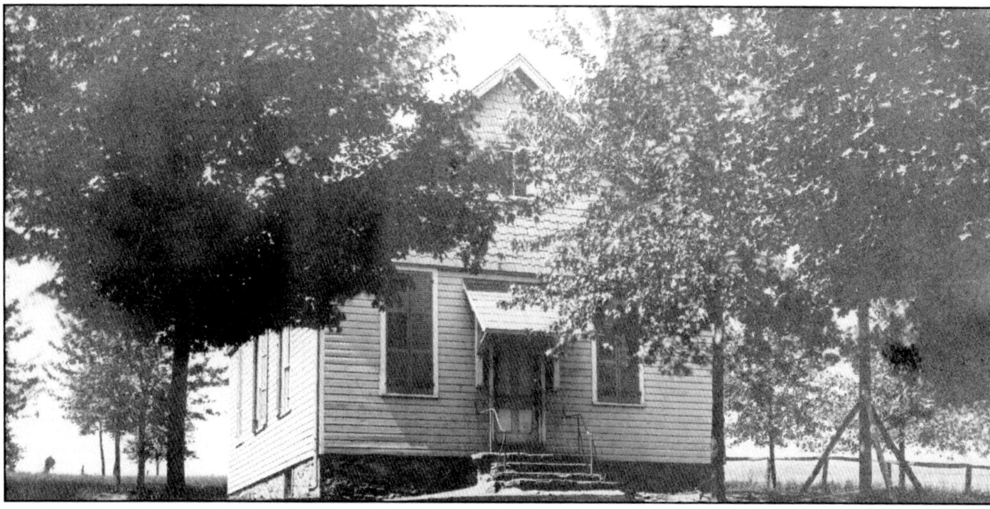

The Kendall School in Sergeantsville, which today is across from the Sergeantsville Grain and Feed store on Route 523, is shown here. It has been remodeled into a residence.

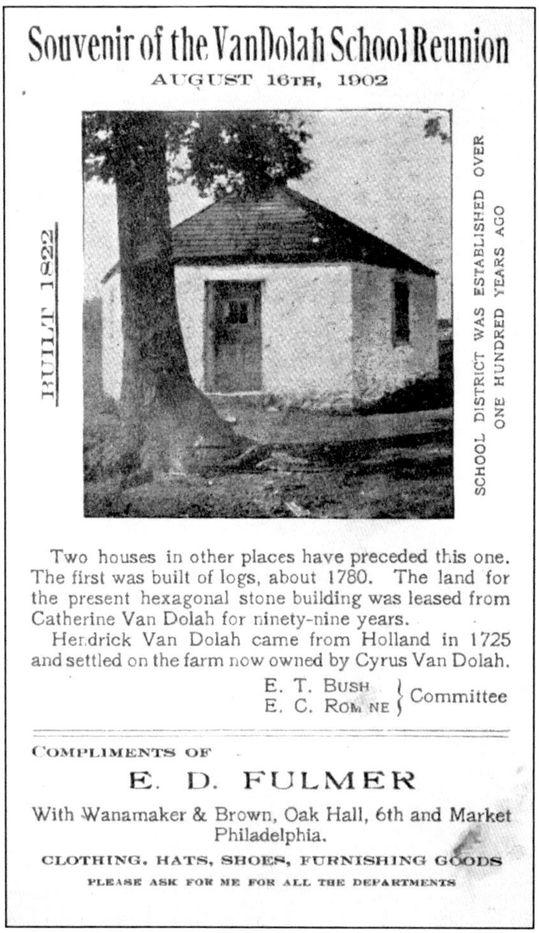

Souvenir of the VanDolah School Reunion

AUGUST 16TH, 1902

BUILT 1822

SCHOOL DISTRICT WAS ESTABLISHED OVER ONE HUNDRED YEARS AGO

Two houses in other places have preceded this one. The first was built of logs, about 1780. The land for the present hexagonal stone building was leased from Catherine Van Dolah for ninety-nine years.

Hendrick Van Dolah came from Holland in 1725 and settled on the farm now owned by Cyrus Van Dolah.

E. T. Bush } Committee
E. C. Romine }

COMPLIMENTS OF

E. D. FULMER

With Wanamaker & Brown, Oak Hall, 6th and Market Philadelphia.

CLOTHING, HATS, SHOES, FURNISHING GOODS

PLEASE ASK FOR ME FOR ALL THE DEPARTMENTS

This Philadelphia notice from the early 20th century gives the full particulars on the Van Dolah School. Notice the date of building is 1822, and the school committee proudly signed the statement.

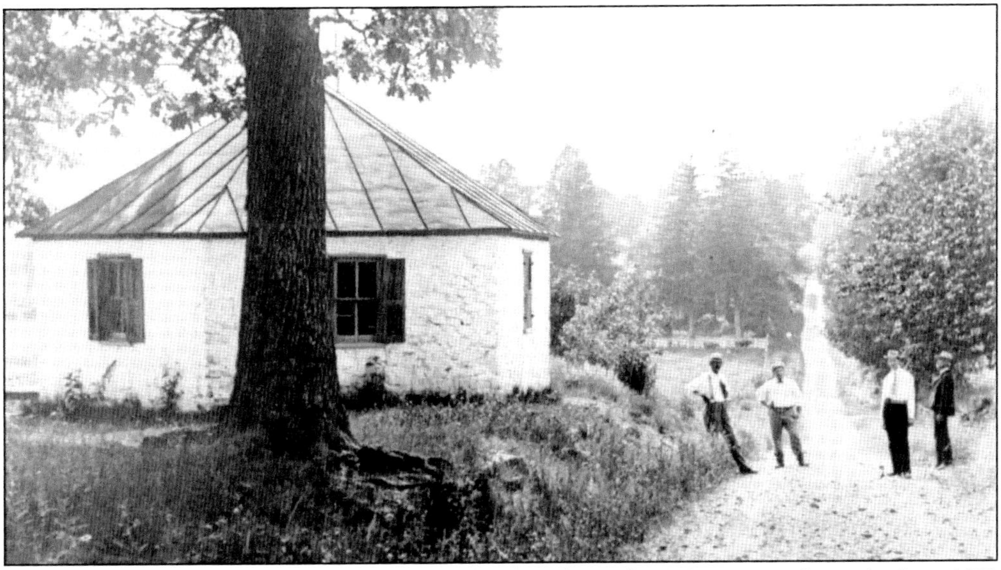

A great photograph shows the Van Dolah School in the early 20th century. It was built in 1822 and demolished in 1908. Edgar Van Dolah is shown on the left talking with Prof. E. T. Bush. The Sandy Ridge Church lies at the top of the hill, and the Van Dolah farm was just across the road. The road is the present Mount Airy-Sandy Ridge Road with the photographer looking from the Dilts Corner area toward the church.

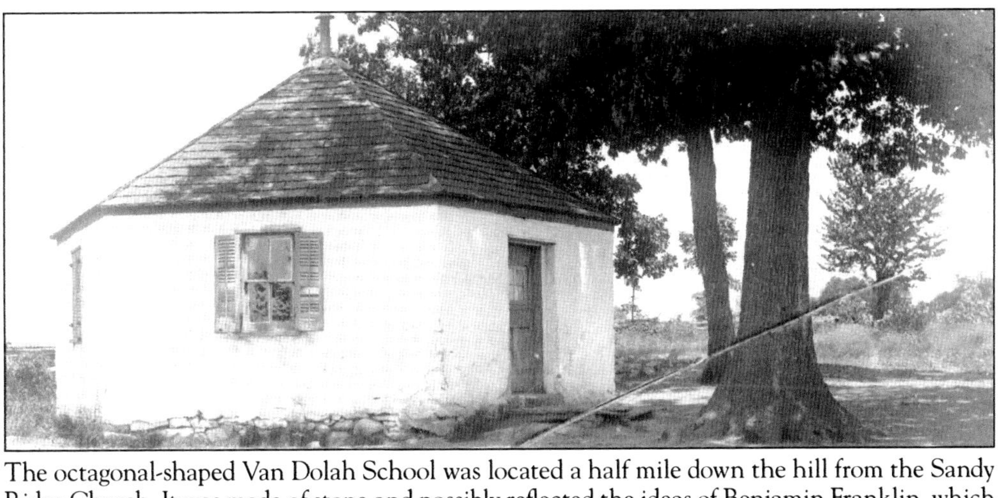

The octagonal-shaped Van Dolah School was located a half mile down the hill from the Sandy Ridge Church. It was made of stone and possibly reflected the ideas of Benjamin Franklin, which emphasized the practical arts, such as bookkeeping, as well as traditional academic subjects. Academies often were built in an octagonal shape, which was emphasized by Franklin.

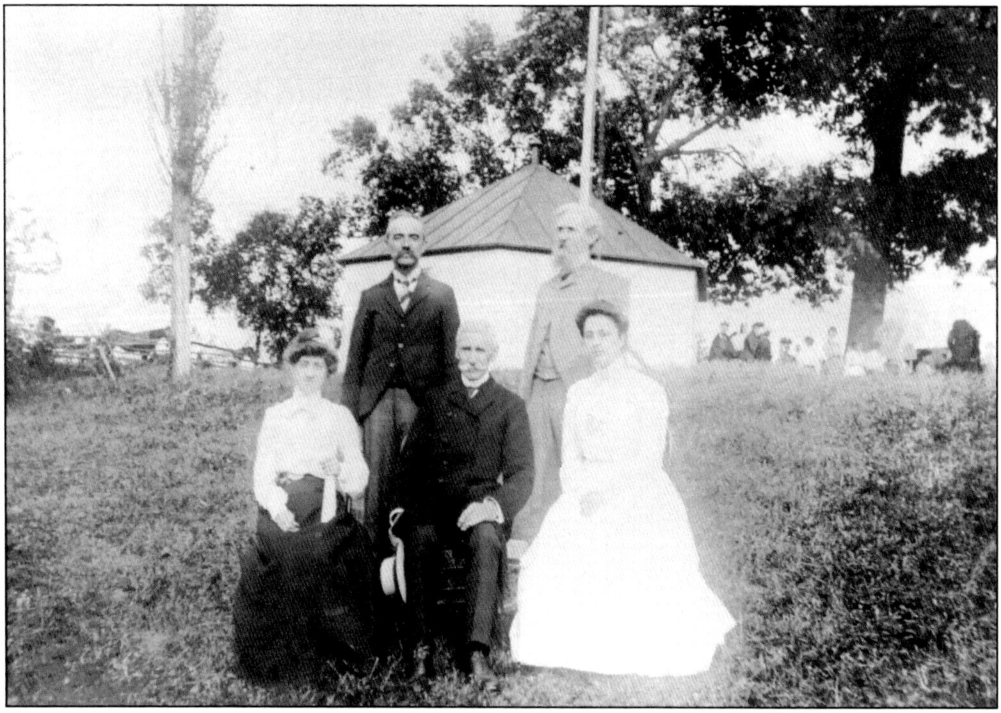

Another view of the Van Dolah School from the early 20th century shows some adults from the nearby Sandy Ridge community. The Van Dolah family owned a farm across the road from the school.

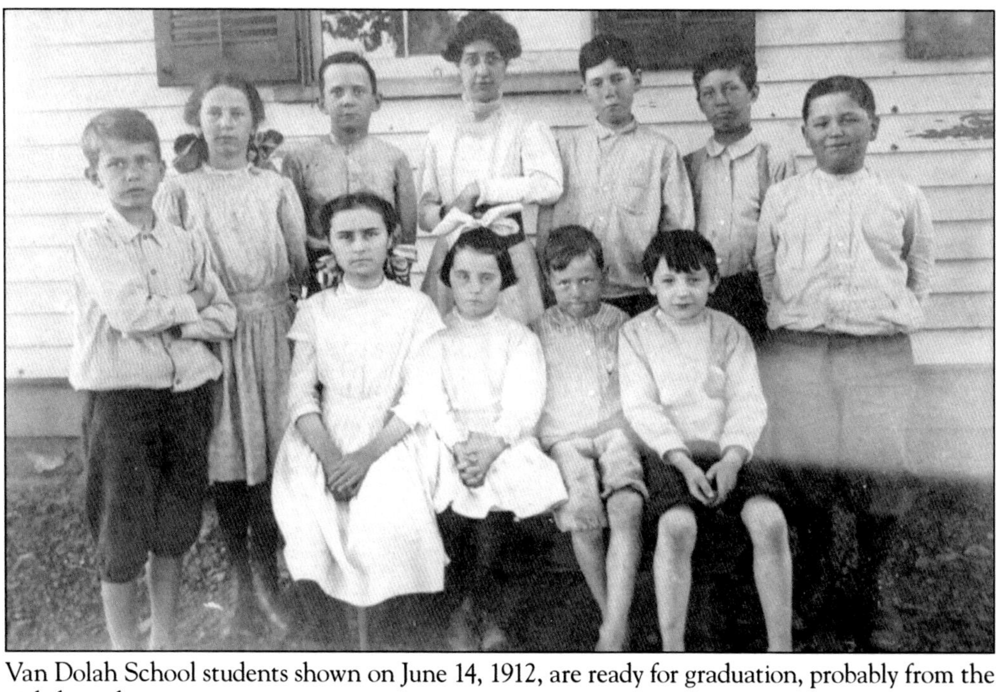

Van Dolah School students shown on June 14, 1912, are ready for graduation, probably from the eighth grade.

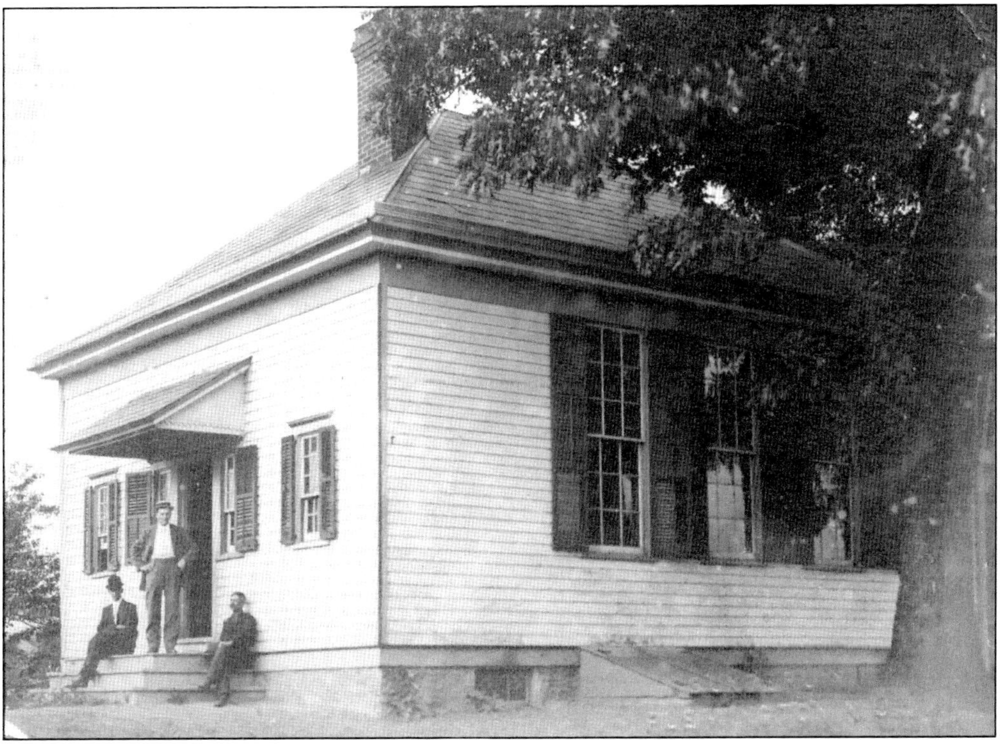

The new Van Dolah School built on Brookville Hollow Road is shown in the early 20th century after the original school was torn down in 1908.

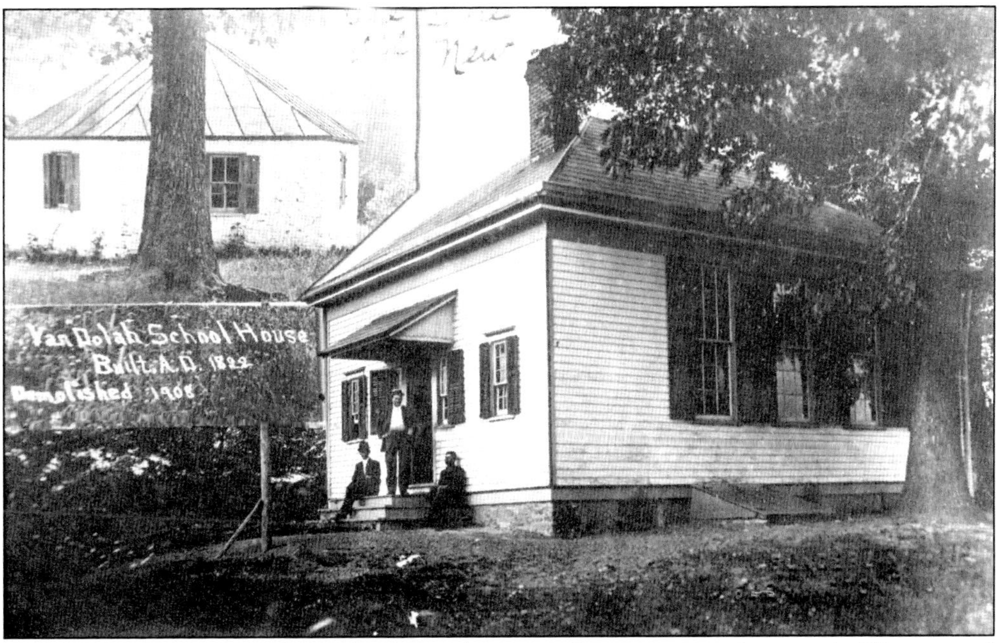

The new and old Van Dolah Schools are shown in this composite photograph. The original school had a chimney thrusting through the top center. This was perhaps the most unique school building in the township.

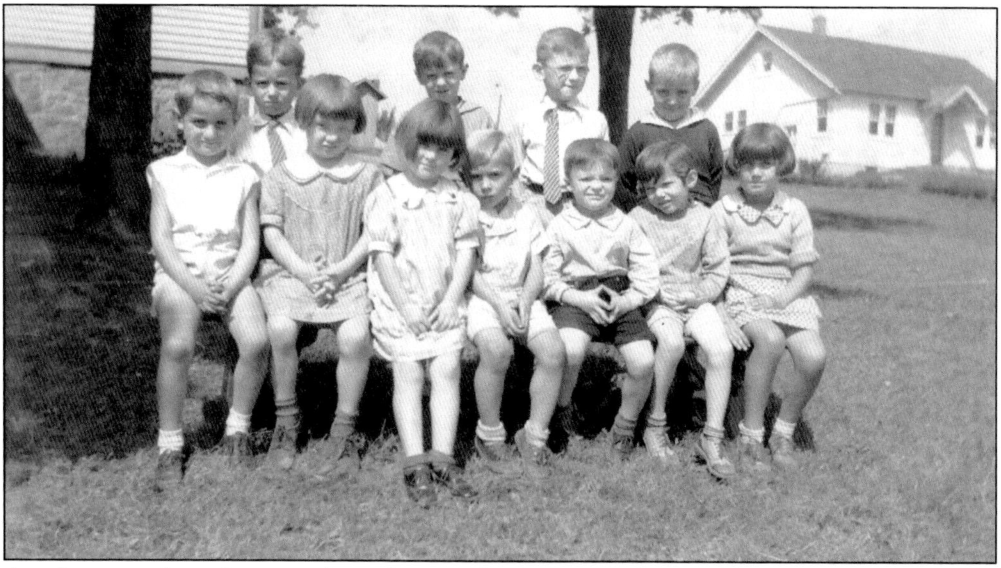

Another view shows lower-grade students at the Sergeantsville Kendall School in 1936. Notice the very put-together dress of these farming community children. The haircuts on the boys and the girls are particularly interesting.

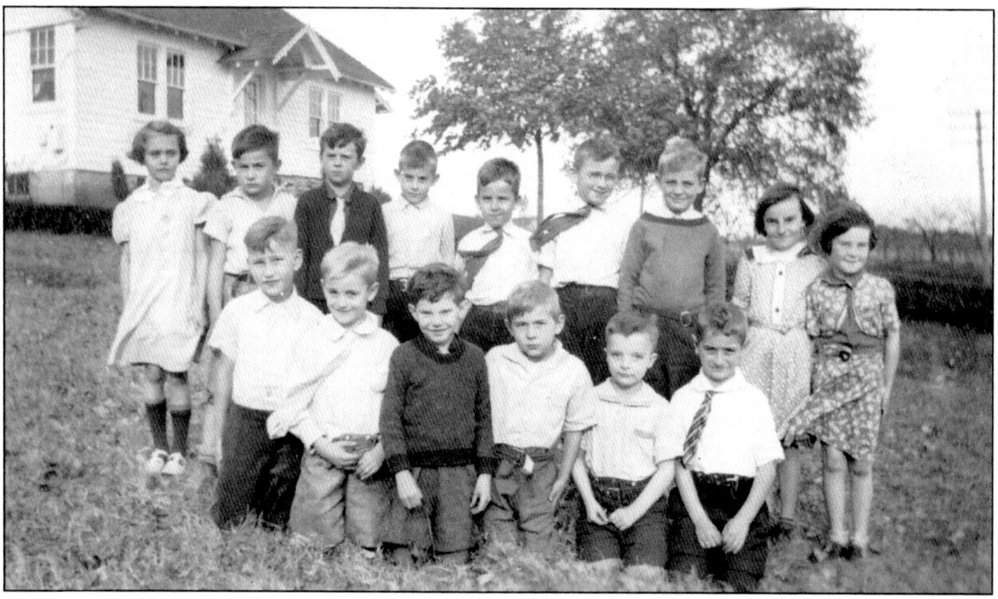

A Sergeantsville Kendall School second-grade class is shown in 1937; Dora H. Hoppock was the vividly remembered teacher. Hoppock was from a long-established Delaware Township family, and here again the pattern of old township families as teachers in the schools is evident.

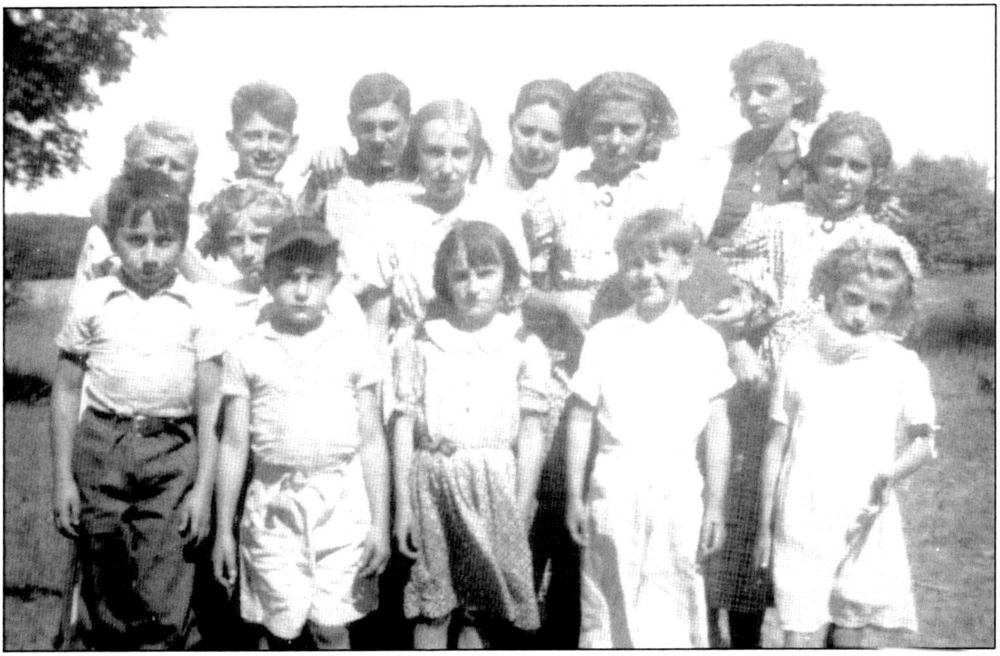

Moore School scholars are shown in this 1930s photograph. The Moore School building, located on the Sergeantsville-Ringoes Road, still exists as a residence that is now located on the corner of Sand Brook and Ringoes Roads (directly across from the Delaware Valley Horsemen's show facility).

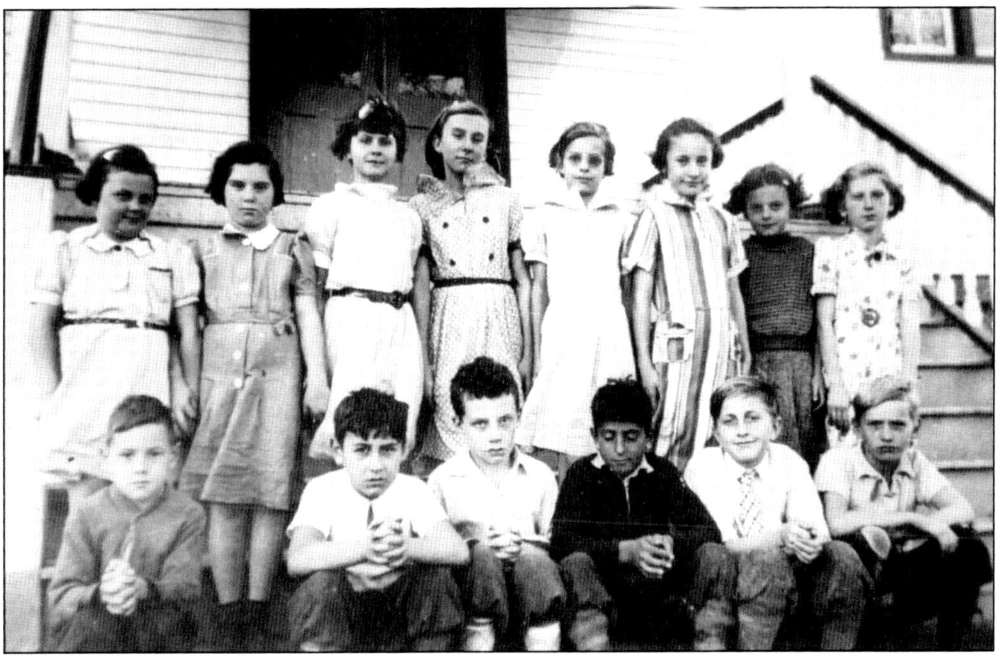

Sergeantsville Kendall School students are shown in the 1930s. Notice the uniformly folded hands and fingers of the boys and girls with their arms at their sides; the teacher was in charge here.

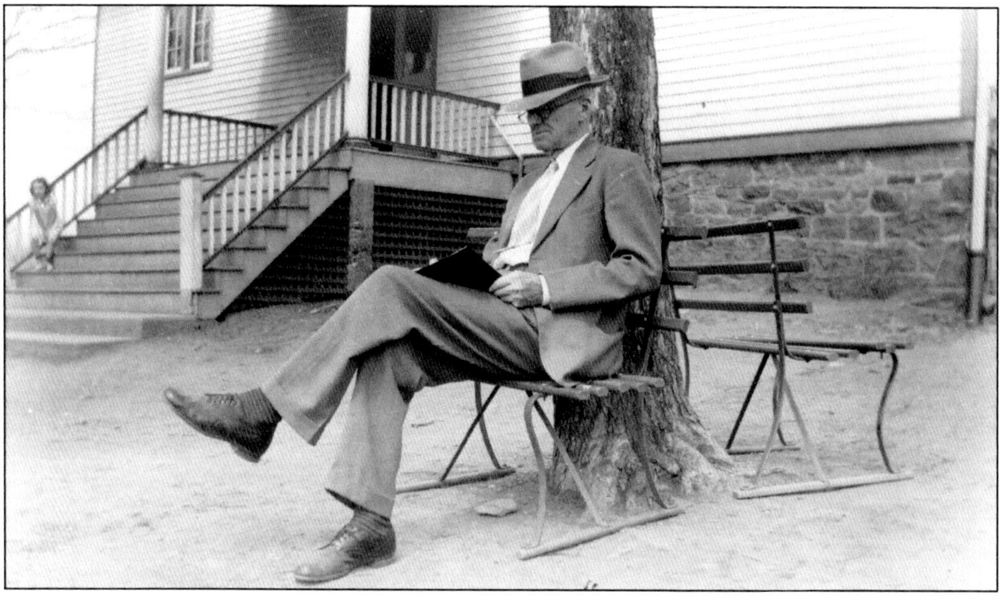

A classic photograph from the 1930s of "Mr. Myers, Boys Teacher" shows a self-possessed, hat-wearing professional. He obviously was in charge, as he is seen checking his roll book.

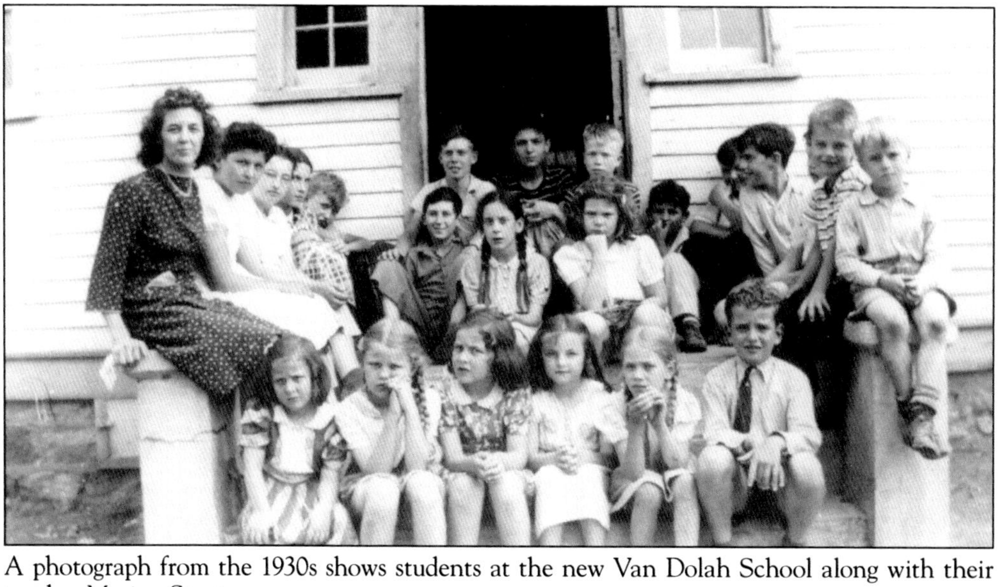

A photograph from the 1930s shows students at the new Van Dolah School along with their teacher Marian Staats.

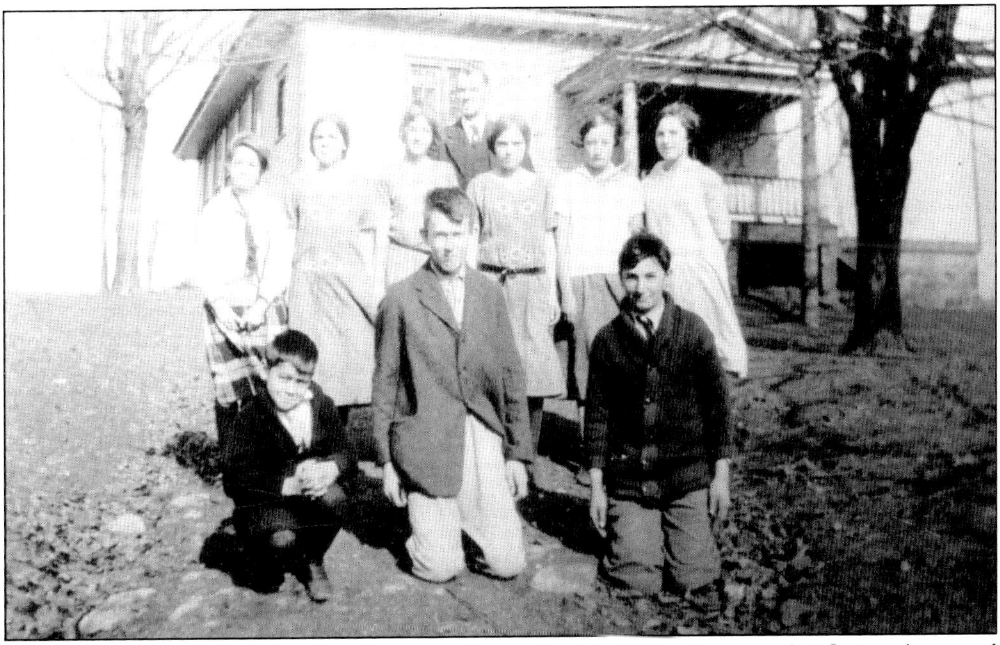

Sergeantsville Kendall School students are shown in this 1930s photograph. Notice the proud teacher in this Depression-era atmosphere.

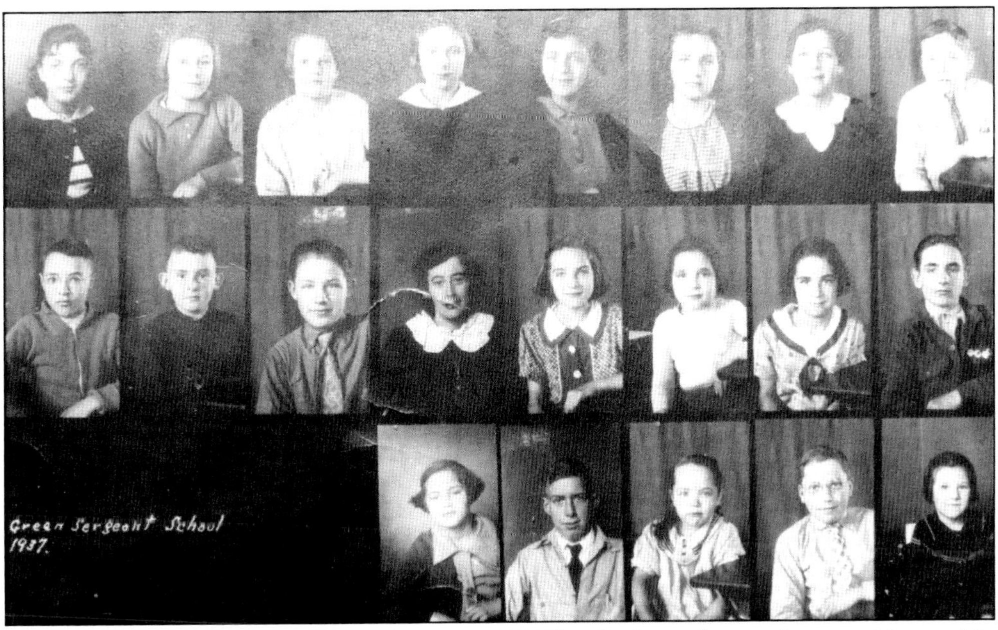

Green Sergeant School students are shown in 1937. Ellen Bodine, who was from an old township family, was the teacher during the 1936–1937 school year. The following year, Clint Wilson, who ran the general store in Sergeantsville, took over in this one-room schoolhouse and taught there through the 1941–1942 school year. He had attended a program at Rutgers University in order to qualify to teach. His amazingly productive life helped build the Delaware Township community; he was also responsible for recruiting and training people for the first police and fire departments.

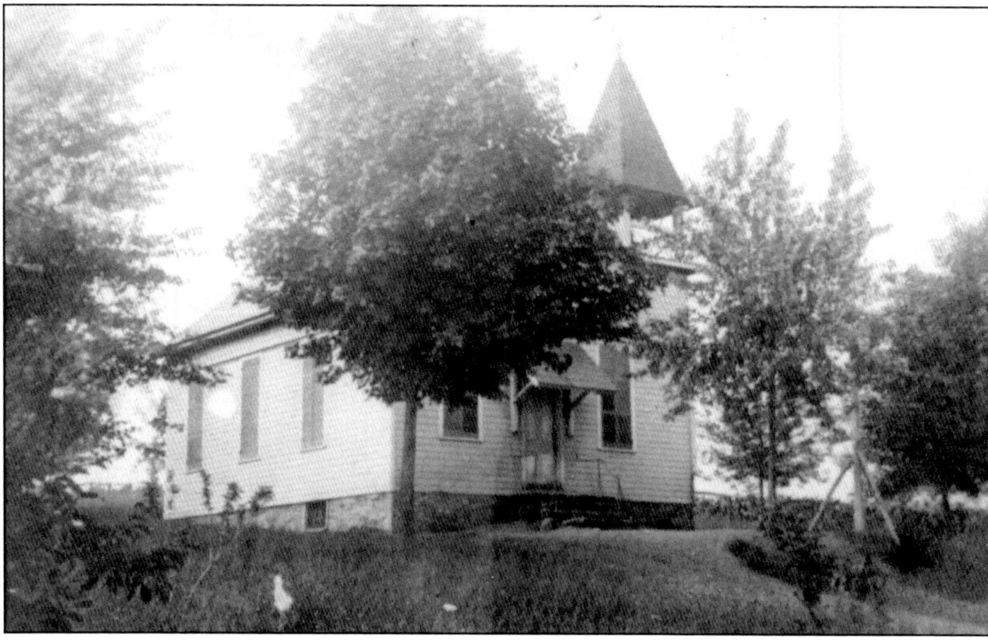

The Sergeantsville Kendall School is shown here in the summer during the 1930s. Notice the large bell tower.

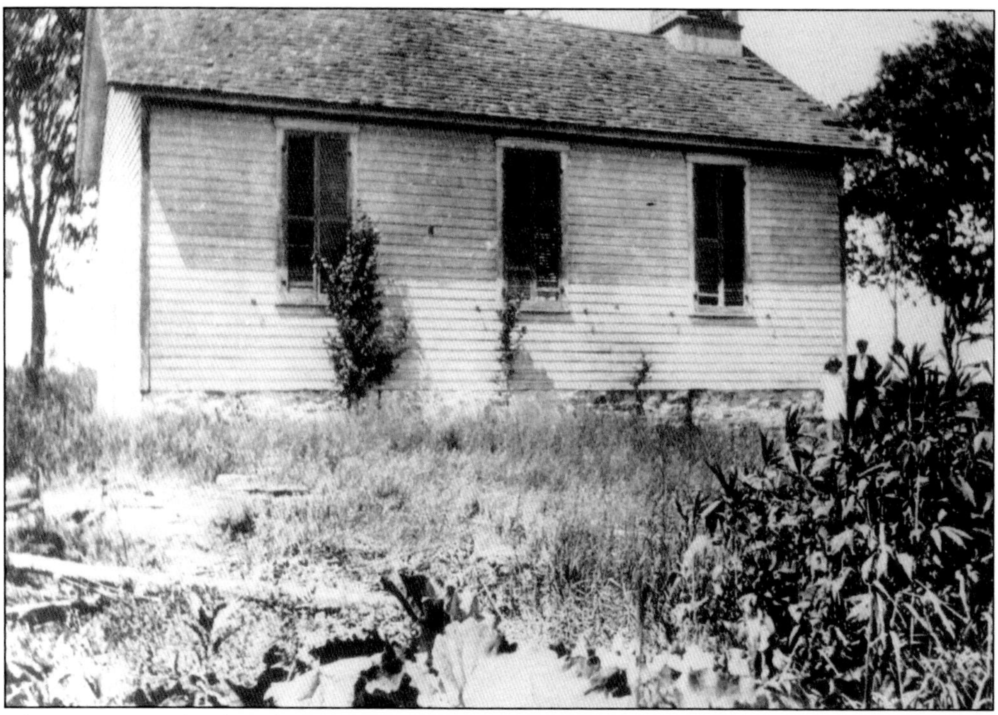

The Higgins School and yard are pictured in the 1930s, and the surroundings have a Depression-era cast.

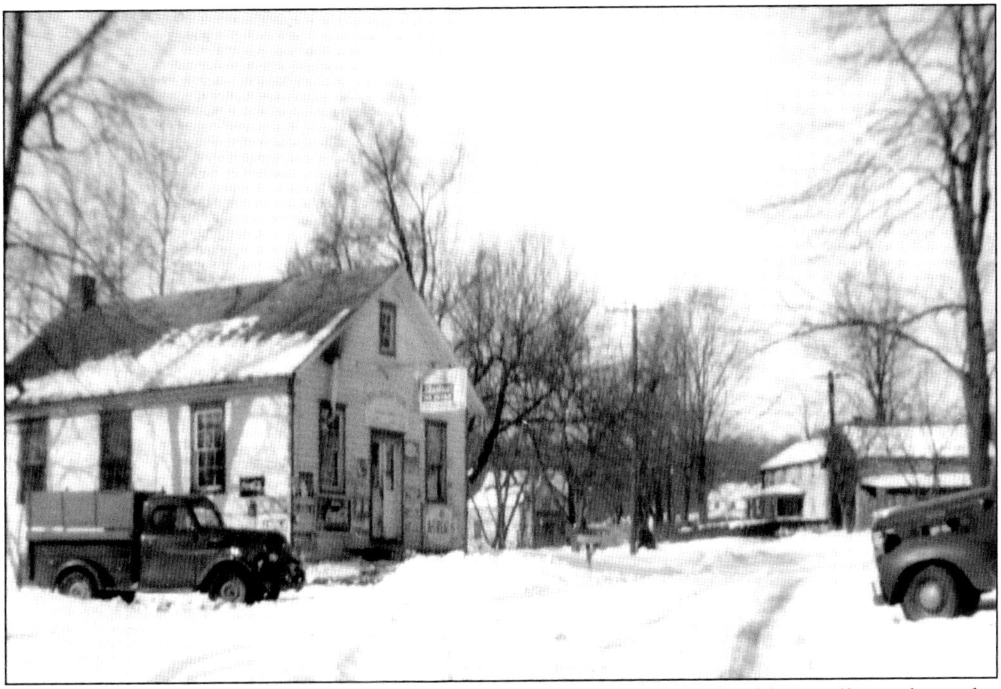

The Sand Brook School is shown during a winter in the 1940s. This building still stands on the left at Sand Brook Road near the intersection with Route 523. It was once utilized as a store that sold sodas, gum, and other small grocery items and was a hangout for some of the local people.

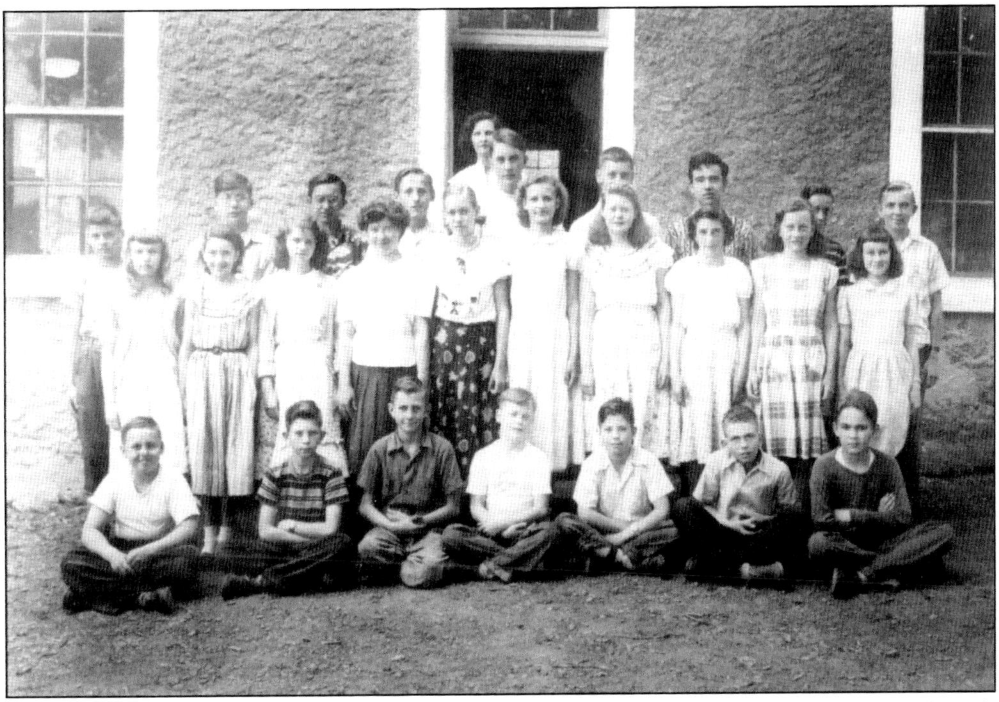

Well-dressed students from the Green Sergeant School are shown in this 1949 photograph with their hands and arms arranged uniformly. The school was located near the covered bridge.

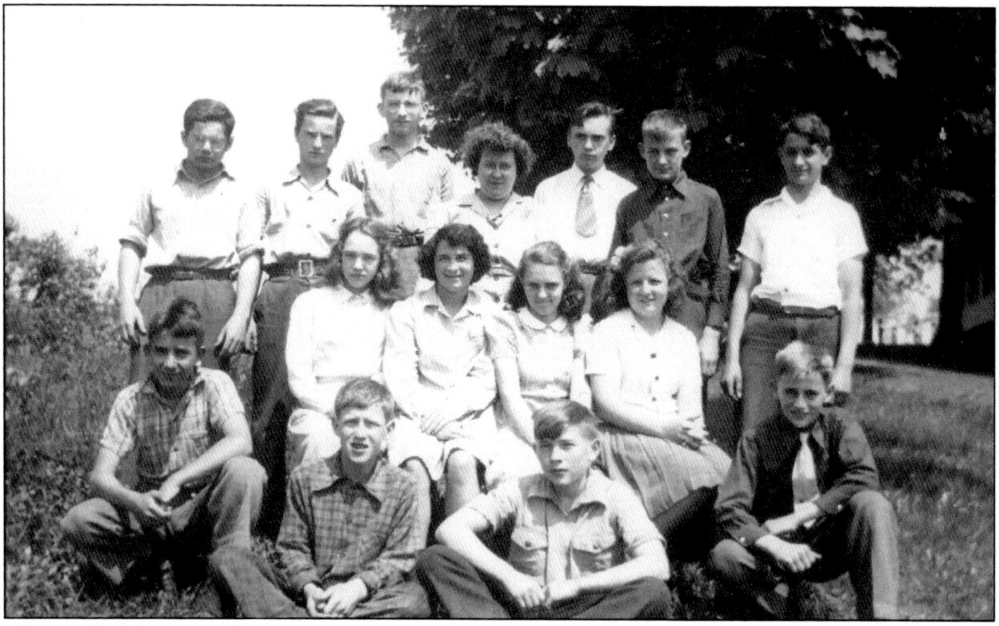

This end-of-the-year photograph from the 1940s shows happy graduates with Paul Kurzenberger on the lower right "decked out" in a stylish dark shirt and white tie.

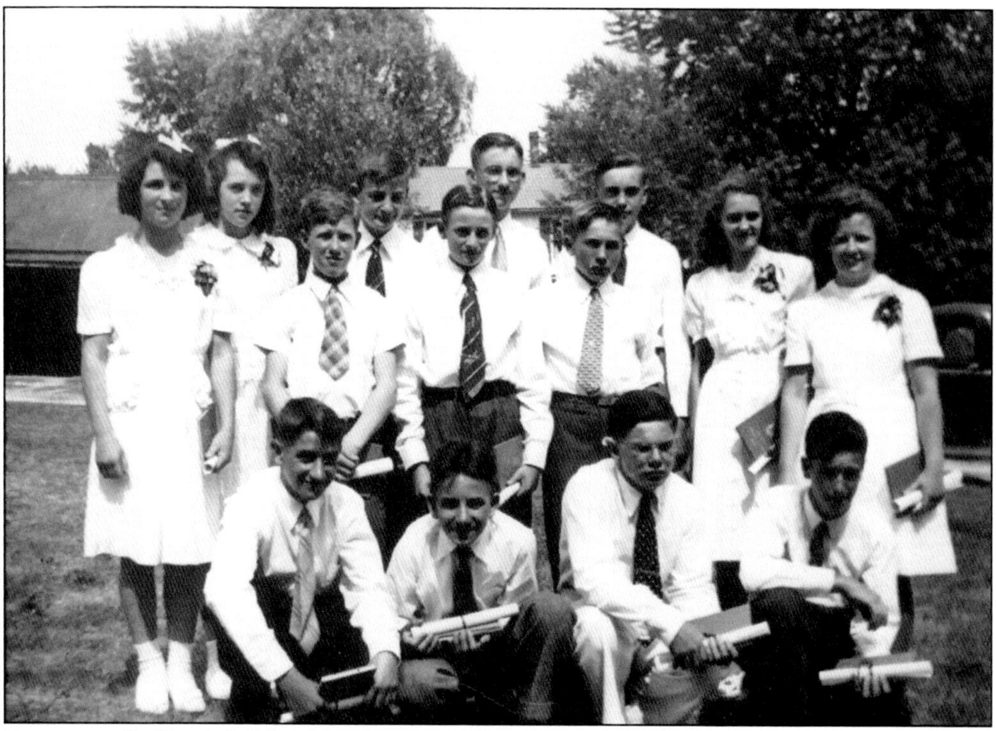

Sergeantsville Kendall School graduates are shown in 1944. The obviously proud students are ready to go on to high school.

Four

The Churches

The impact of churches and religion on life in the township has been quite pronounced. Some of the most important churches historically were the Locktown Baptist Church, Sandy Ridge Baptist Church, Locktown Christian Church, Sergeantsville Methodist Episcopal Church, German Baptist Church, Sand Brook German Baptist Church, Rosemont Methodist Episcopal Church, and Croton Baptist Church.

A number of these churches had a membership in the hundreds during the 19th century. The first church meetinghouse in the township was built in 1750 in Locktown, was made out of logs, and measured 30 by 38 feet. The present stone structure was built in 1819 on a lot nearby.

The Amwell Church of the Brethren celebrated its 275th year in 2008. This church (after which Dunkard Church Road is named) originally started as a German-speaking congregation in 1733 and met in a rotation of homes until the first meetinghouse was built in 1811 on the present church site. It was originally called the Amwell German Baptist Church, but the name was changed in World War II to the Amwell Church of the Brethren. The present vitality of this church is emblematic of many churches in the township. Each of the township's churches has been distinguished by the longevity of their tenure in the community, often starting from a very small initial group.

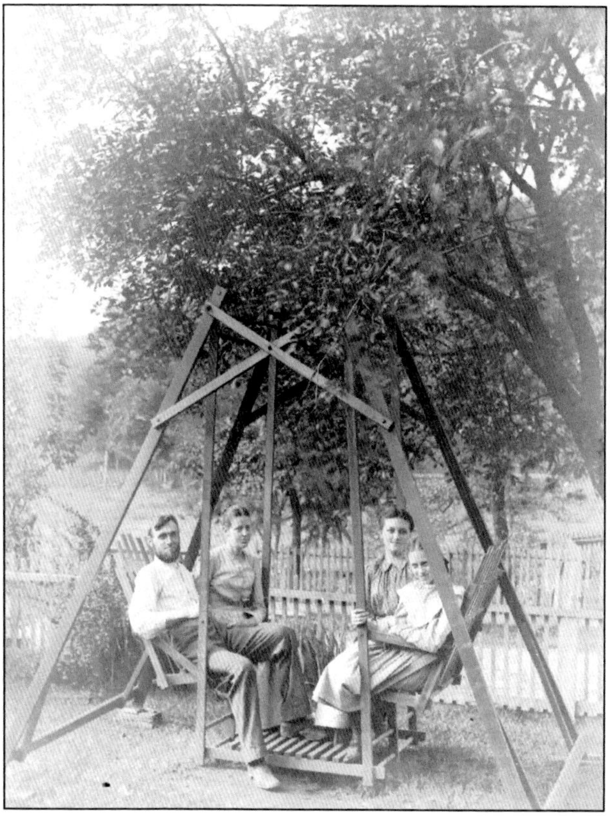

Rev. Henry T. Horne, pastor of the Sand Brook Brethren Church, and his family are shown relaxing on a swing in the early 20th century.

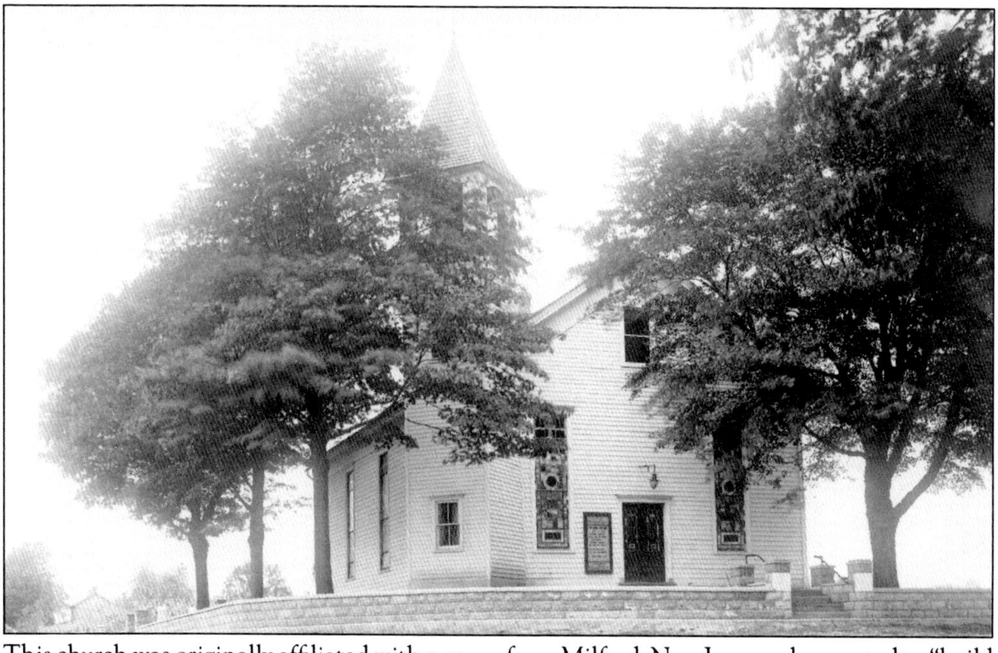

This church was originally affiliated with a group from Milford, New Jersey, who wanted to "build a local church" and did so in Locktown in 1829. The present building, part of the Presbyterian church today, was erected in 1864. The steeple placement, set at an angle, is quite unusual.

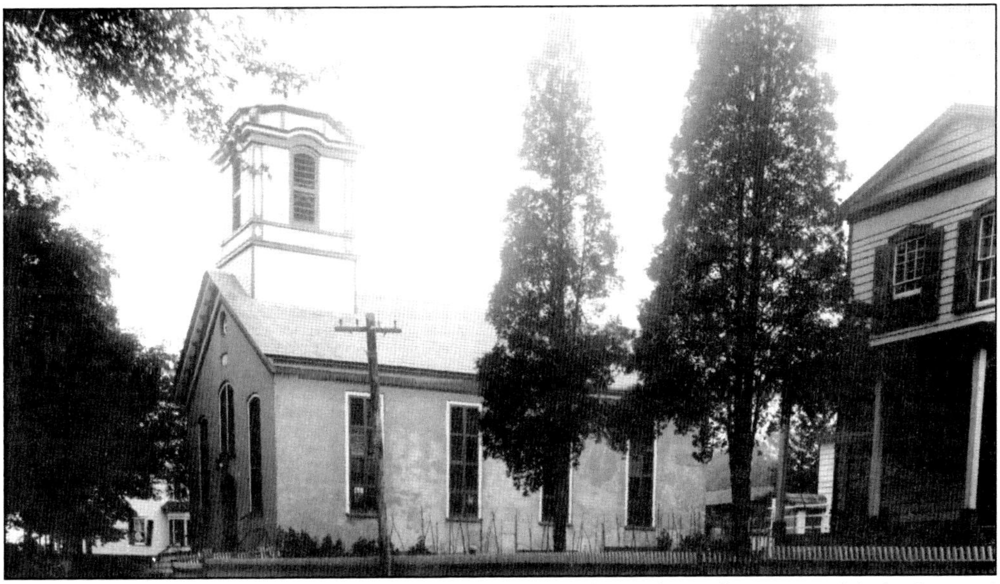

The Methodist church in Sergeantsville is shown in the early 20th century. Methodist and Baptist churches have predominated in Delaware Township, partly because early religious workers from those groups were very active in evangelizing the area and the two Protestant denominations appealed to the middle-class farm culture that made up most of the township's population historically.

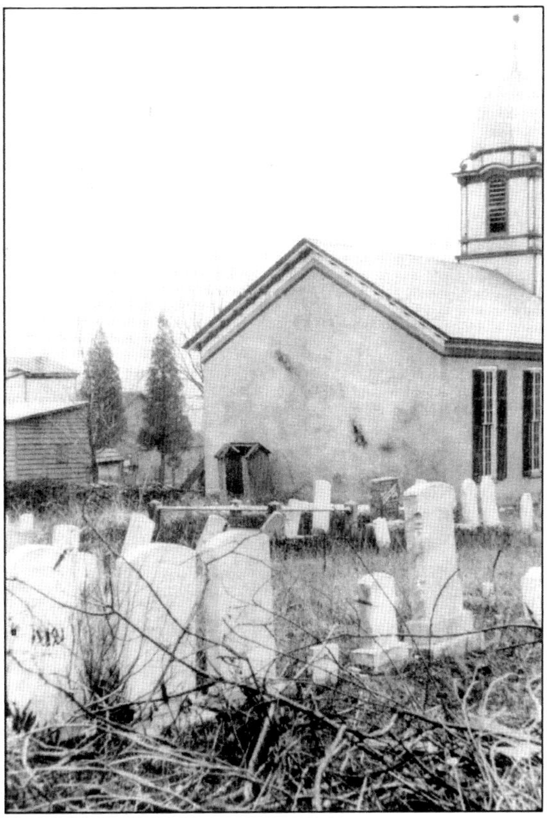

Shown in this early-20th-century photograph is the back of the Methodist church, the cemetery, and an outhouse in Sergeantsville.

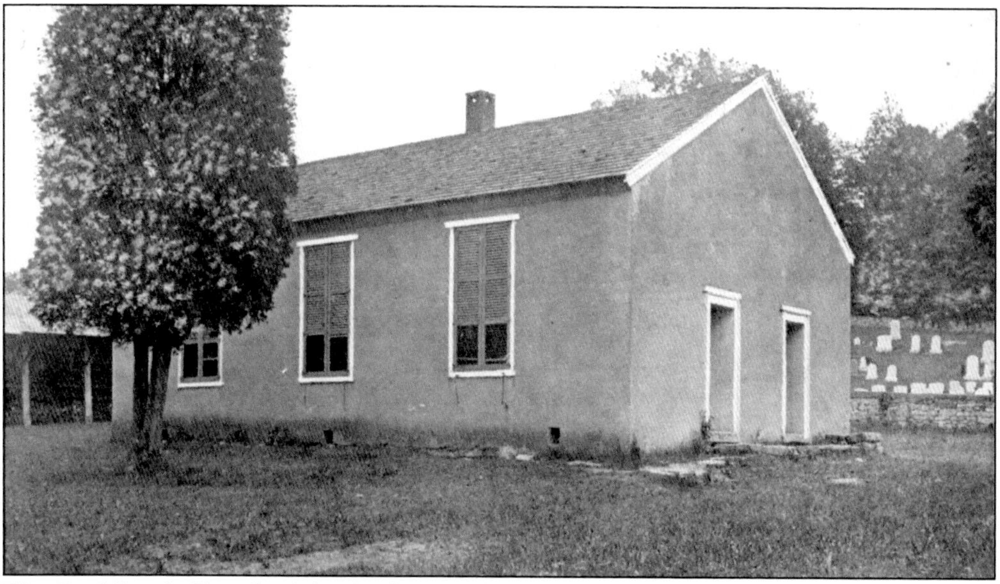

The Sand Brook Church of the Brethren is shown in the late 19th century. This church was formed by a breakaway group from the Amwell Church of the Brethren in 1849. The churches are located about one mile apart on Sand Brook Road. The Amwell Church came to be known as the Dunkard Church, and the Sand Brook Church was known as the United Christian Church. The two congregations reconciled in 1913, and services were held in both churches until 1920, when the Sand Brook Church closed.

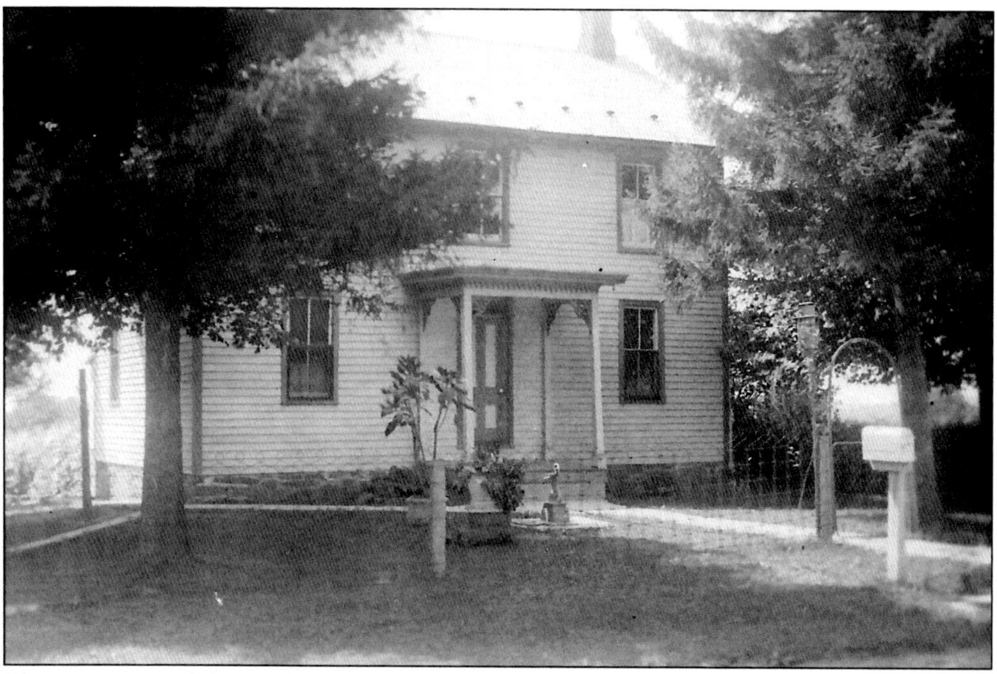

The parsonage of the Locktown Baptist Church is shown in this photograph in the early 20th century.

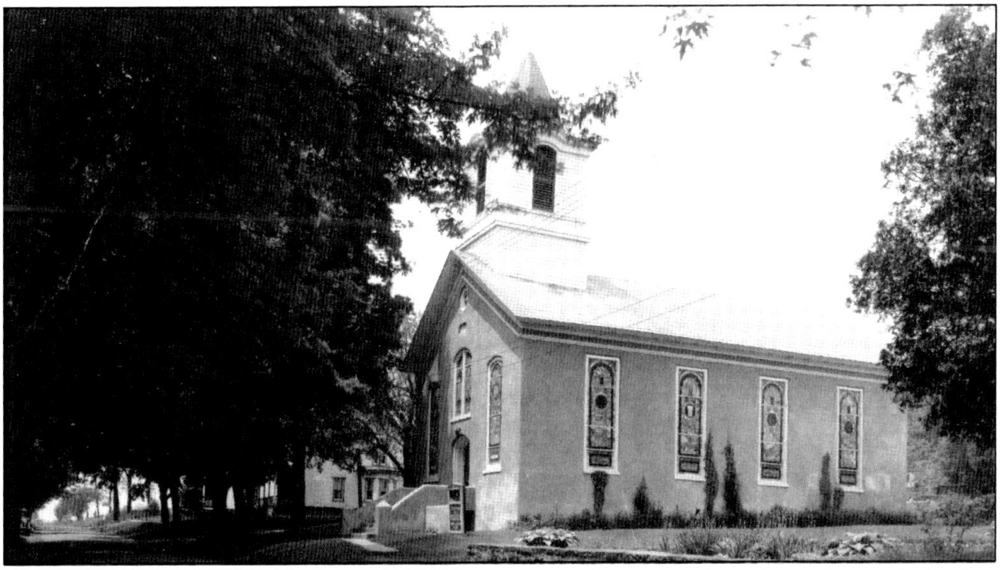

The Methodist church in Sergeantsville is shown as it looms up the hill on Route 604 a few doors west of today's general store. This photograph was taken in the middle 20th century.

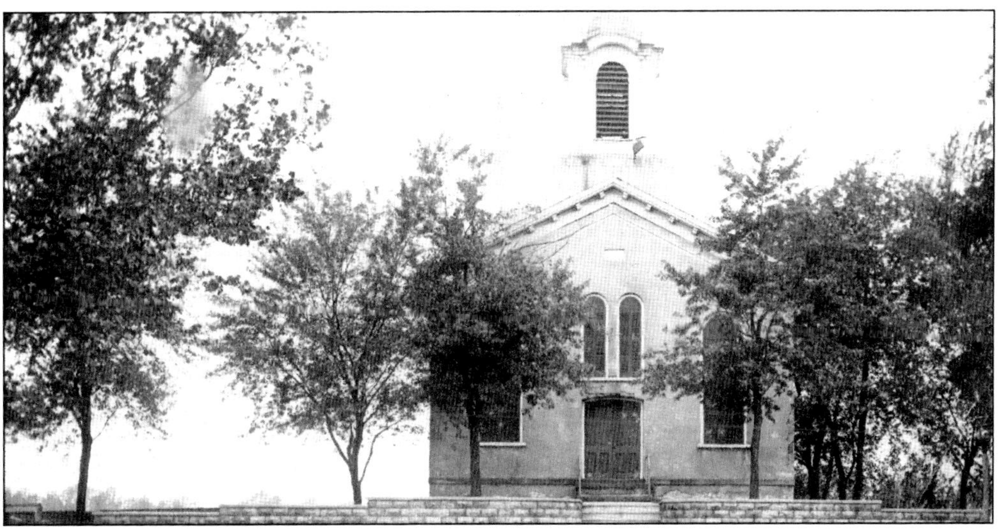

The Sandy Ridge Baptist Church is shown in the early 20th century. This church was formed as an offshoot of the Flemington Baptist Church and was served by that pastor, as he did a circuit during its early days.

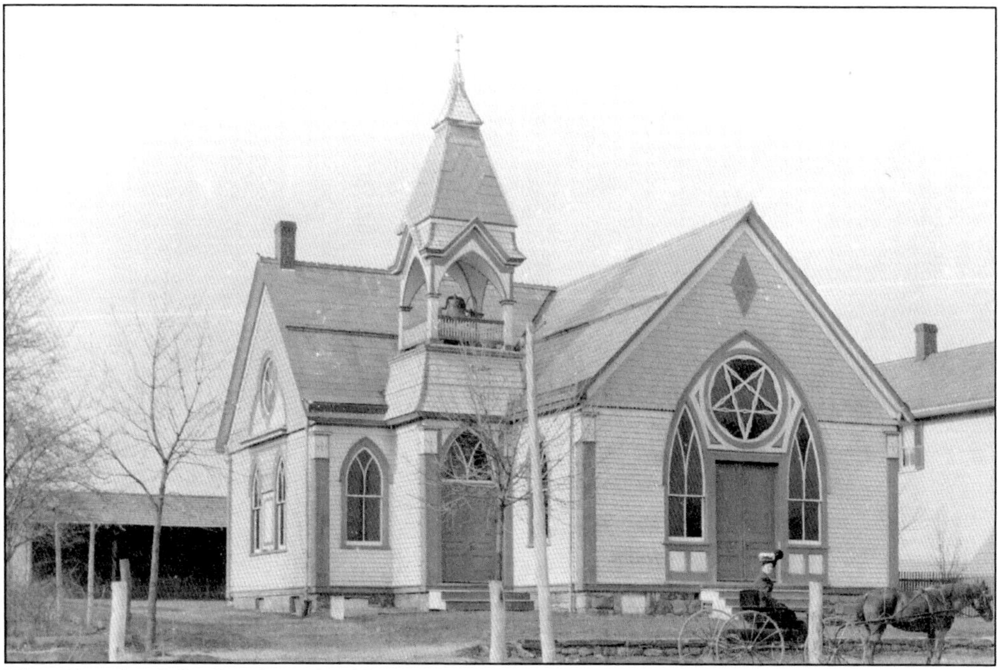

The Church of the Brethren building in Sergeantsville is shown in the early 20th century; it was originally established by a group that left the Amwell Church of the Brethren. This church ceased operating in 2007, and the building was put up for sale in 2009.

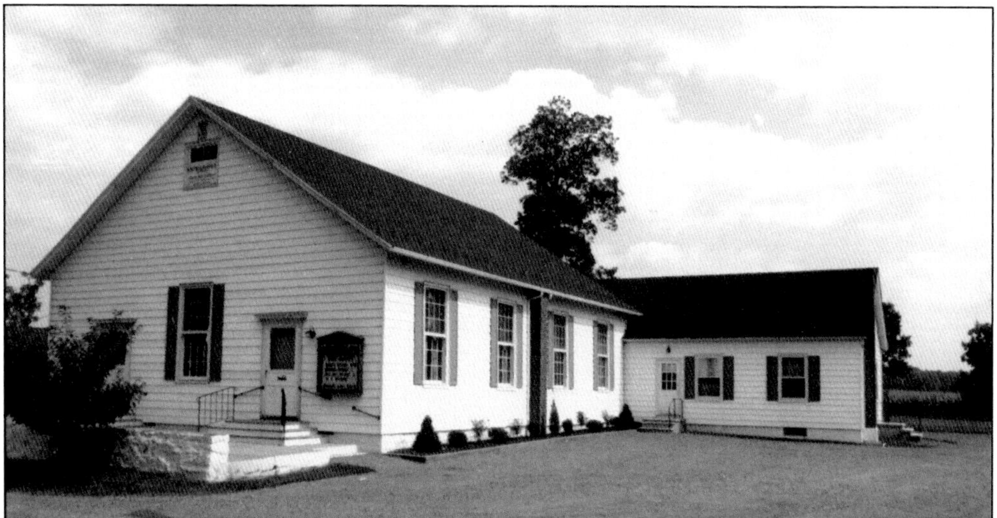

The Amwell Church of the Brethren is shown in 1989 after the successful rebuilding of the edifice. The almost miraculous rebuilding of this church structure is good evidence of the congregation's strong faith and community spirit. (Courtesy of the Amwell Church of the Brethren.)

The Croton Christian Church is shown in an early-20th-century winter scene. This building, minus the steeple, is situated next to the Wickecheoke Creek along Route 579 (the old Trenton-Easton Turnpike) and is now a lawn mower shop.

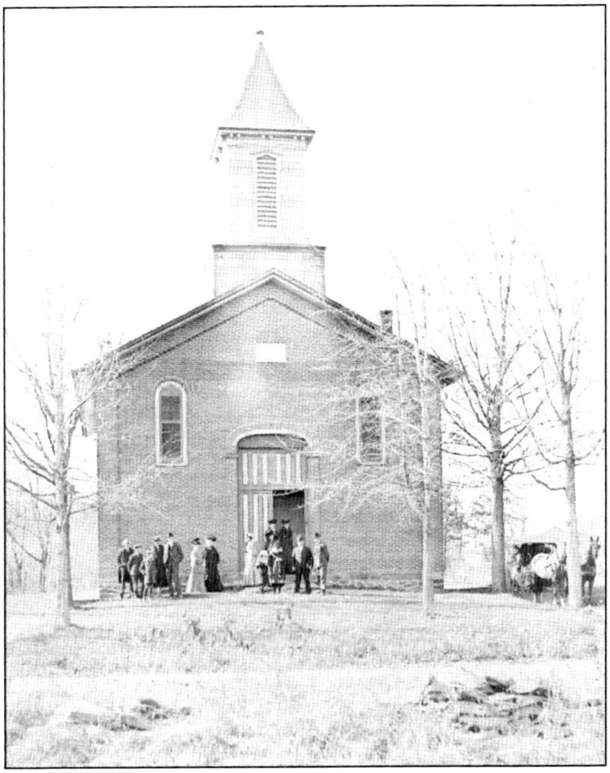

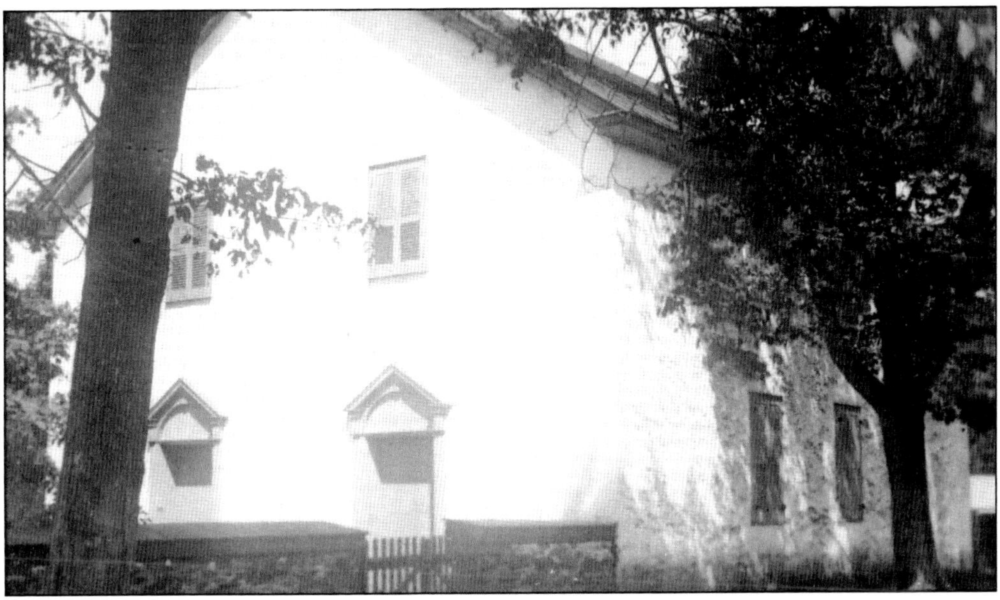

The Locktown Baptist Church is shown after extensive remodeling and preservation was done by the Friends of the Stone Church group. It was formerly the Old School Baptist Church. The congregation had a split at one point in earlier days, and one group put a padlock on the door, which the rival group then cut. The name of the town comes from that incident. The interior of this church is classic in its design with the pulpit raised to a 10- to 12-foot height in the front of the church.

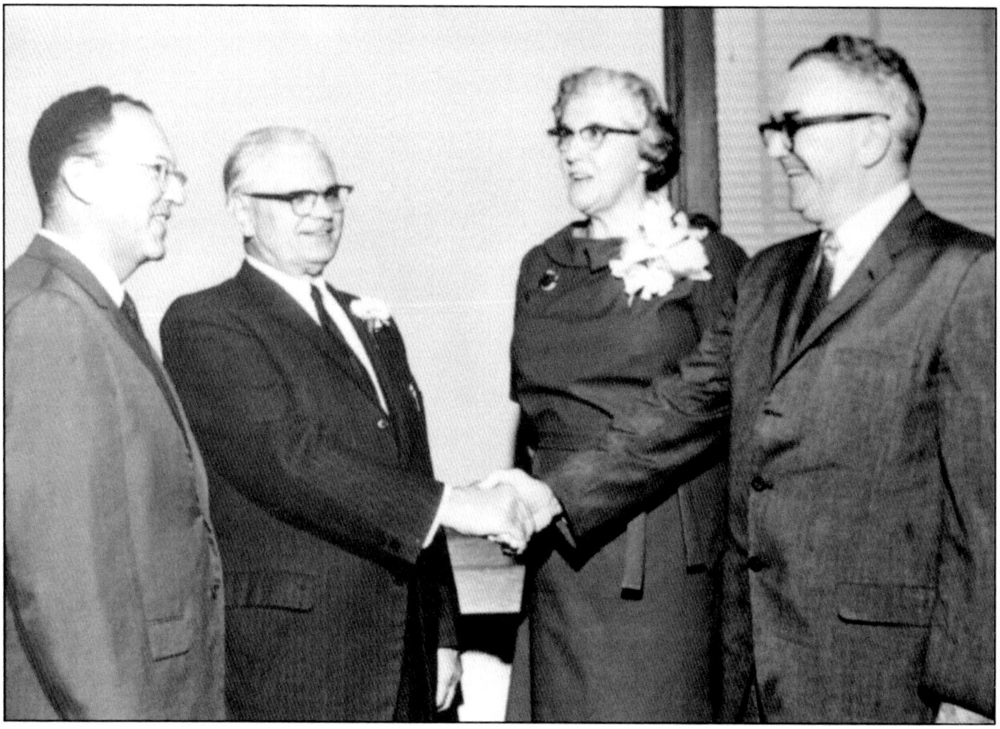

Rev. George Landis of the Amwell Church of the Brethren and his wife are shown in the center. Landis led the congregation in the mid-20th century and brought strong vitality to the church. (Courtesy of the Amwell Church of the Brethren.)

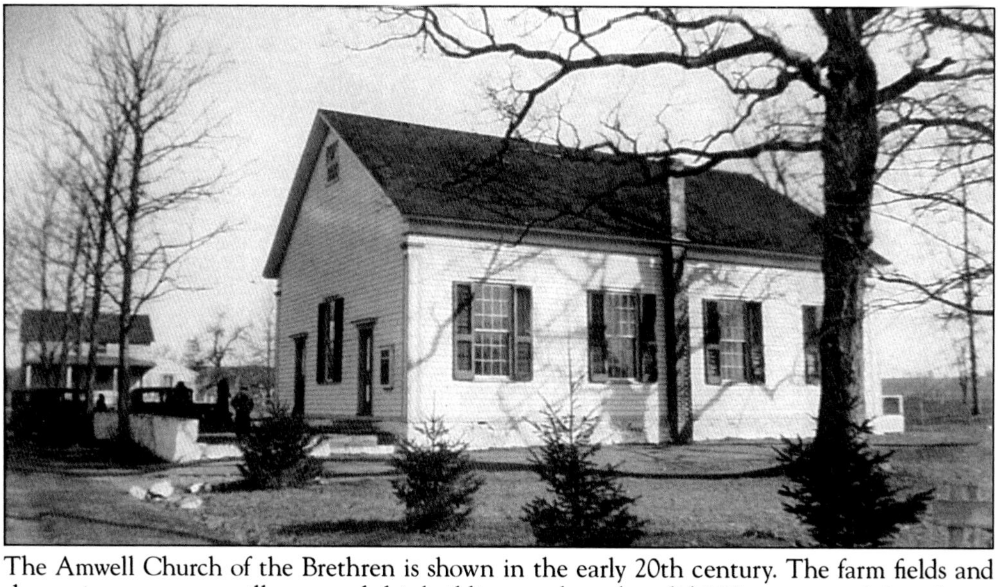

The Amwell Church of the Brethren is shown in the early 20th century. The farm fields and the ancient cemetery still surround this building much as they did 200 years ago. A long horse shed in which congregants hitched their horses is still standing on the other side of the building. (Courtesy of the Amwell Church of the Brethren.)

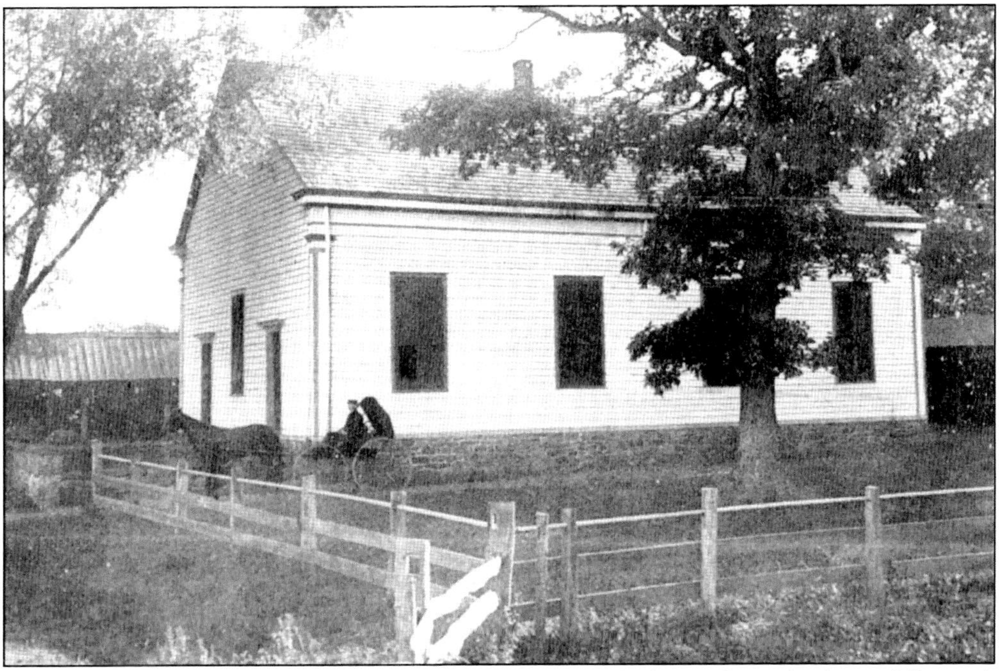

The Amwell Church of the Brethren is shown in 1915 before a fire. The beautifully stark functionality and simplicity of design is evident. (Courtesy of the Amwell Church of the Brethren.)

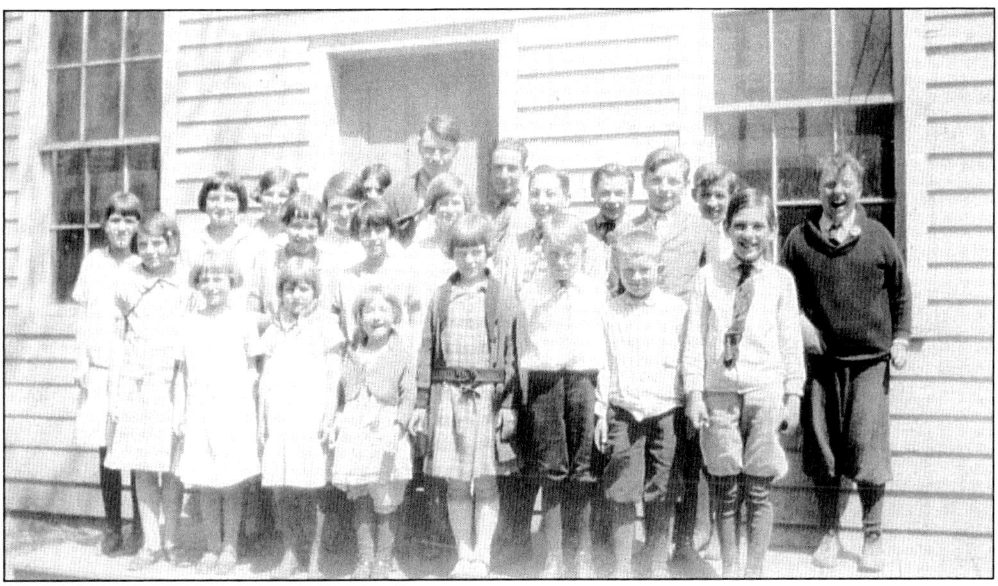

Seen here in 1926 are young people from the Amwell Church of the Brethren. Note the knickers on the boys and the bobbed haircuts on the girls. (Courtesy of the Amwell Church of the Brethren.)

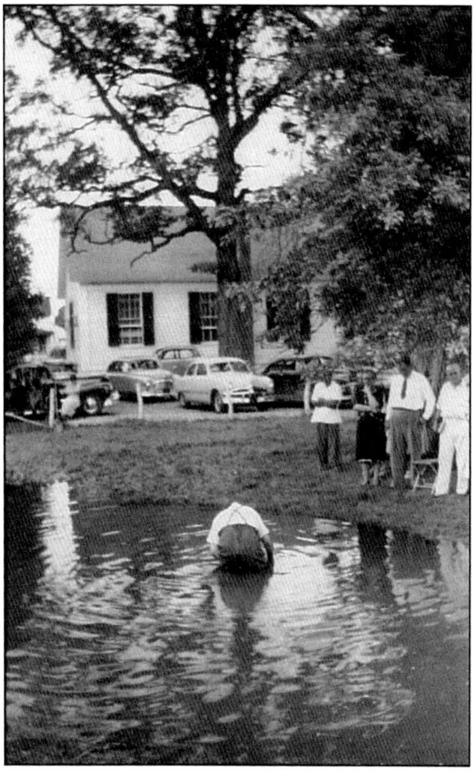

A baptismal event is seen in the stream next to the Amwell Church of the Brethren in the 1950s. The simplicity of this ancient ceremony is graphically exhibited in a manner very similar to early baptisms from 2,000 years ago. This church still practices foot washing as a ceremonial event, which is directed toward humility in its membership. (Courtesy of the Amwell Church of the Brethren.)

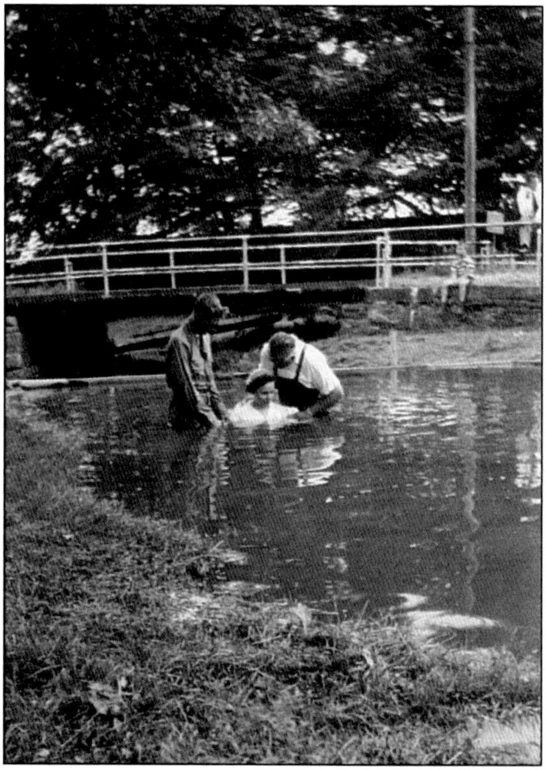

The pastor of the Amwell Church of the Brethren baptizes a parishioner in the stream next to the church in the 1950s. The bridge on Dunkard Church Road can be seen in the background with spectators viewing the ancient ceremony from it. The State of New Jersey has restricted the church from damming up the stream in recent years, and baptisms are no longer held there. (Courtesy of the Amwell Church of the Brethren.)

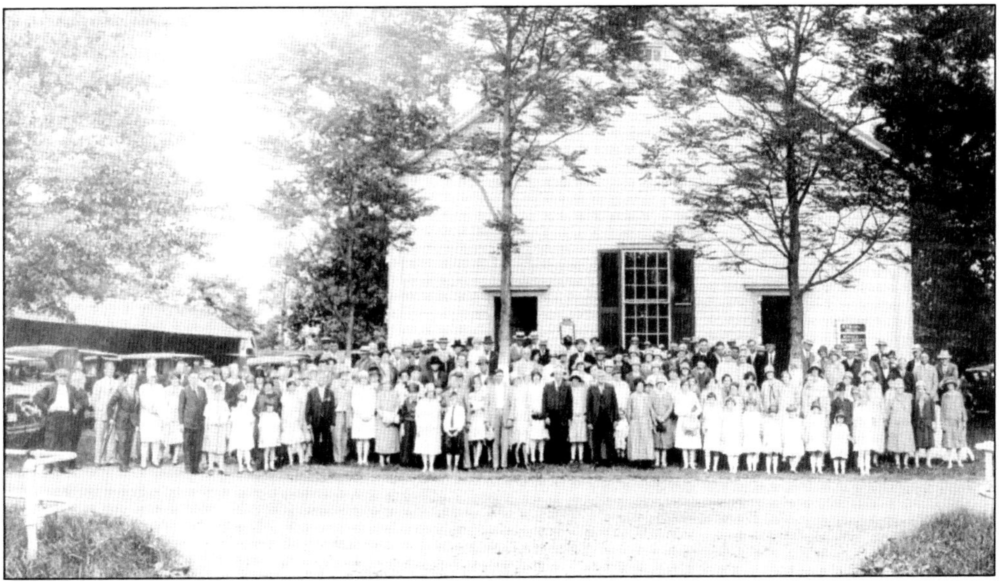

The Amwell Church of the Brethren had a large reunion in the 1920s. The strong community spirit that has been a part of this church over the centuries is evident here. (Courtesy of the Amwell Church of the Brethren.)

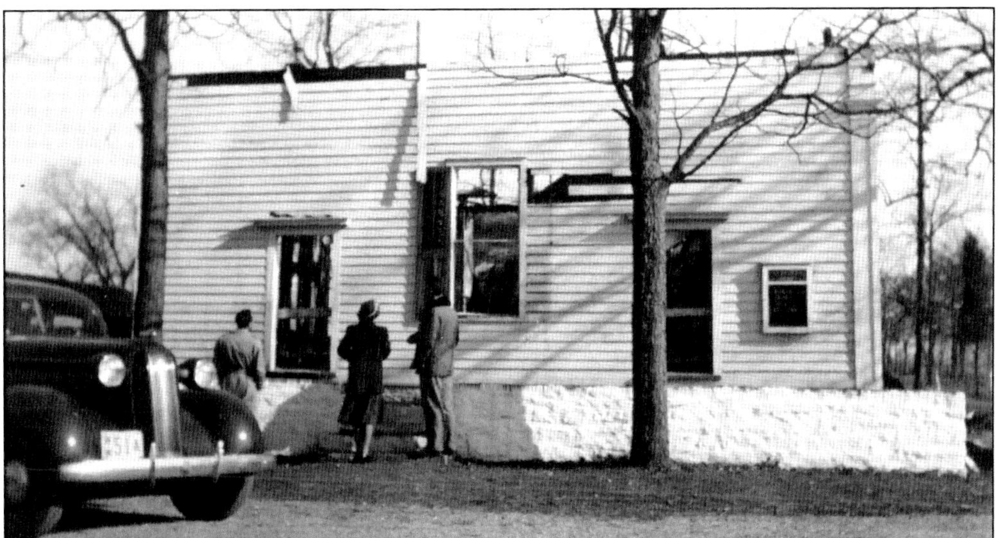

Members of the Amwell Church of the Brethren survey the damaged church after a fire in November 1950. Fire companies from Ringoes and other surrounding communities had to be utilized to fight the blaze, and the seed was planted that Delaware Township needed its own fire company. (Courtesy of the Amwell Church of the Brethren.)

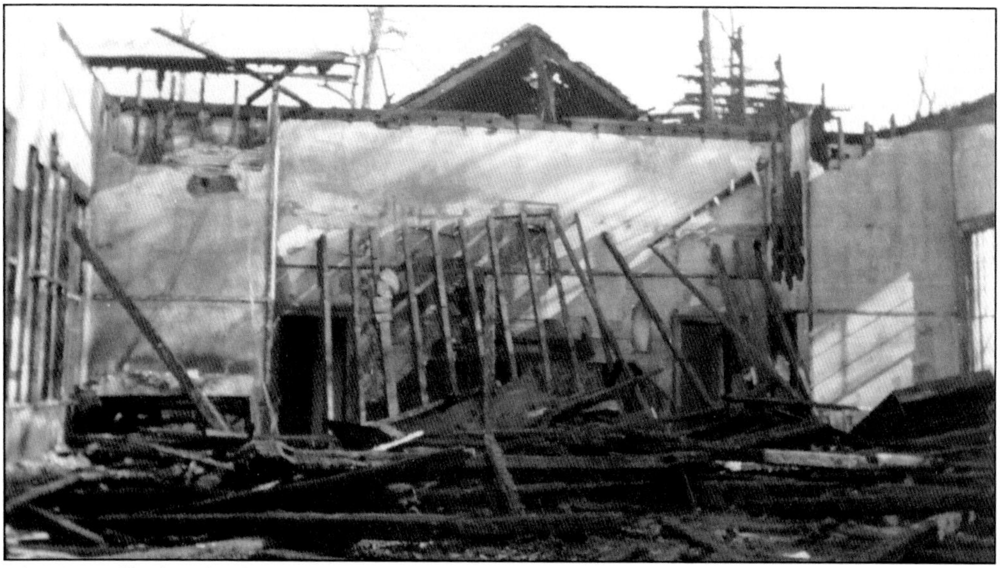

The Amwell Church of the Brethren suffered extensive damage from the fire in 1950. The level of devastation and the almost-miraculous rebuilding bear testimony to the commitment and determination of the members of this venerable old church, and it is evidence of their strong faith and community spirit. The church building seen today came from that heroic rebuilding. (Courtesy of the Amwell Church of the Brethren.)

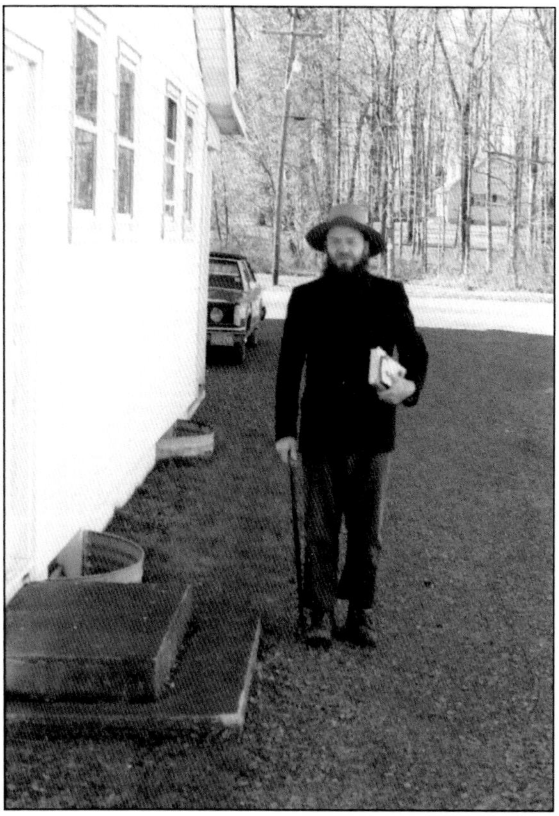

This winter 1986 photograph shows Brother Clarence Kulp of the Amwell Church of the Brethren. Kulp was a faithful member of the church. (Courtesy of the Amwell Church of the Brethren.)

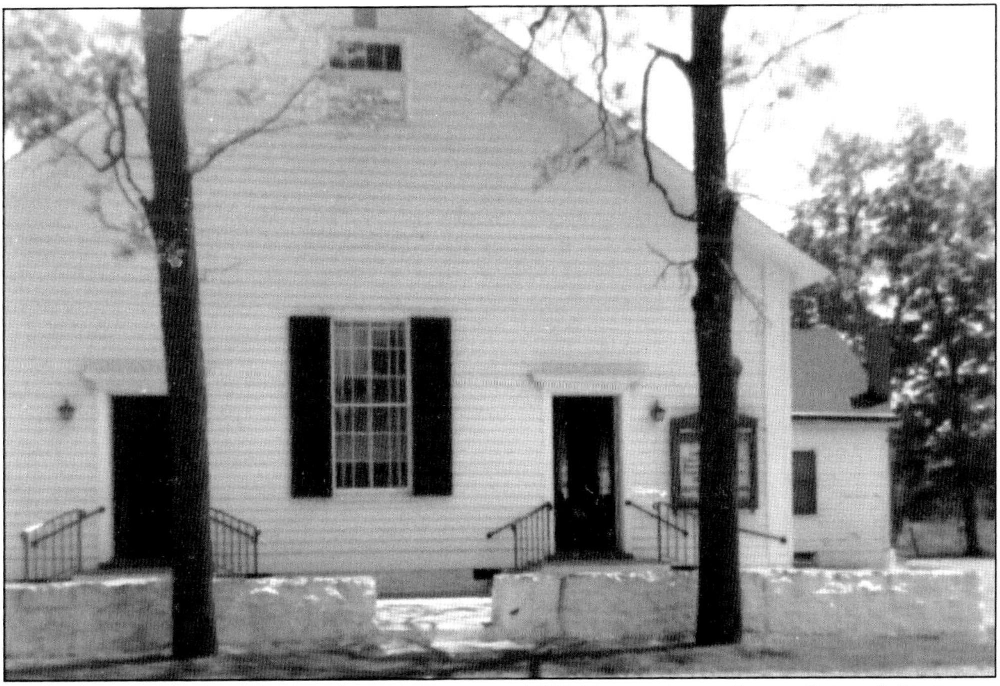

The Amwell Church of the Brethren is shown in 1972. Notice the stark simplicity of this house of worship as it reflects the functional, living nature of religion in the Delaware Township countryside. (Courtesy of the Amwell Church of the Brethren.)

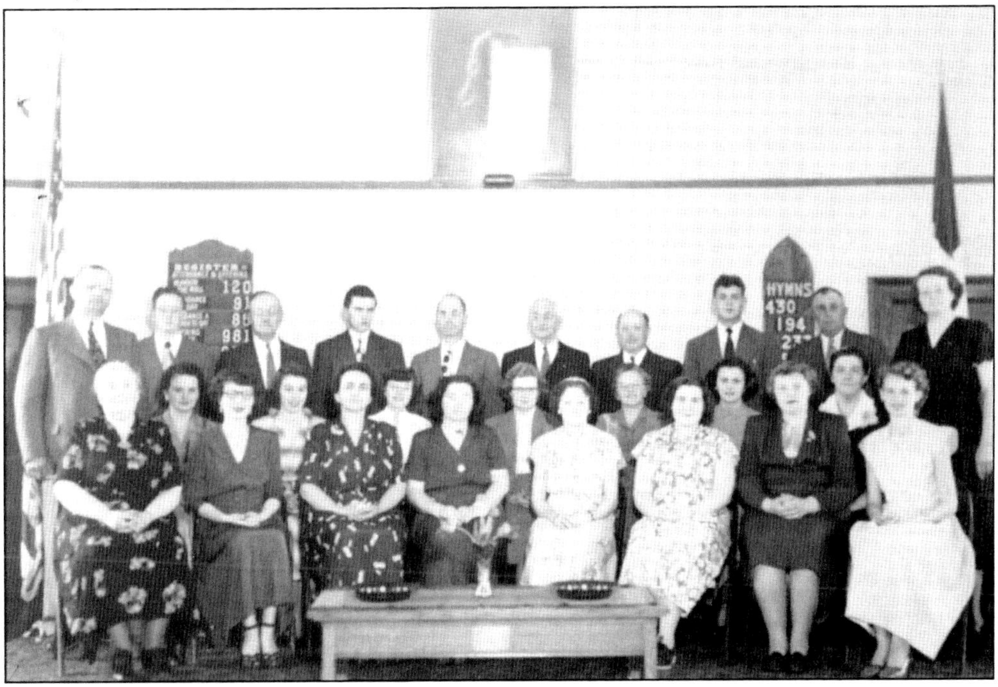

The Amwell Church of the Brethren is shown with some members of the congregation in 1940. Notice the dressed-up style of clothing worn by all the members. Attendance shows 120 for the current week on the board to the left. (Courtesy of the Amwell Church of the Brethren.)

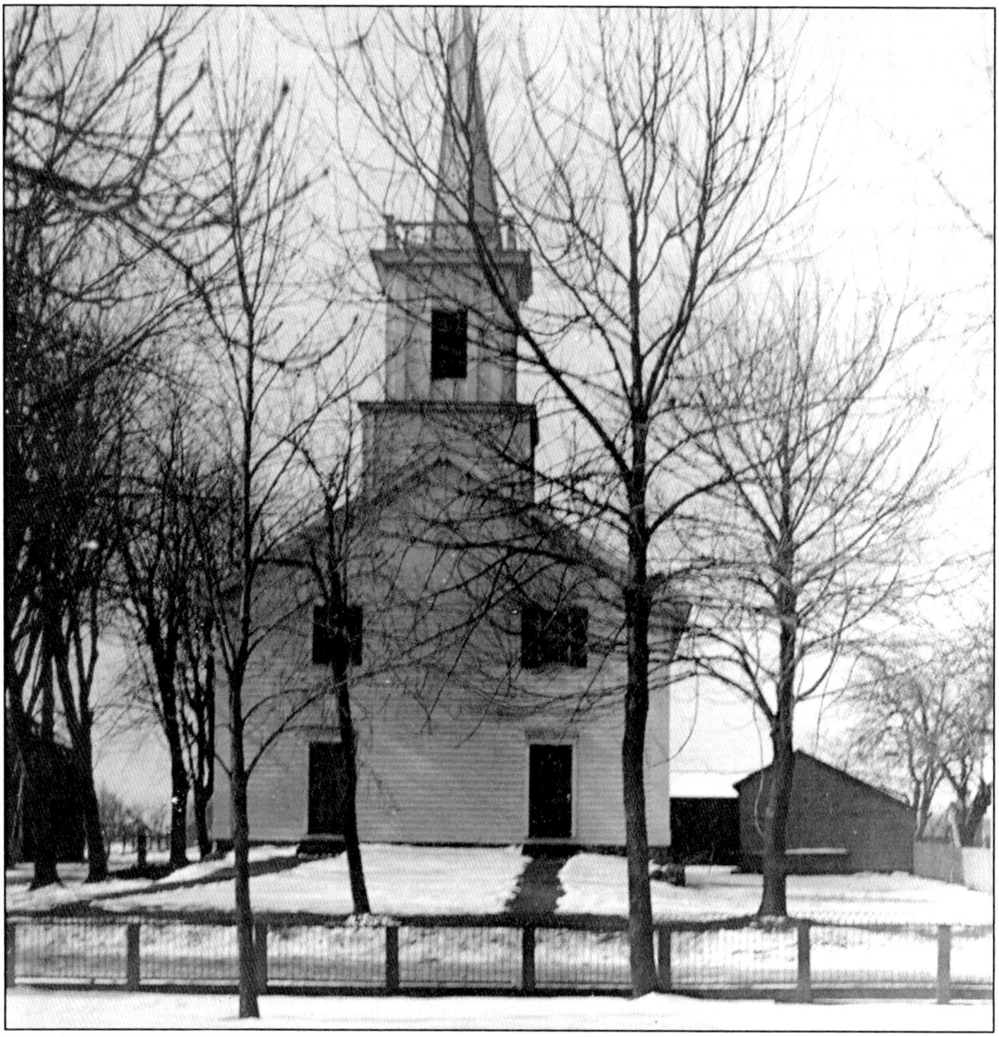

The former Methodist Episcopal church in Rosemont is shown in a winter scene during the early 20th century. This classic structure with its striking steeple is quite reflective of the early Protestant emphasis on simplicity and function in architecture. The building has been remodeled into a residence today, and the beautiful steeple has been taken down.

Five

THE PEOPLE

Historically the people of Delaware Township have been influenced in their patterns of living by their relationship to the land and the cycles of nature, climate, seasons, and the recurring regularity of growth and change occasioned by that natural world. The pattern of life lived by the late Prall Bodine can in many ways be duplicated in the lives of countless others who have lived over the years in the township.

Bodine owned a farm (that his family lived on and farmed for generations) located on the left as one leaves Stockton and climbs the hill going toward Sergeantsville. He was a descendant of the Pralls, after whom the local village Prallsville was named, and the Bodines, a local family going back generations. The striking relationship that Bodine had to the land, the animals, and the buildings, including the great barn that his father constructed, and to the general pattern of living on that land is emblematic of how many others have lived in the township over the years.

Bodine seldom took a vacation and worked seven days a week as he cared for over 100 dairy cattle. He named each of the cows and could identify all of them individually as he tended to them day by day. His fields were as well tended as the animals and flourished as he and his brother Wesley worked the land year after year.

There were other patterns of life in the township besides farming; however, the same facets of life tended to be part of those who lived in the towns. For example, Clint Wilson, the proprietor of Wilson's Store in Sergeantsville, was the initiator and founder of Delaware Township's fire department and police department. He had interested candidates meet in the back of his store for two years and used the state standards for training police and firemen as a guideline in tutoring them. The fire and police departments soon took shape through his tutelage, and today the township has strong, functioning protective services because of Wilson.

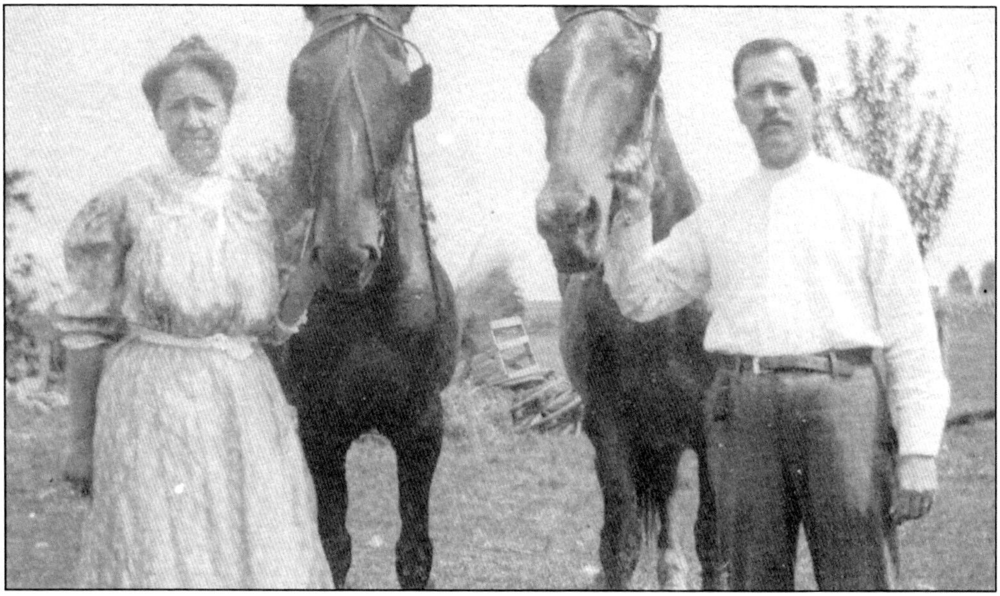

A Delaware Township couple is shown with their team of horses in 1907. Notice the determination and strength of character showing in their stance and facial expressions. This has a quality much like Grant Wood's famous painting *American Gothic*, minus the pitchfork.

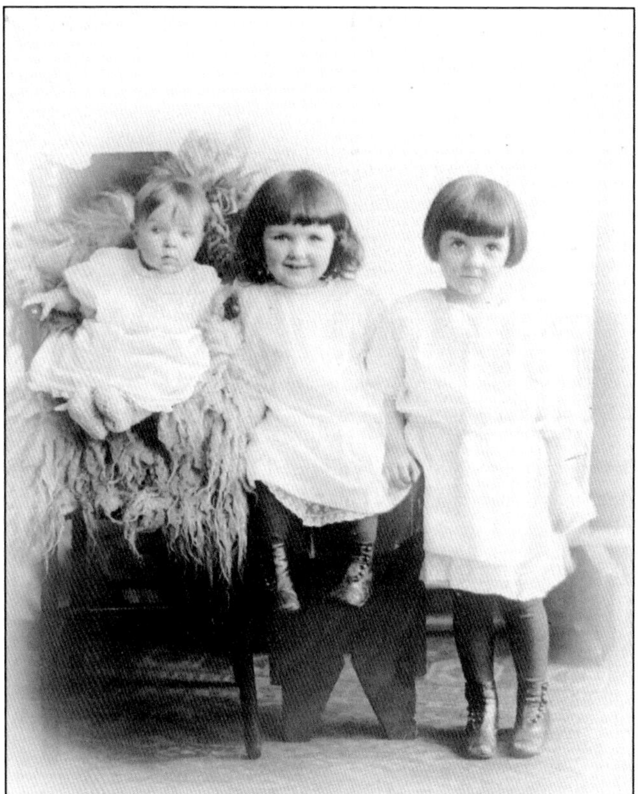

The Wagner girls in 1917 are, from left to right, Margaret, age 2; Rhoda, age 3; and Katherine, age 5. Wagner Road, where the family's farm was located, was named for them.

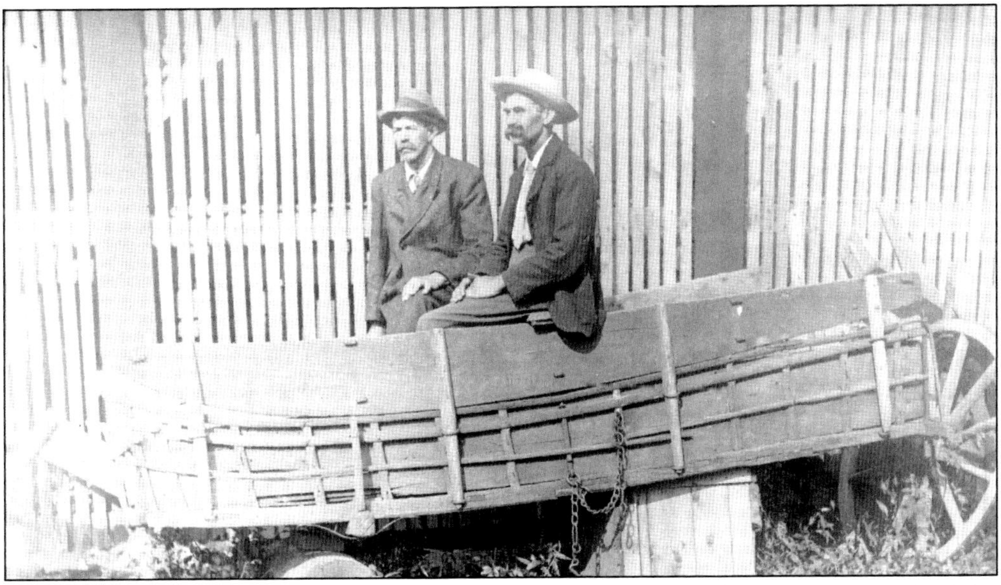

H. Miller (right) and a friend are shown in 1907 sitting in a wagon body at Sandy Ridge. The wagon was constructed in 1795 by Henry Van Dolah, who lived just down the hill near the Van Dolah School. Note the great mustaches and beautifully cut suits.

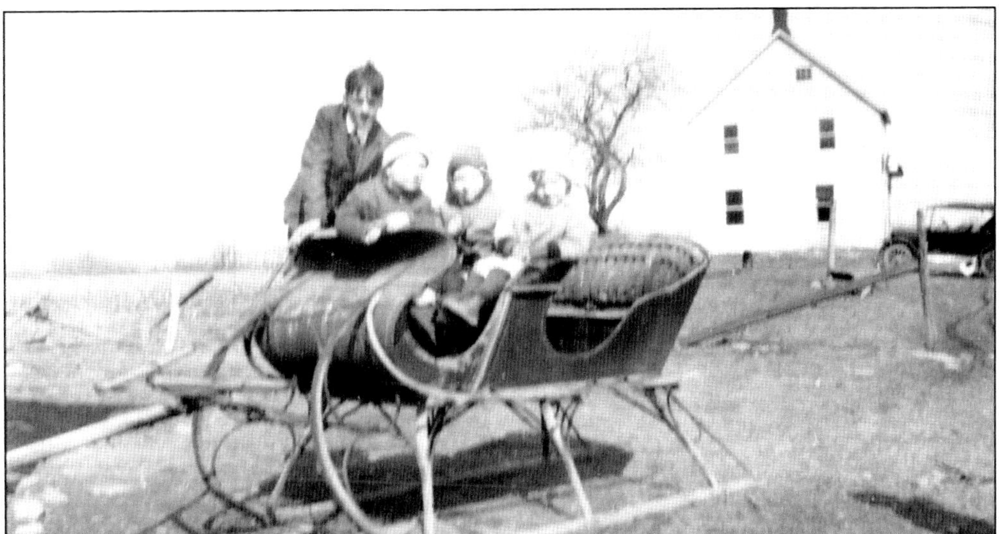

George Spain (on the left above) is seen in this photograph from the early 1920s as he visits his farm relatives, the Roadenbaughs (from left to right, Herbert, Madeline, and Dora). They are trying out the farm's horse-drawn sleigh. The house in the background was built in the early 1700s and is on Sanford Road above the covered bridge. (Courtesy of Blanche Carl.)

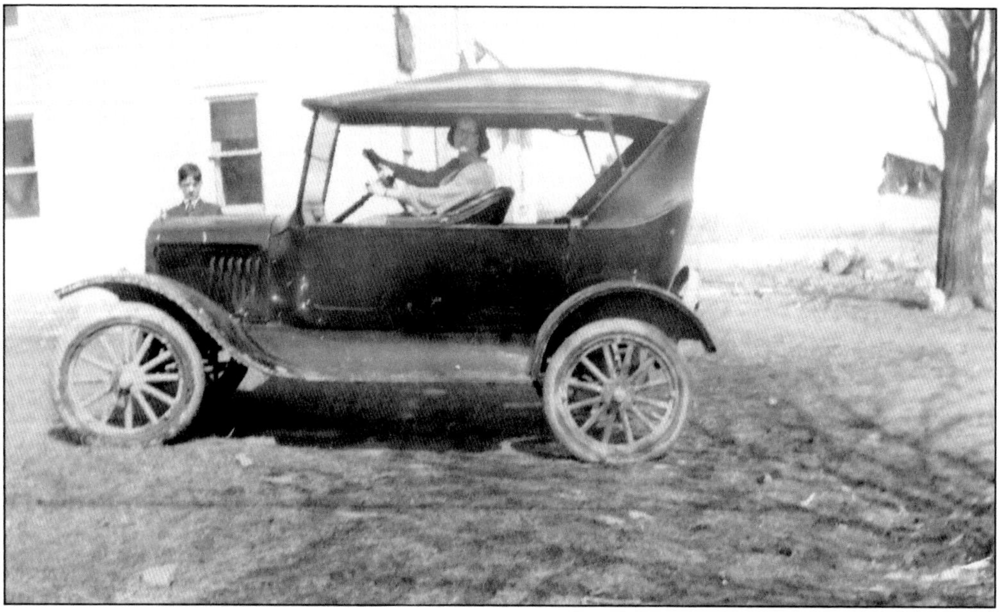

Dora Spain in the driver's seat and her brother George, standing nearby, are shown as they visited their Delaware Township relatives, the Roadenbaughs, in the early 1920s. This Sanford Road farm is at the second curve, and the house in the background was built in the early 1700s. (Courtesy of Blanche Carl.)

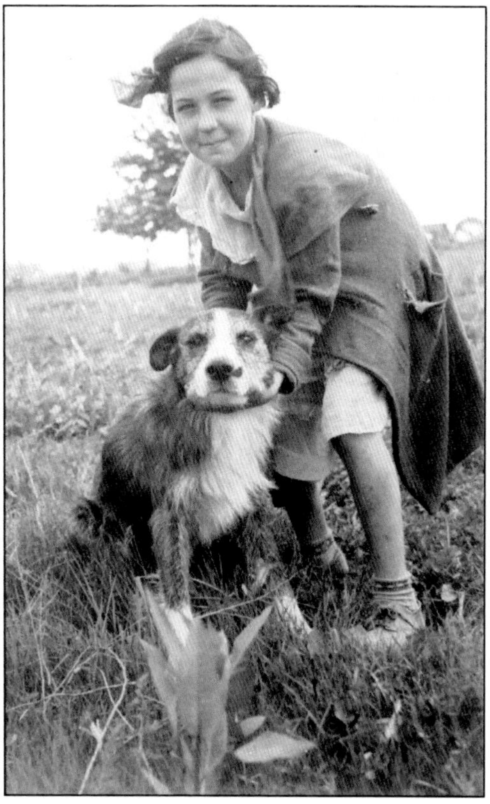

Blanche Carl is shown playing with her dog Tippy on the Roadenbaugh farm in the mid-1930s. Notice the wide-open expanse of fields behind her. Carl recently pointed out that the township is more densely covered in hedges in 2009 than it was in the 1920s and 1930s because the township then employed three workers all summer working with hand scythes to trim back the hedges. For example, in the 1930s, Bowman's Tower, miles away in Bucks County, Pennsylvania, could be seen from the Roadenbaugh farm a couple of miles above the covered bridge. (Courtesy of Blanche Carl.)

The Roadenbaugh children are shown on the Sanford Road farm in the 1930s: from left to right, (first row) Blanche and Harriet; (second row) Madeline (Peggy), Herbert, and Dora. They are a typically wholesome group of children who lived in the township in those earlier days. (Courtesy of Blanche Carl.)

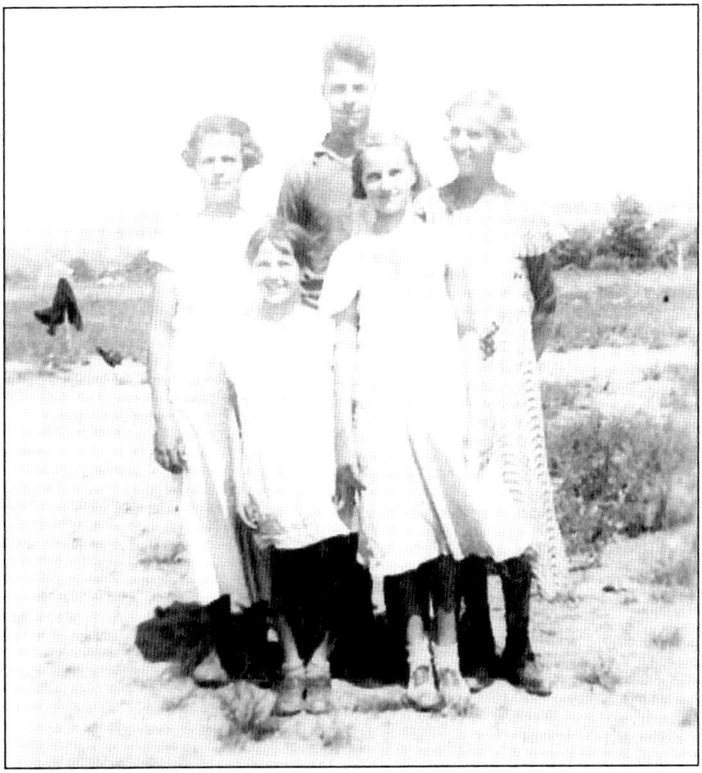

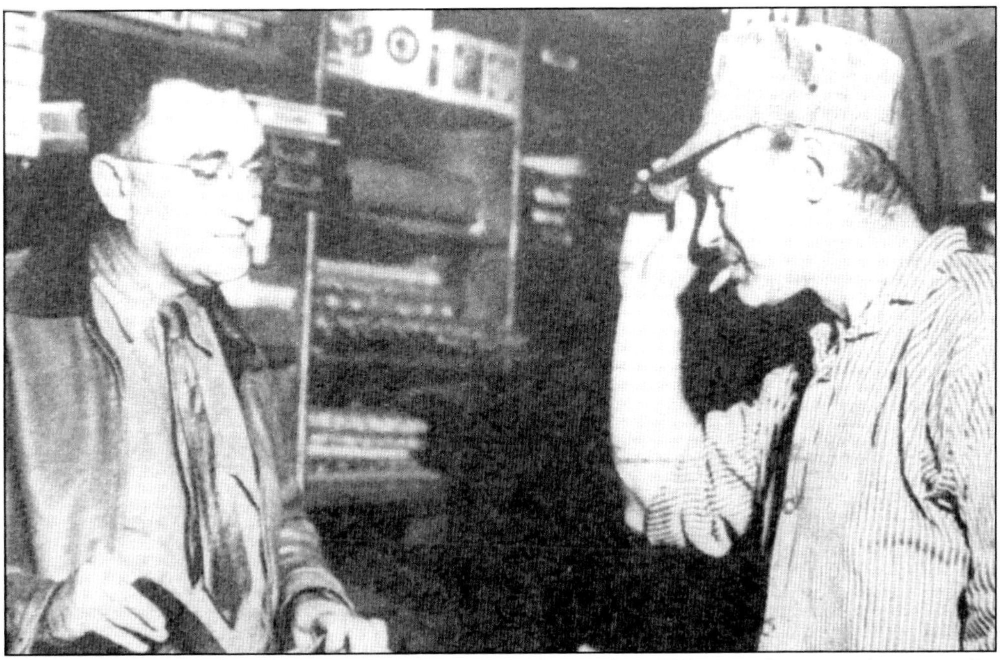

William Lohmann of Sandy Ridge purchases a cap from Clint Wilson at the general store in the 1930s. Wilson appears to be quite an astute storekeeper, as he watches the transaction carefully and fingers the books.

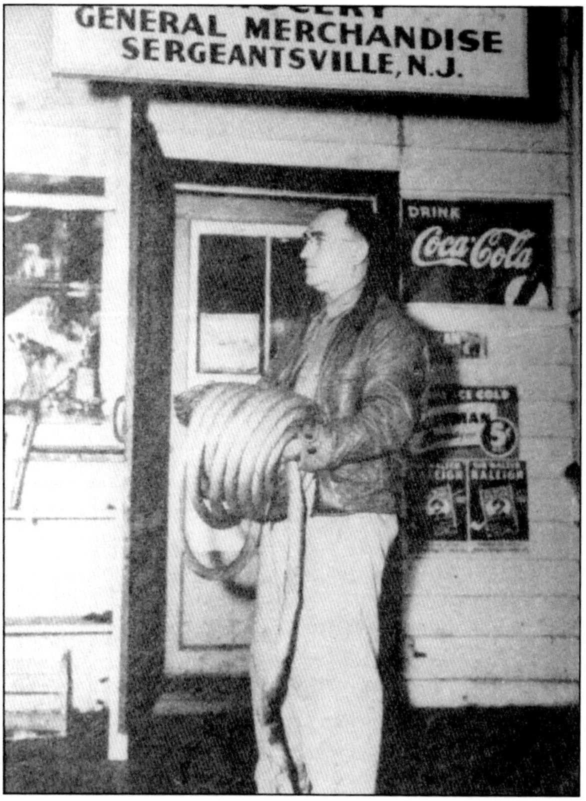

The C. B. Wilson General Store, commonly called Wilson's Store, in Sergeantsville is pictured in the 1930s, and owner Clint Wilson is ready for business. He is holding a roll of tar rope that was used to bind corn shocks (smaller strands would be pulled from the larger rope). The cornstalks were still cut by hand using a corn knife (similar to a machete). The post office was established in this store in 1827. The building is the second one from the corner on Route 604 across from the municipal hall. Notice the sign indicating that Coca-Cola was available in the store.

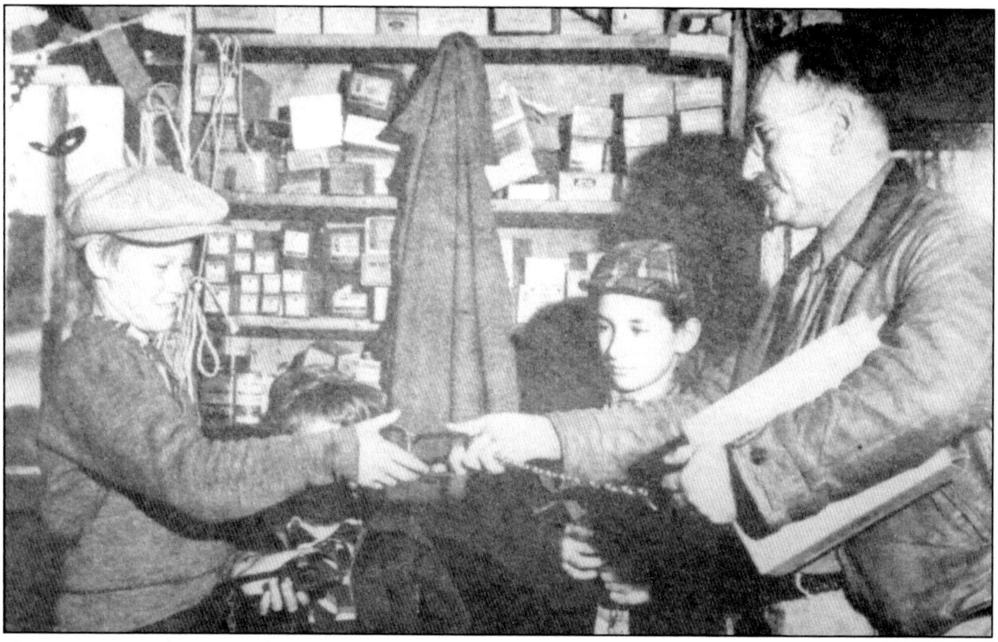

Customers are shown with Wilson in his store in the 1930s. Wilson was a mover and shaker in Delaware Township, as he initiated the first training for police and firemen, organizing those departments, and he taught school as well as running his store.

Gussie Harned, the blacksmith in Sergeantsville, is shown in the 1930s. Note the bib overalls and the horseshoe being formed. Harned is wearing a leather apron for protection from the hot implements.

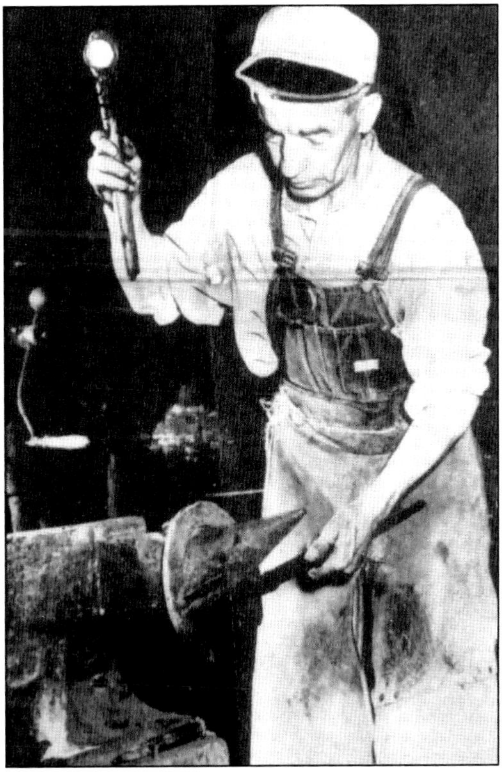

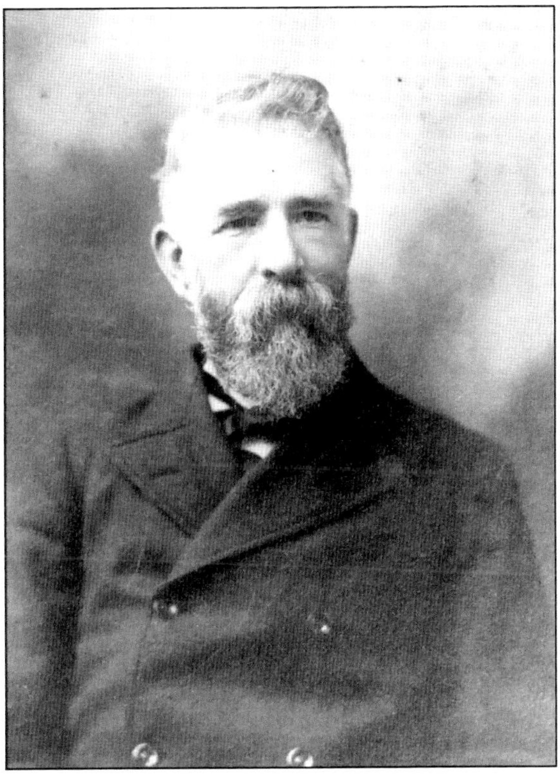

Highly respected local physician Dr. George Best of Rosemont is shown in this photograph from the early 20th century.

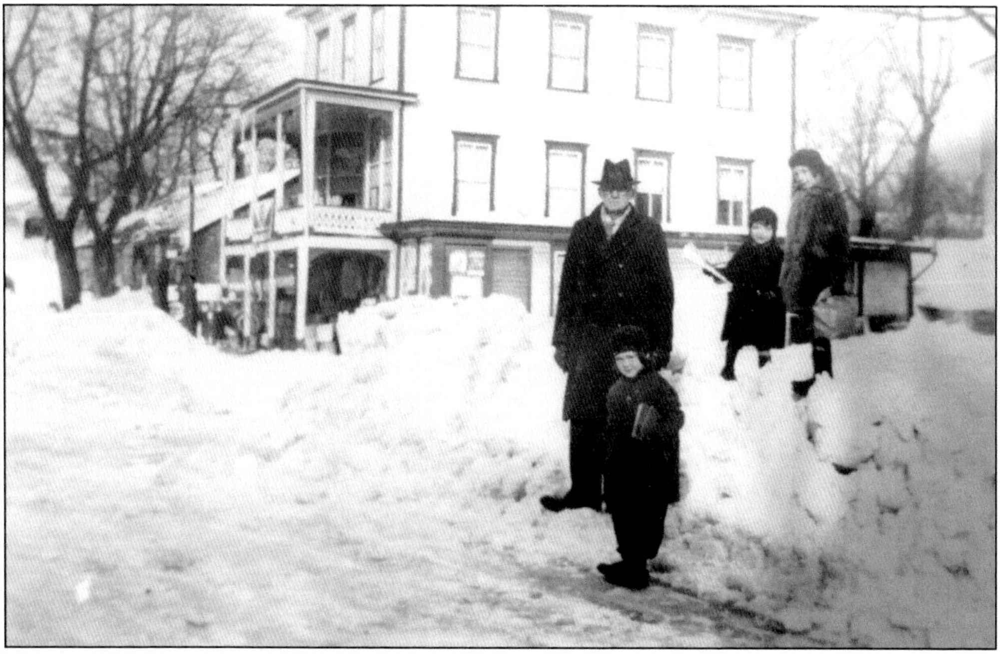

Newton V. Myers, a noted local teacher, is shown in a winter scene in the mid-20th century across Route 523 with the general store in the background. Note his blocked hat and the quite put-together clothing he is wearing.

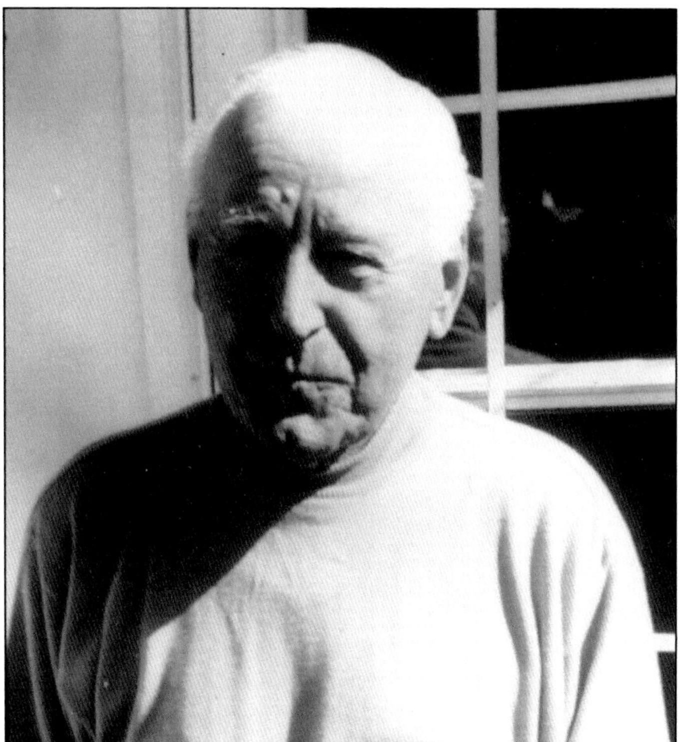

A mid-20th-century photograph shows Henry Burgett, a previous owner of the Sergeantsville Grain and Feed Store. Burgett lived in a house near the Methodist church in Sergeantsville.

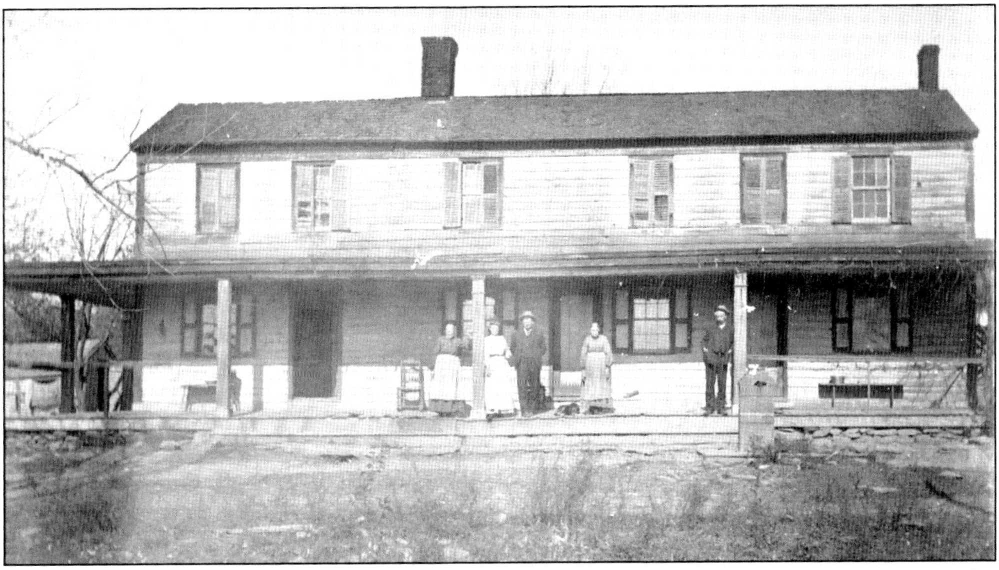

This building, which was a hotel directly across from the Edzel store in Croton on the Trenton-Easton Turnpike (Route 579 today), has a family on the porch in the early 20th century. The Edzel store was next to this building. It was a stagecoach stop on the turnpike during the early 1800s.

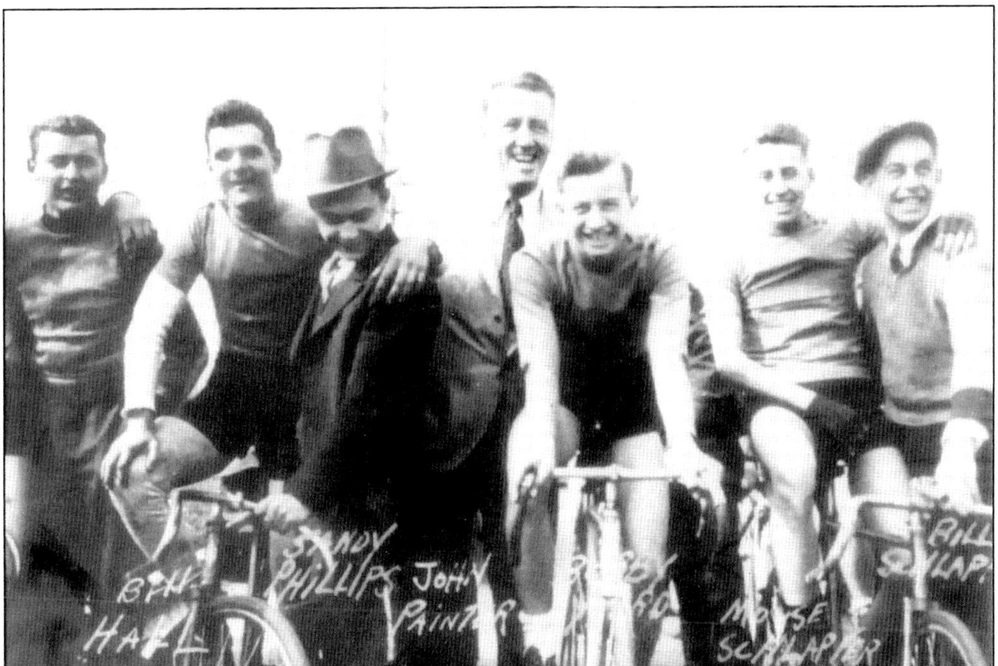

Bicycle racers are ready for the next event at the velodrome in Sergeantsville. The velodrome had originally been built and operated in Madison Square Garden, New York City. When that venue ended, it was torn down and reconstructed on Route 523 about a mile north of Sergeantsville in 1932. A riding stable and farm occupy the site in 2009.

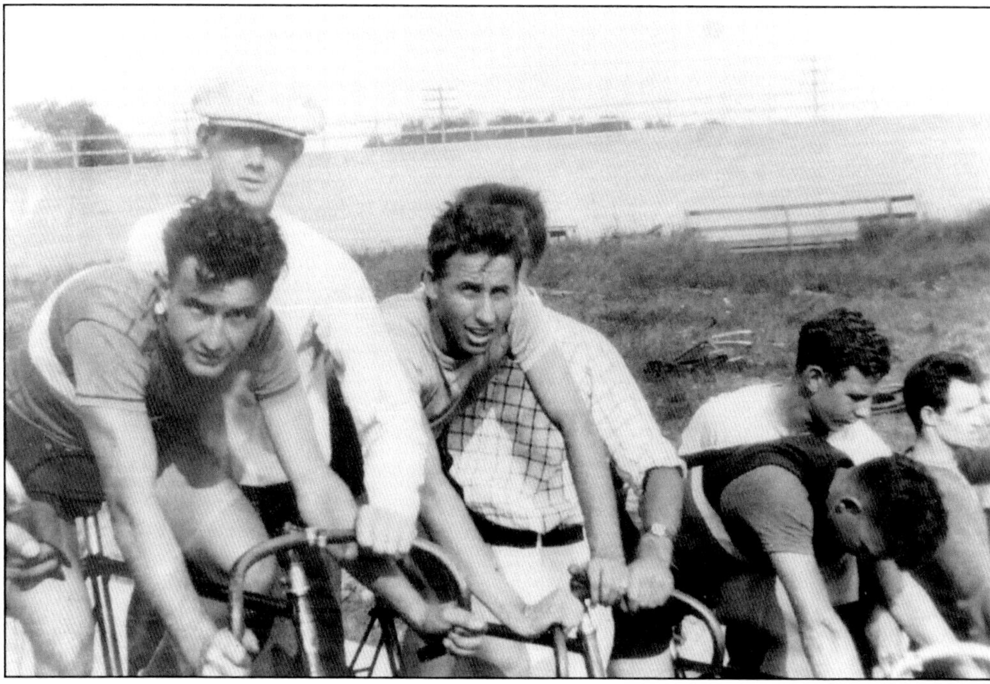

The bicycle velodrome was constructed in Sergeantsville on the Flemington-Sergeantsville Road in the 1930s. Bob Yard, one of the local racers, is shown on the left. It is interesting to note that the whole Delaware Township area is a prime bicycling place with cyclists coming from far and near to travel the township roads and paths in the year 2009.

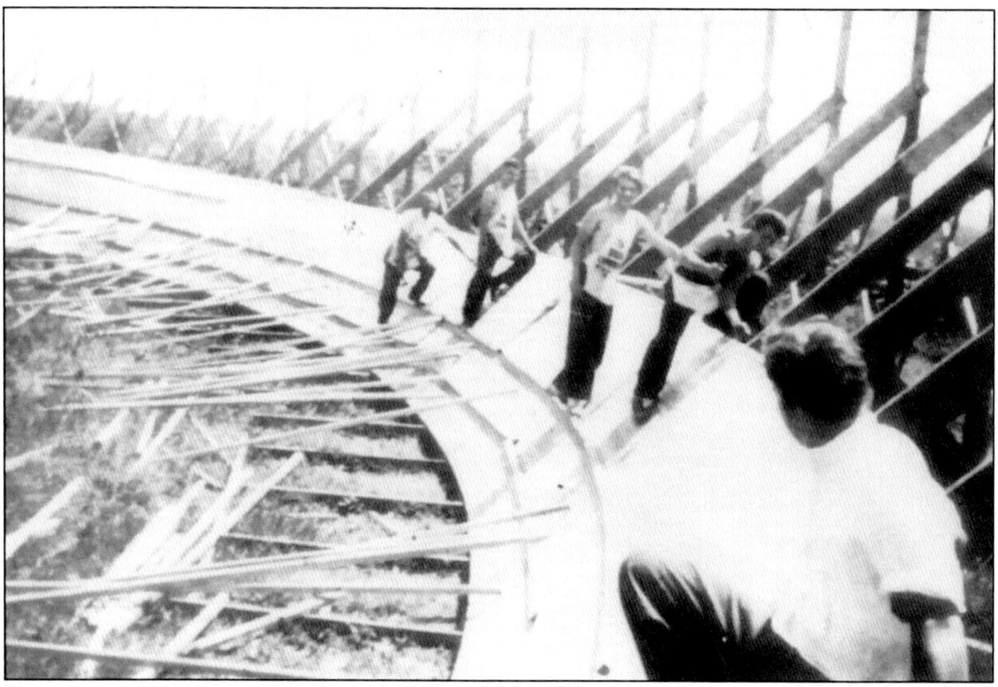

Here the velodrome is in the process of being constructed. Yard, the local racer, is shown on the left aiding the construction effort.

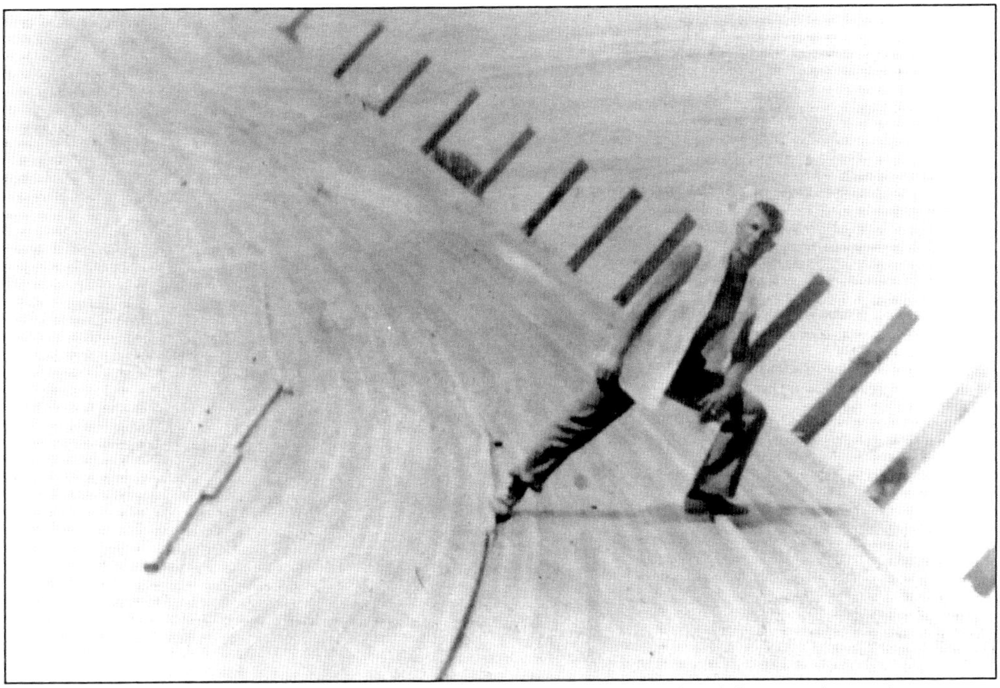

The velodrome is nearing completion in the 1930s. Note the angle of the circular surface meant to keep the speeding bicycles on the track as they raced around it. These velodromes were quite popular all over the United States in the 1920s and 1930s.

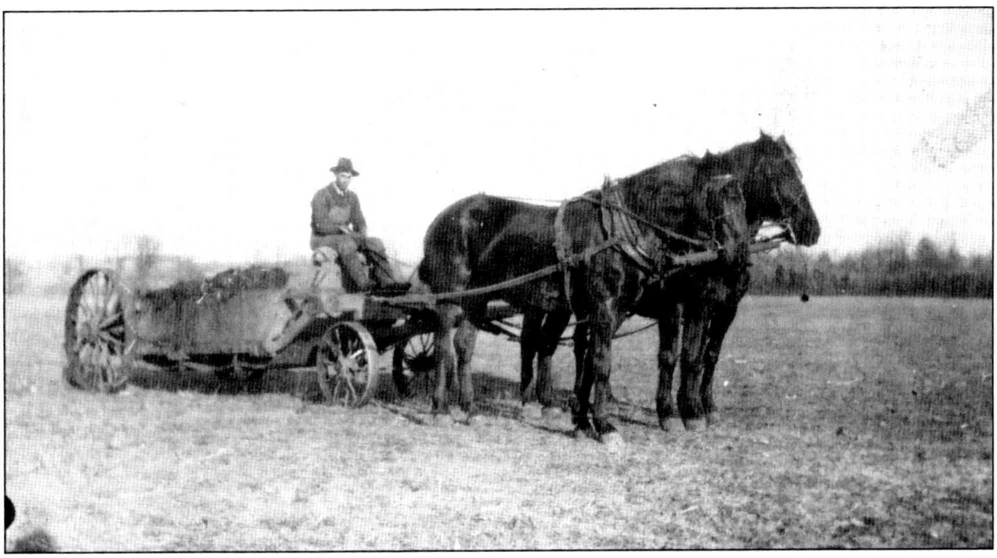

Irvin Shepperd in 1922 is shown spreading manure with a two-horse team. Horses were often used for such chores in the township through the 1940s. (Courtesy of Dave Bond.)

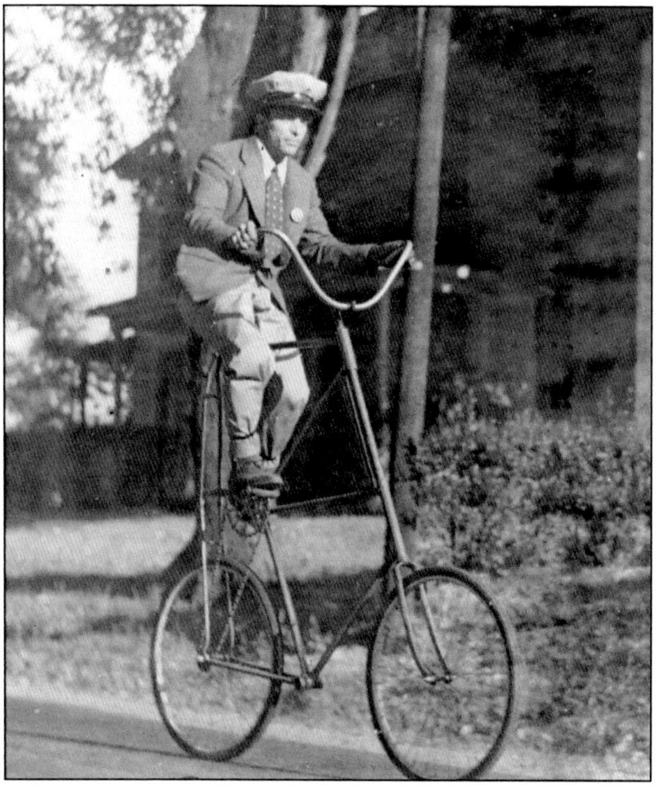

Albert Newcomb is shown in the 1940s on a bicycle he constructed. He also put together his uniform outfit. He had an artificial hand that he attached at times. His family owned the gasoline station and garage on Route 604 across from today's post office.

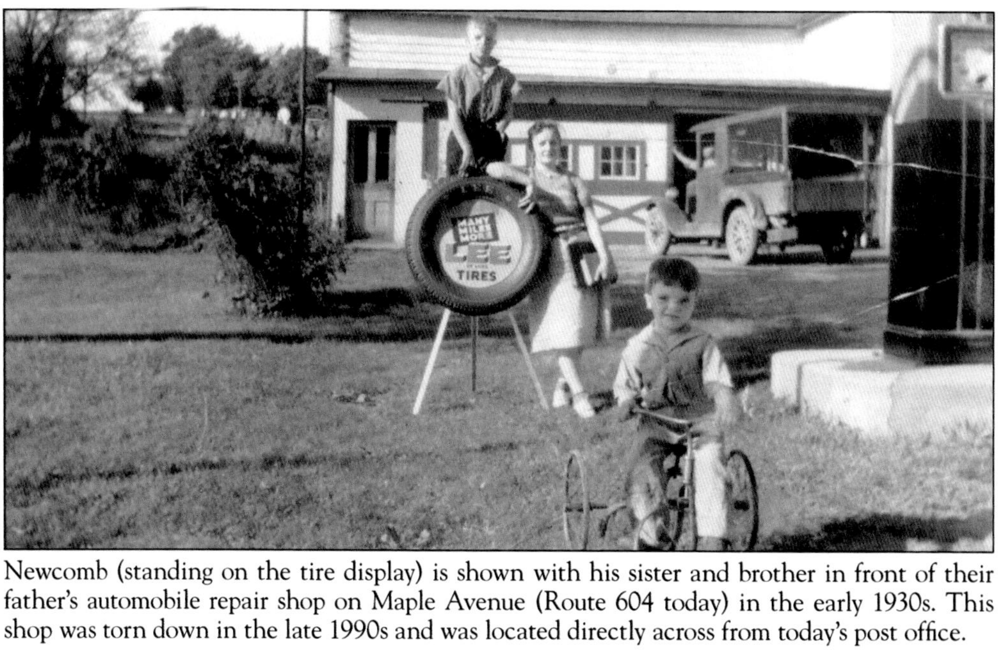

Newcomb (standing on the tire display) is shown with his sister and brother in front of their father's automobile repair shop on Maple Avenue (Route 604 today) in the early 1930s. This shop was torn down in the late 1990s and was located directly across from today's post office.

Otto Maresca is shown in front of his meat market. The Marescas owned a local farm and were butchers. They still sell prepared meats, soups, and other foodstuff to take home or eat at their shop.

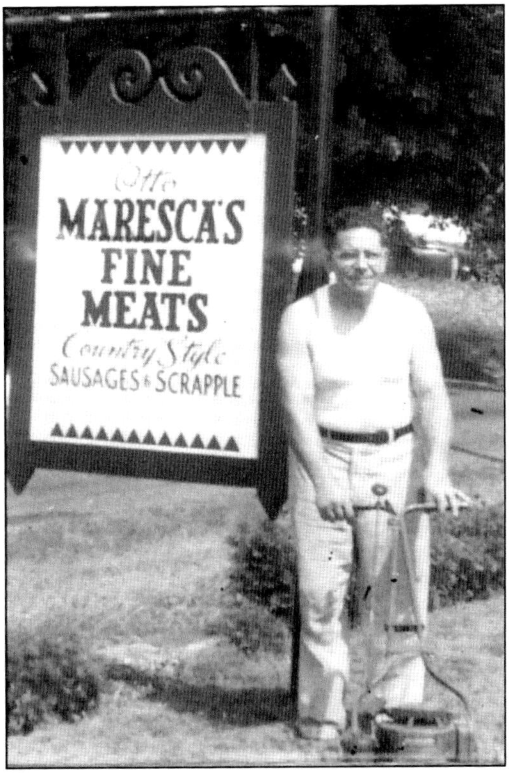

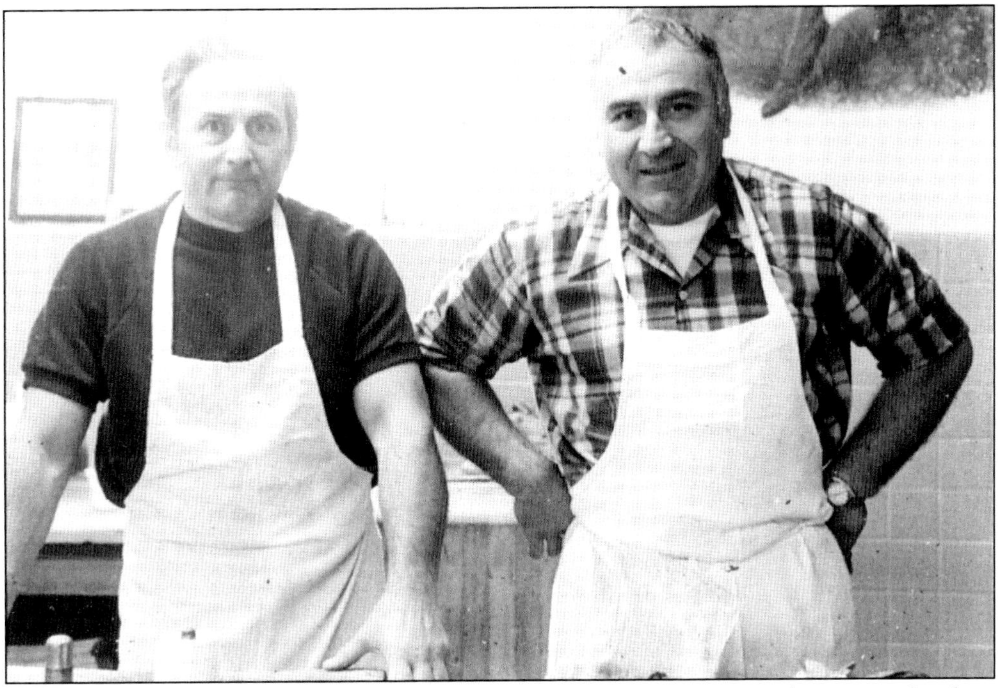

Joe and Emil Maresca greet a customer in their meat market in the 1960s. The Maresca brothers took over their father's store and today still prepare special sausages, pâté, and house-smoked meats in their Sergeantsville meat market.

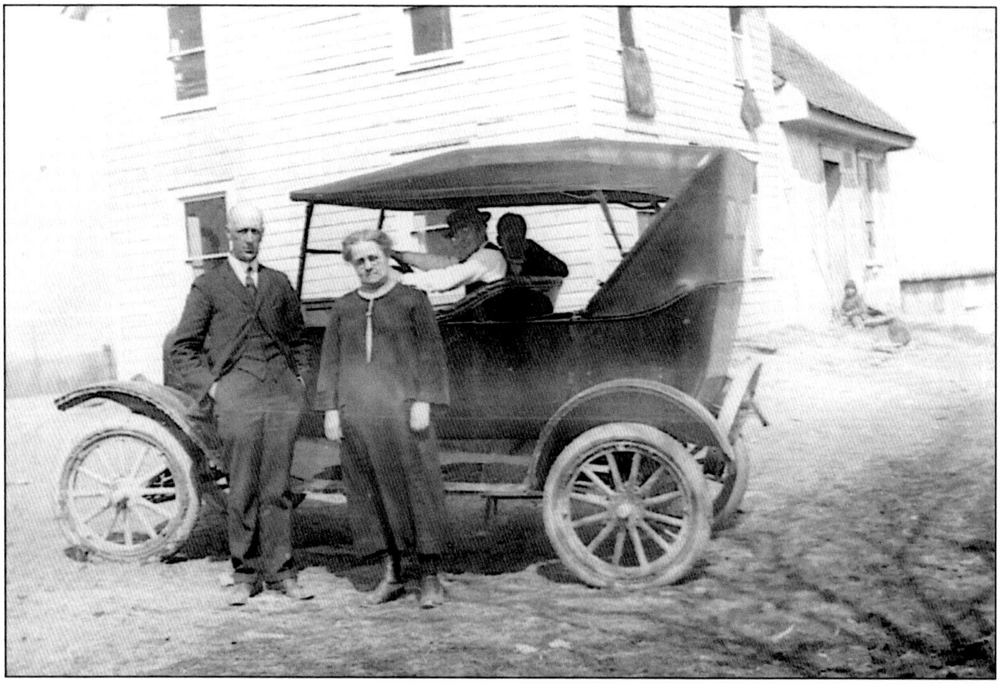

Harry Lester and Madeline Spain are shown standing beside their Model T in the 1920s. They were members of a family visiting their relatives the Roadenbaughs on Sanford Road. (Courtesy of Blanche Carl.)

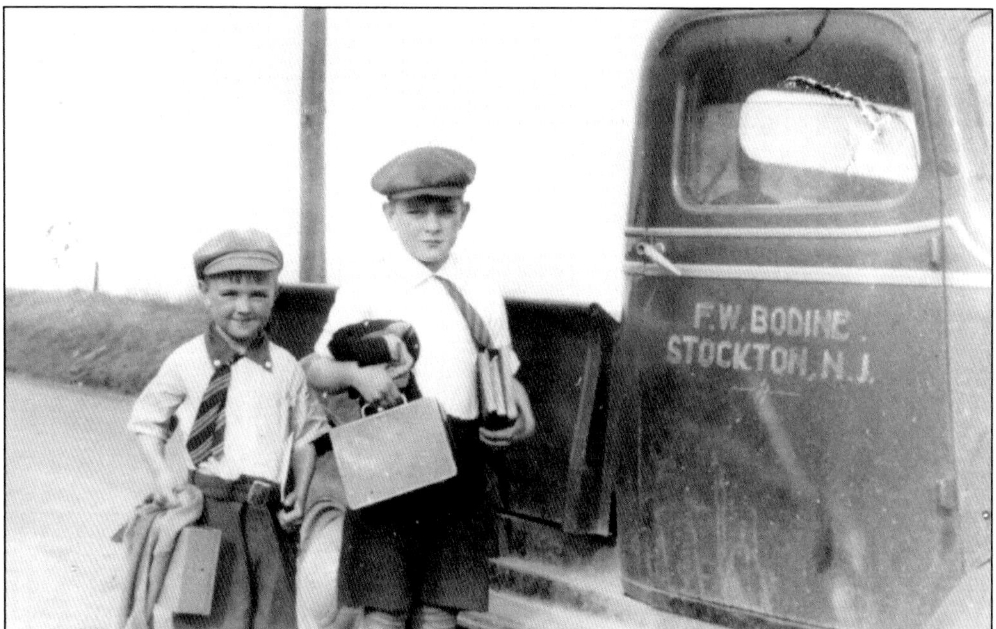

Wesley (right) and Prall Bodine pose in 1938 next to their father's pickup truck before they went to school. The Bodines have lived in Delaware Township for generations, and their farm (on the left as one leaves Stockton going toward Sergeantsville) is on some of the best land in the township.

Mr. and Mrs. Fisher, the parents of Bill Fisher, are shown in quite fashionable attire in the 1930s. The Fisher family has farmed in the township for generations, and their farm was just west of the Delaware Valley Horsemen's Association showgrounds on Route 604 near Headquarters. The parents later lived in the house next to the Amwell Church of the Brethren on Sand Brook-Headquarters Road.

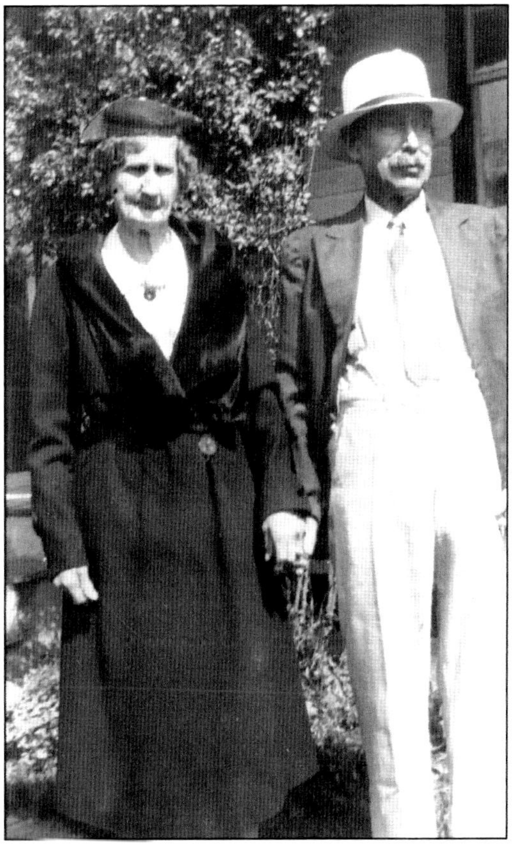

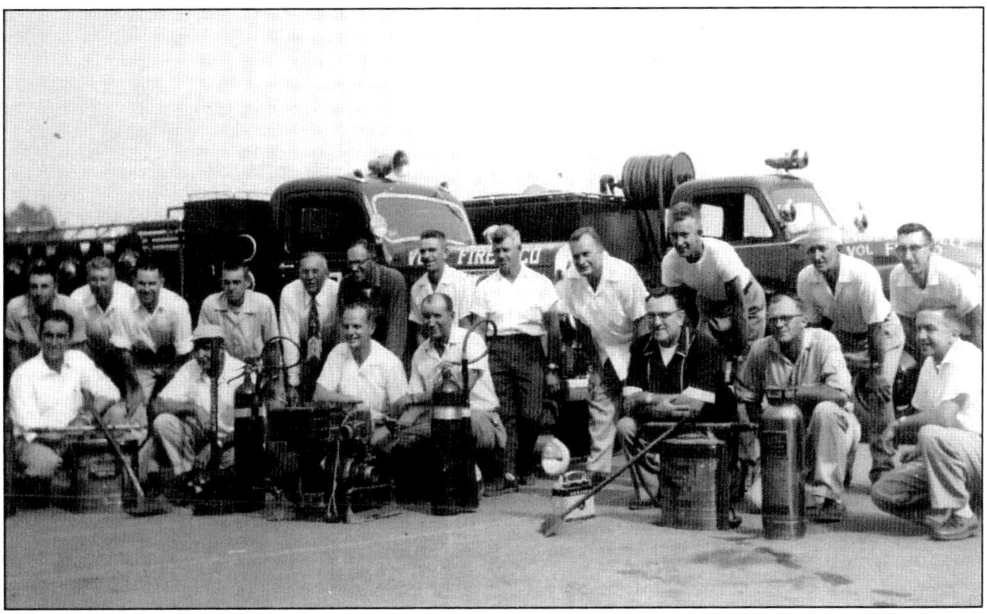

Members of the Sergeantsville Fire Company are shown in the early 1950s soon after its founding; Clint Wilson is third from the right in the first row. Notice the vintage fire trucks and the firefighting equipment ready to go.

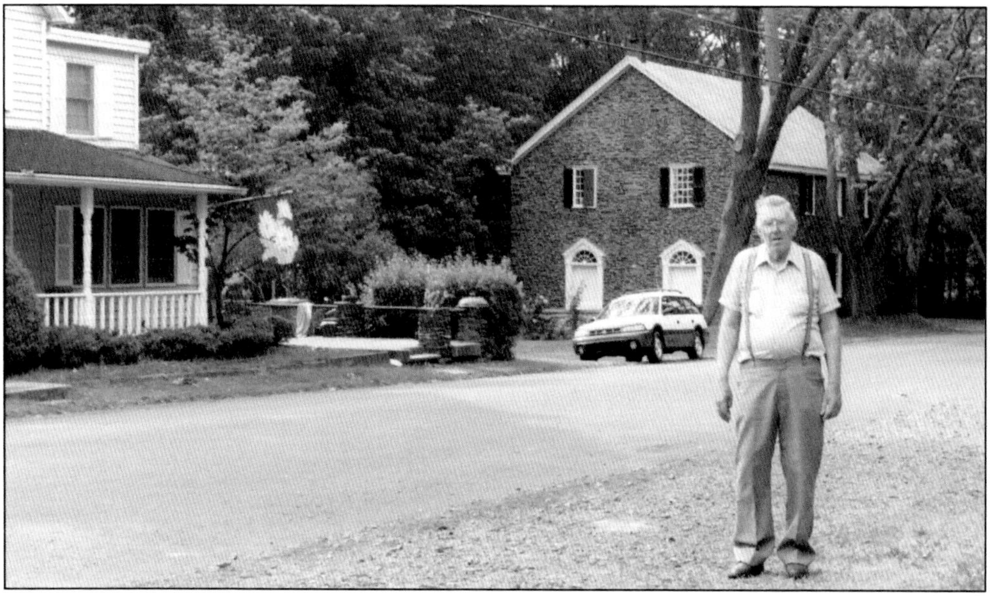

The Locktown Baptist Church lies in the background, with Milt Smith, former mayor of Delaware Township, standing in front of his house across the road in Locktown. This is near the spot where the problematic streetlight was located that was originally installed by a private group who eventually wanted to sell it to the township. There was some controversy over the sale (New York and Philadelphia newspapers picked up the story), which Smith facilitated while he was mayor.

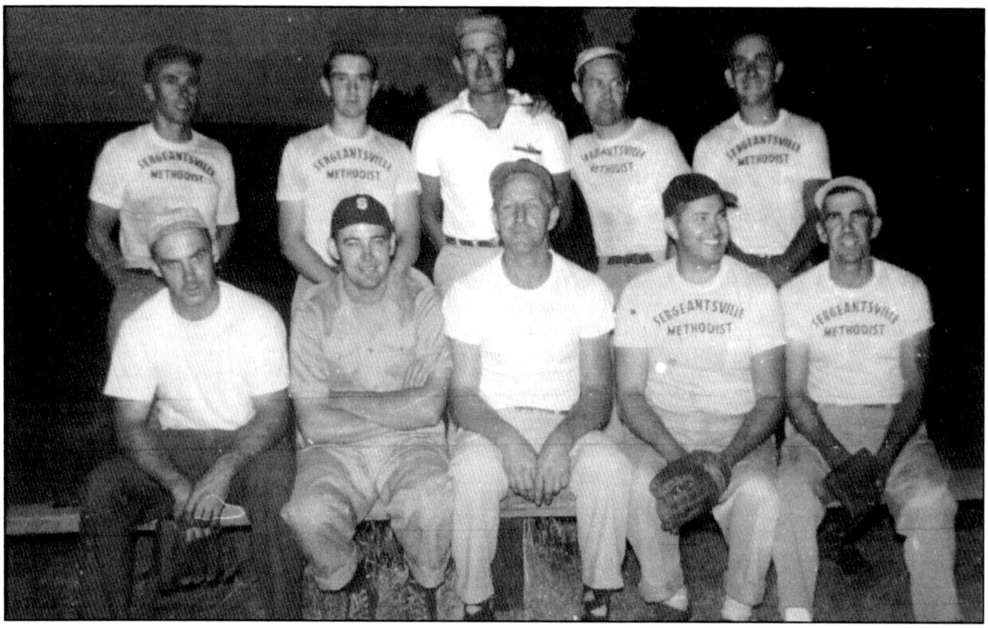

The Sergeantsville Methodist Episcopal Church softball team is shown in the 1930s. A number of those pictured descend from families that have been in the township for generations. From left to right are (first row) Dick Brown, Henry Fisher, Walter Burgett, Henry McAlone, and Bob Culbertson; (second row) Arlie Emmons, John Johnson, Orville Emery, Bob Forest, and Bill Emery.

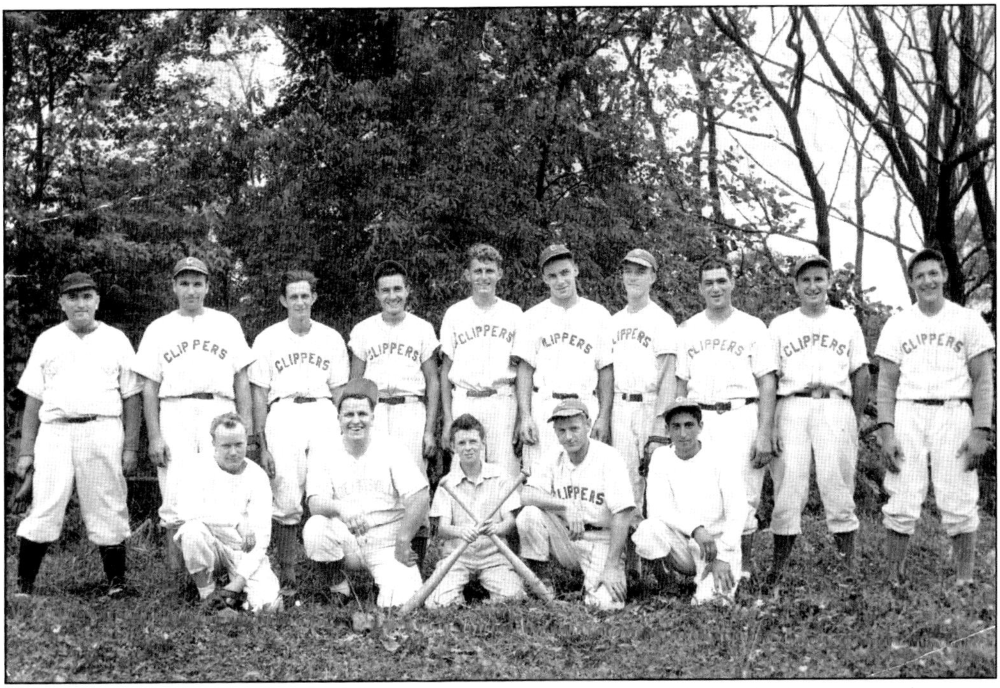

The Sergeantsville Clippers, another of the competitive township baseball teams, is shown in the 1930s. Clint Wilson, the manager, is the first person on the left in the back row and appears to be ready for action.

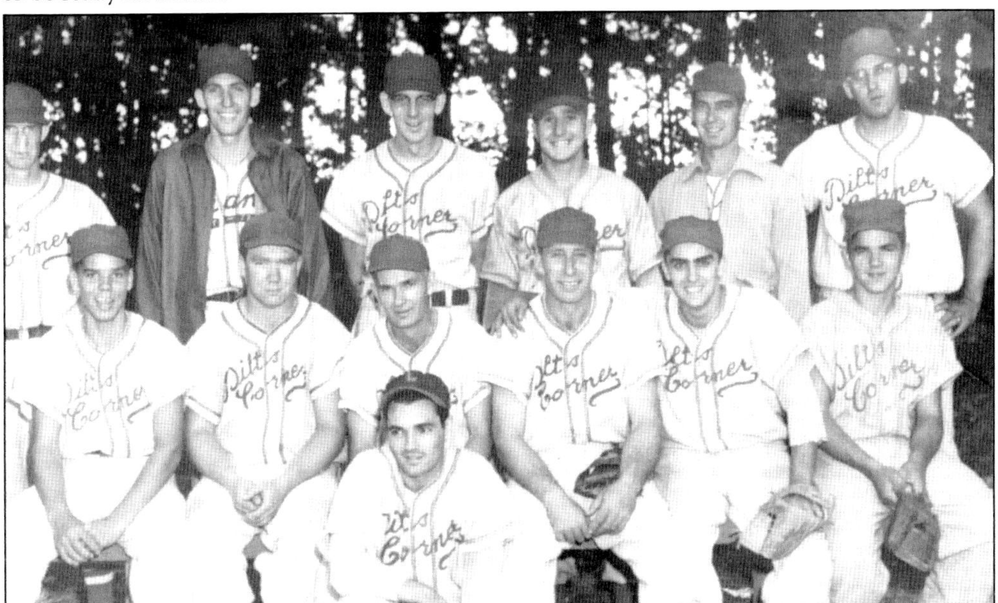

The Dilts Corner baseball team is suited up for a game in the 1930s. Note the obvious physical fitness and clean-cut demeanor of the players. There were several local teams and playing fields around the township in the 1930s. Some of the playing fields could still be seen around the township at the beginning of the 21st century. It is interesting to note the almost professional level of suiting reached by these essentially local teams.

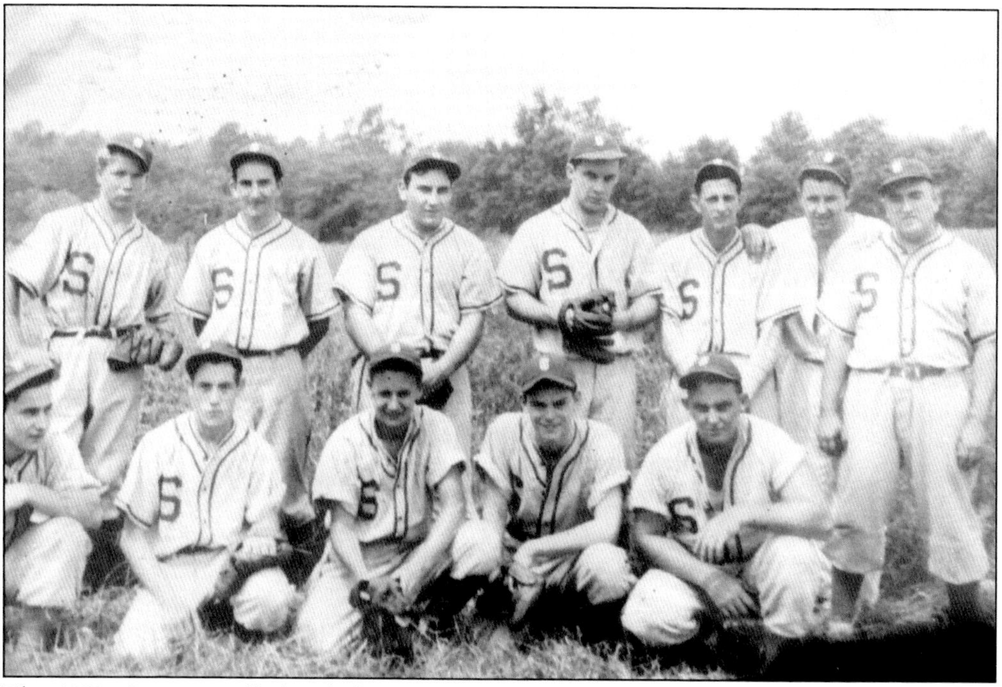

The 1930s Sergeantsville baseball team is ready for a game and looking quite competitive. The team is completely outfitted with full uniforms, as were many of the 1930s and 1940s township teams.

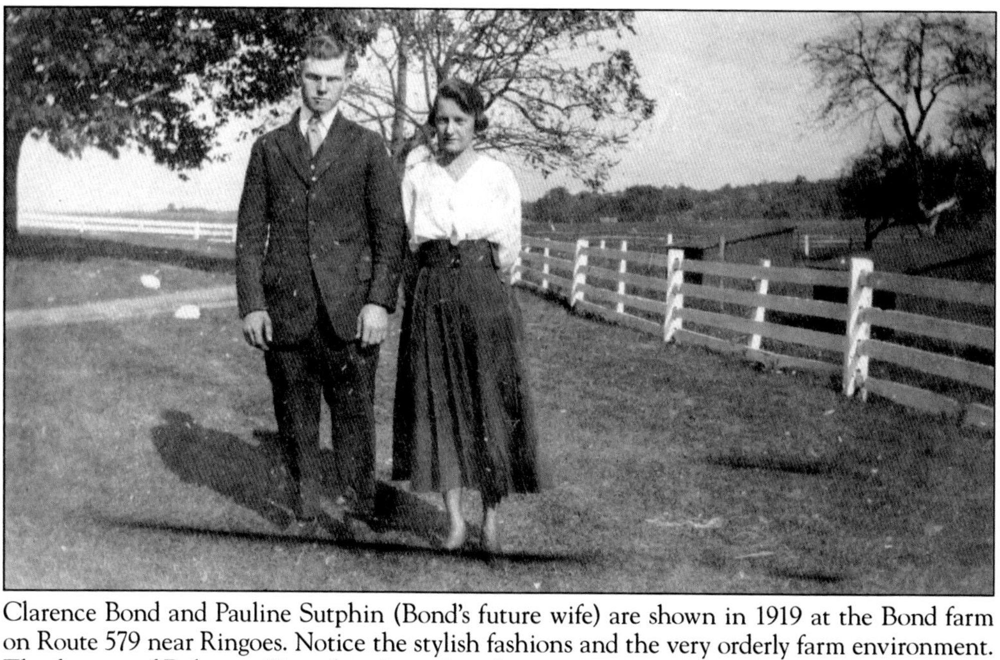

Clarence Bond and Pauline Sutphin (Bond's future wife) are shown in 1919 at the Bond farm on Route 579 near Ringoes. Notice the stylish fashions and the very orderly farm environment. The farmers of Delaware Township dressed up for most occasions. One farmer in the township even went into his house and put on a tie before taking his milk to the market. (Courtesy of Dave Bond.)

Young Paul Kurzenberger is shown in 1944 holding one of six geese from his family's farm. The farm is on Lambert Road near the Amwell Church of the Brethren. Notice the barn that was built in 1846 and was used to house wagons.

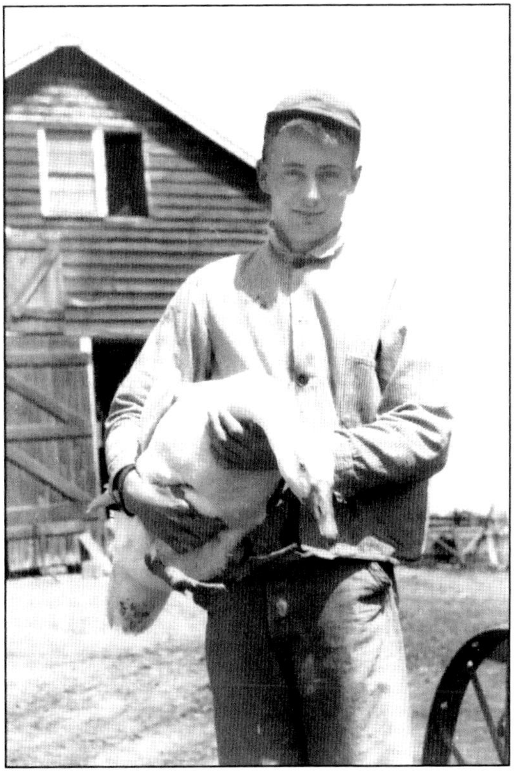

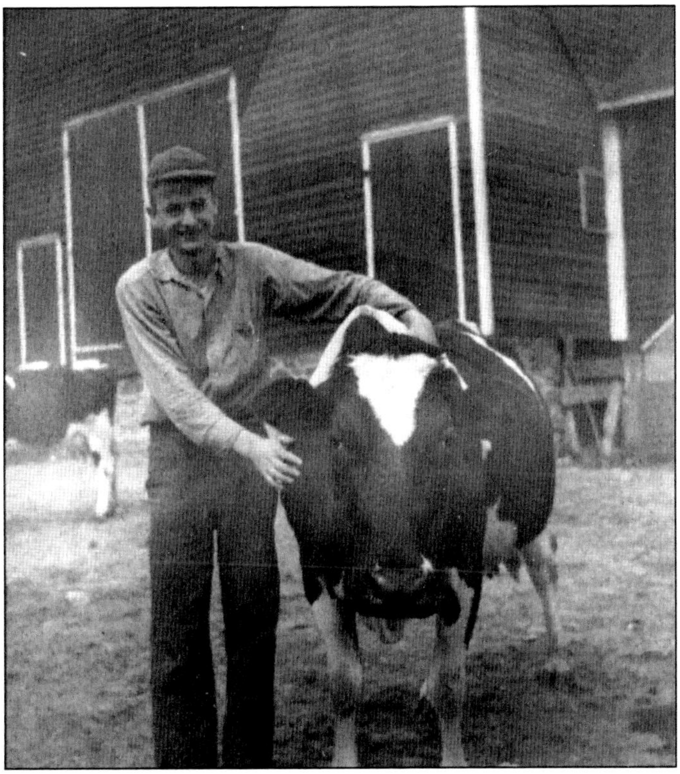

Kurzenberger is shown in 1944 with one of the farm's Holstein cows. Many of the Delaware Township dairy farms had Holstein cows because they produced significantly more milk than other breeds.

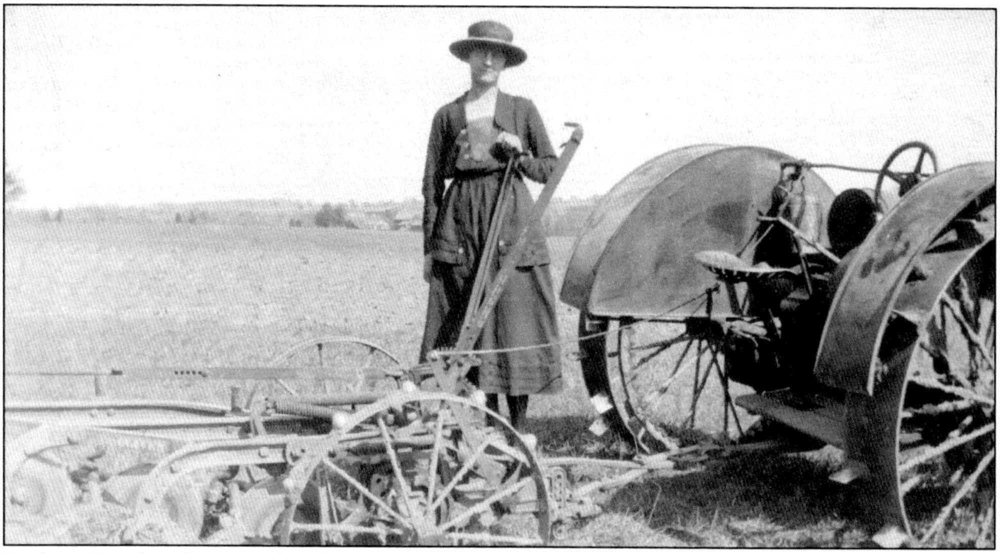

Pauline Bond is shown in her finery with a new tractor in the early 1920s. Delaware Township people kept up with changes in fashion, technology, and culture, partly because of the geographic placement of the township in the middle of the cultural flow along the eastern seaboard. (Courtesy of Dave Bond.)

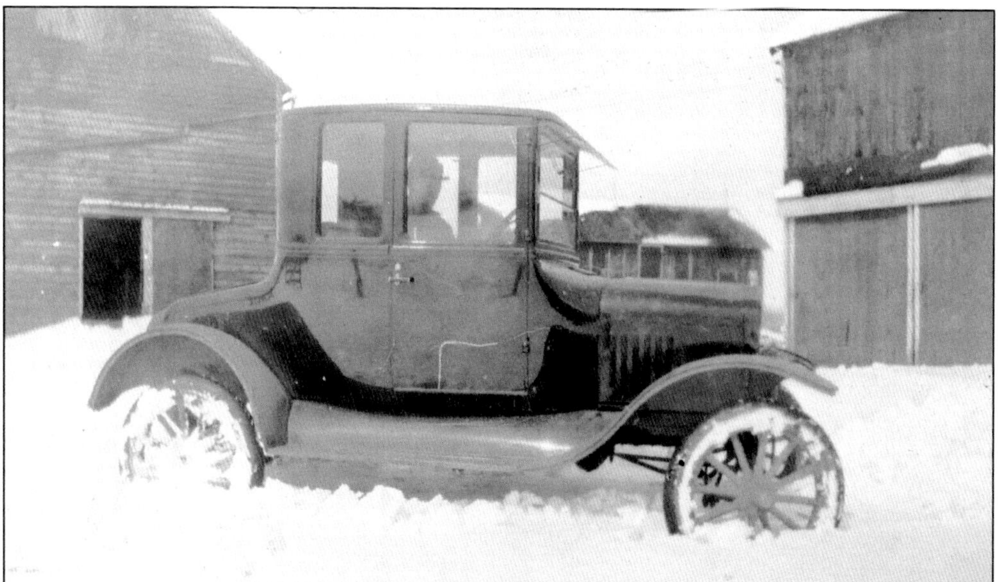

A new Model T coupe is shown in the winter of 1924 on the Bond farm. The family usually got a new car each year, as Clarence Bond was able to work a good deal with his cousin William Bond, the Ford dealer in Newtown, Pennsylvania. (Courtesy of Dave Bond.)

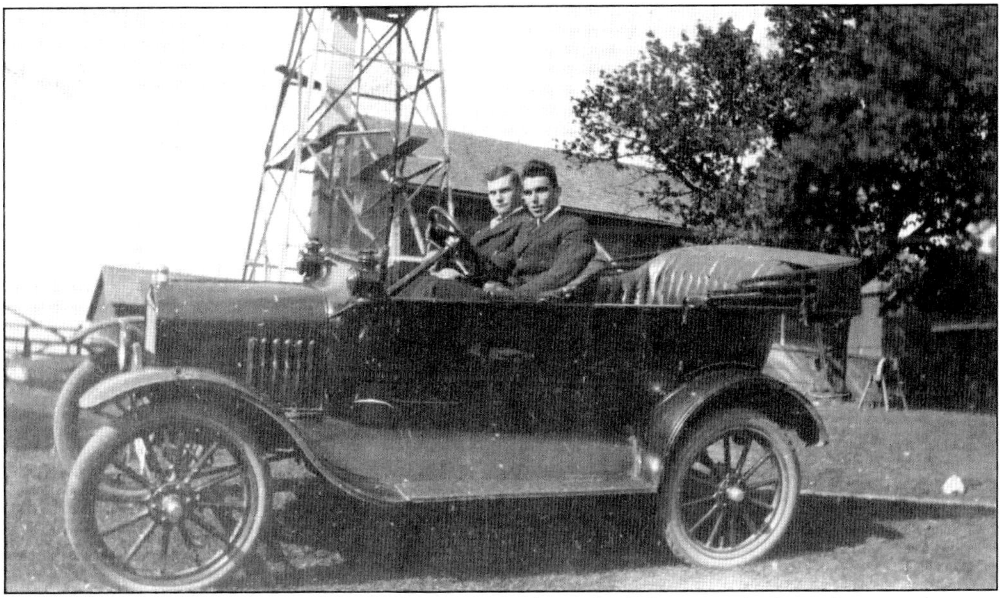

John Frizzel in the driver's seat and Clarence Bond on the left are ready for a drive in the new touring car in 1919. Notice the water tower in the background. (Courtesy of Dave Bond.)

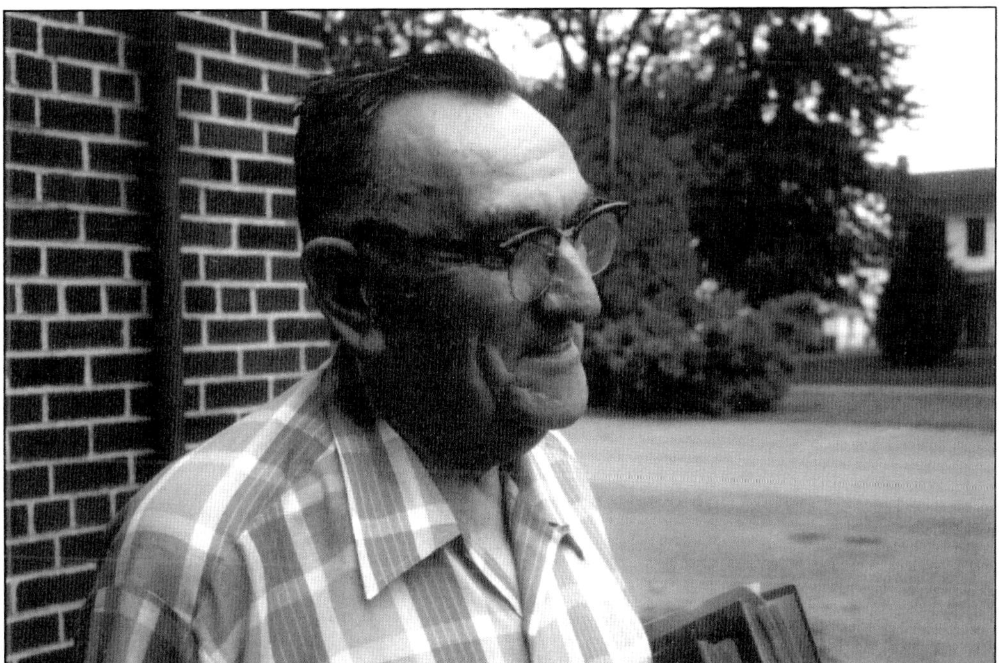

Shown here in the 1950s is general store owner Clint Wilson, who took over operation of the business from his mother and father. He was also quite involved in the local sports scene and coached some teams.

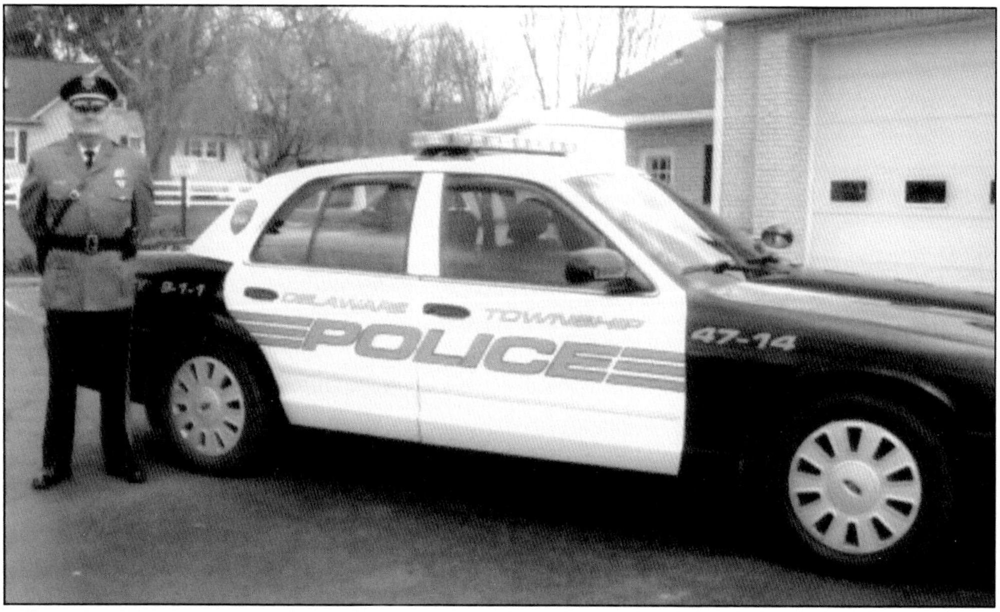

Police chief Bruce Mast is shown beside one of the township's 2009 police cars. Mast is the son of an airline pilot who spotted Delaware Township from the air in his approach to New York City and decided to move to the township since it showed "more green" than any other area around the city. Chief Mast grew up in the township, rose through the ranks, and now heads the department.

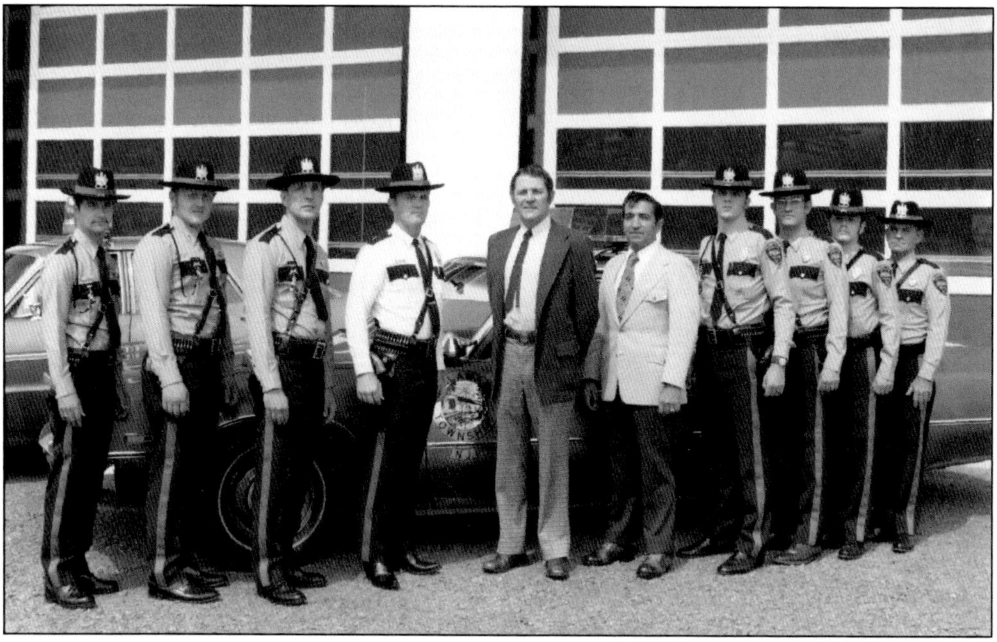

Delaware Township's finest are shown in a photograph taken in 1976. Shown are, from left to right, Lee Stelle; Richard Sands; Mike Delcasale; Warren Peterson (who was chief and later became sheriff of Hunterdon County); Harry Copeland, mayor; Andrew Leone, police committee; Edward Fleming (who later became chief); Carl Soltis, officer DeMeo; and Herb Culbertson (who was in the original tutorial group led by Clint Wilson).

Six

THE PLACE

Delaware Township rises from the Delaware River for one and a half miles to a flat, gently rolling countryside and is one of the most fertile farming areas in the region. The soil is of diverse types and easy to cultivate; the water is plentiful with a number of creeks flowing into the Delaware River. There has, consequently, been a tradition of intelligent, strong farmers in the township, which shows in the quality of the farms, the buildings, and a general atmosphere of tidy, orderly symmetry.

Delaware Township is studded here and there with quite spectacular views of 18th- and 19th-century farmsteads, making up a cultural landscape that, according to one authority, "ranks among the finest examples of a rural historic area in the United States." Those places, which can be glimpsed at a distance in journeys through the township, are a strong reminder of Delaware Township's history as a breadbasket to America and even earlier to the British empire.

A great deal of the built environment in the township also has a patina of use over time and still thrives as dwellings, stores, sheds, and storehouses (barns)—all functional tools for life over the centuries. Delaware Township has a total of 455 historic sites located throughout the township.

The town hall is a great testament to the preservation of the built environment, as the old tavern was recycled and meticulously preserved in its historical veracity and yet is amazingly functional as a town focus and meeting place. New construction in Delaware Township is tending to reflect the historical aesthetics and design of the historic buildings that are evident throughout the township.

The sense of history evident in preserving old structures and an open agricultural environment adds a time dimension to space and place. The very identity of and variety within the township has been enhanced with local construction materials and designs from the past.

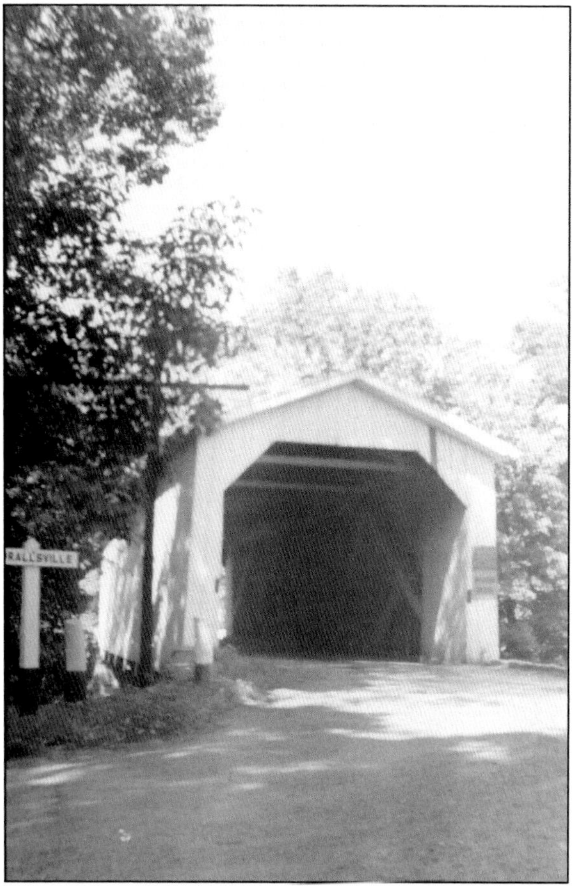

This is a view of the Green Sergeant's covered bridge as it appeared in the early 20th century. Notice the sign pointing to Prallsville, which is called Stockton today.

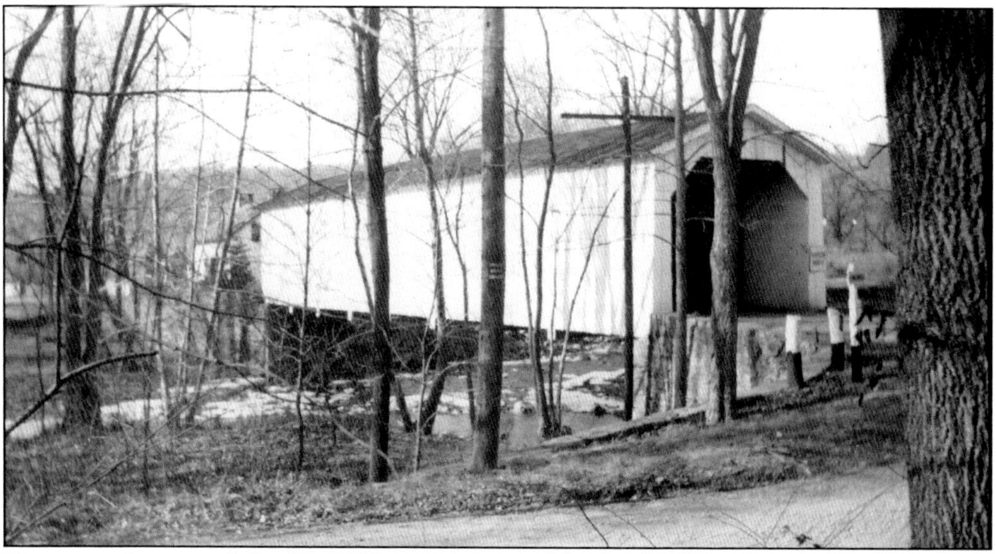

Here is a side view of the Green Sergeant's covered bridge from the winter of 1939, showing its 84-foot length. The bridge was originally built in 1866. (Courtesy of Maggie Clare and Gary Hinesley.)

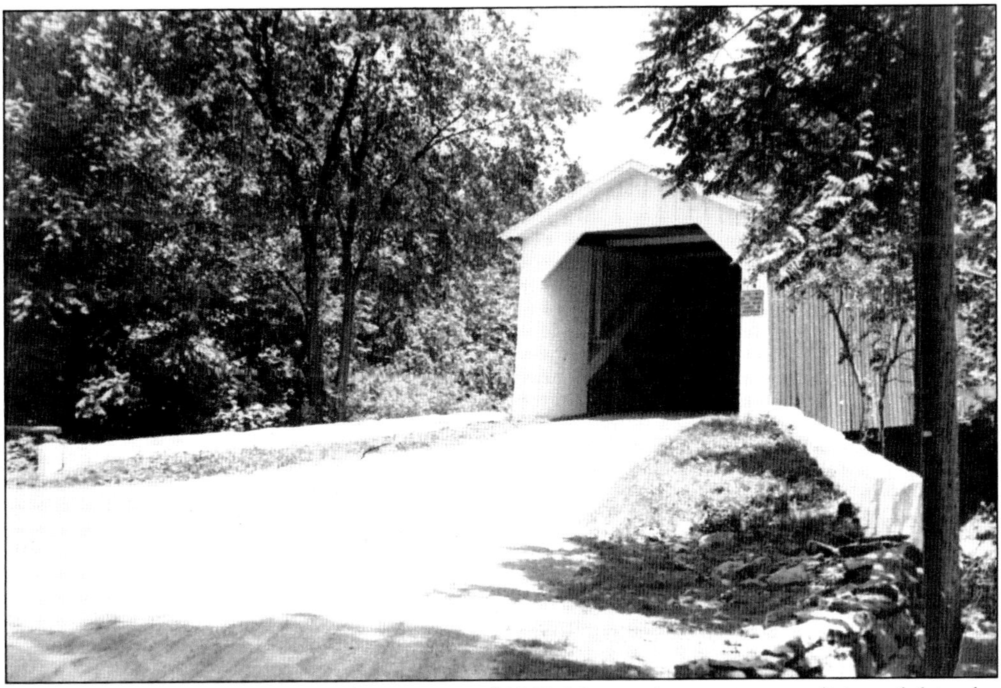

The covered bridge is shown in the summer of 1940. Notice the pristine condition of this, the last historic covered bridge in New Jersey, before it was reconditioned. (Courtesy of Maggie Clare and Gary Hinesley.)

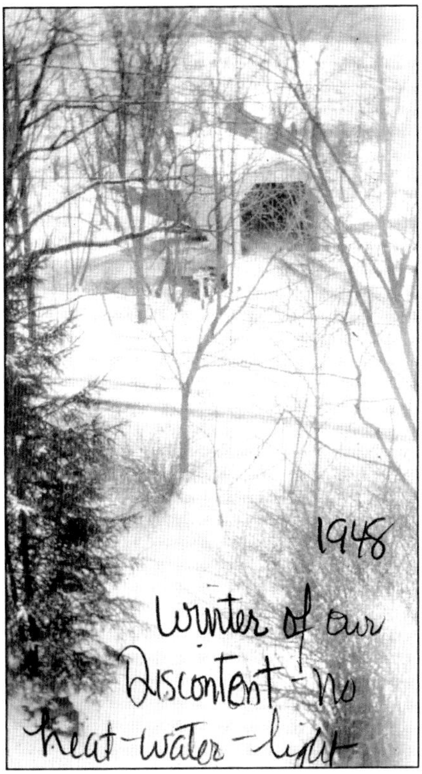

The covered bridge is seen here in 1948 from the Miller's House. The comments on the photograph indicate that early 1948 was the "Winter of Our Discontent," referring to the loss of heat, water, and light, which were knocked out by the weather. (Courtesy of Maggie Clare and Gary Hinesley.)

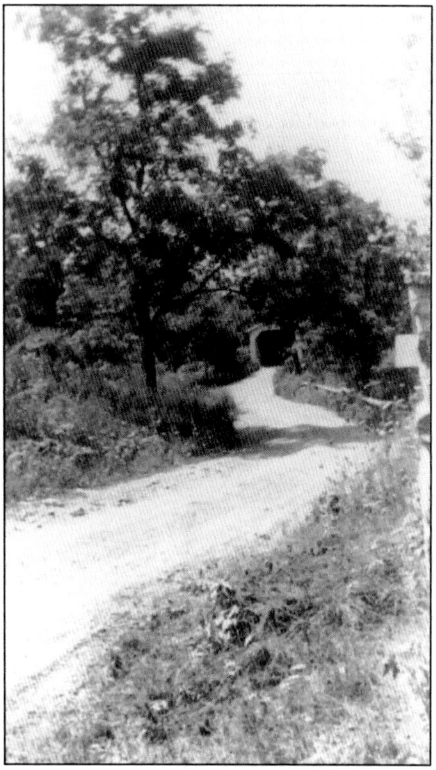

Here is a view of the still unpaved Route 604 as it winds out of sight toward the entrance to the Green Sergeant's covered bridge in the early 20th century. (Courtesy of Maggie Clare and Gary Hinesley.)

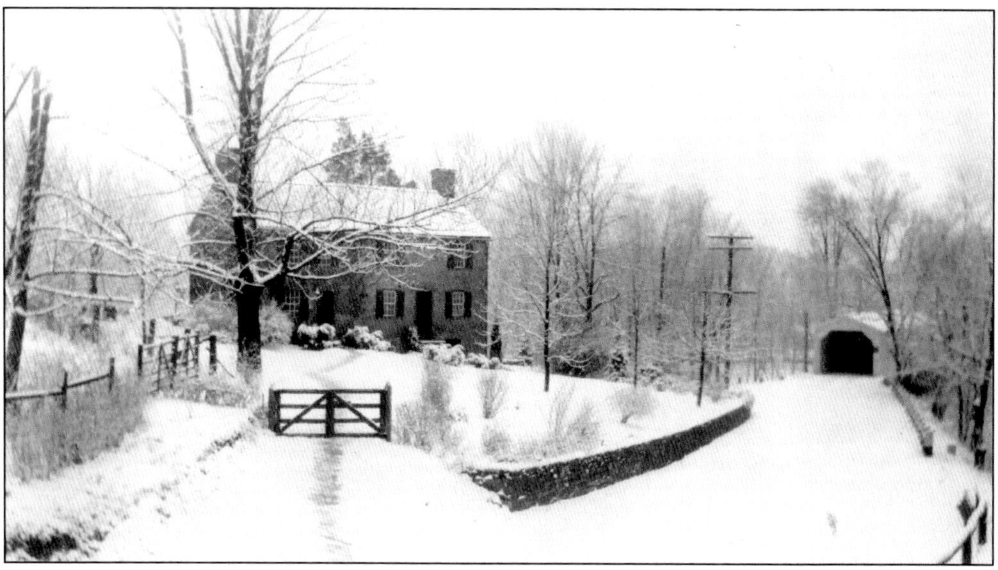

The Miller's House, built by John Opdyke in the 1700s, is shown in the winter of 1940 just above the covered bridge along the Wickecheoke Creek. Opdyke willed the house to his son Samuel in 1777. Samuel's son John sold it to Charles Sergeant in 1805, and Green Sergeant inherited it from Charles in 1823. It was held by the Sergeant family until 1923, when it was sold to the Johnson family. They sold it to Will Cotton, the well-known caricature artist for *Vanity Fair* and the *New Yorker*, in 1923. Cotton lovingly refurbished the house and grounds between the 1920s and 1940s. (Courtesy of Maggie Clare and Gary Hinesley.)

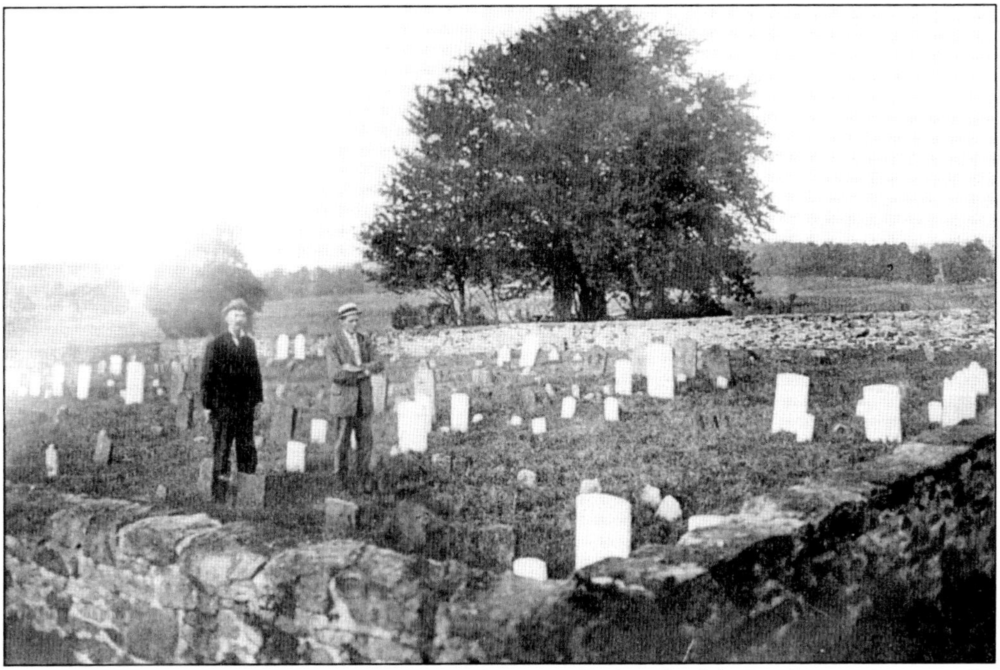

The old Amwell Cemetery off Route 604 near the Amwell Church of the Brethren is shown in the 1920s. Cemeteries were an important part of life in Delaware Township, with departed ancestors buried in the nearby facilities. Cemeteries were spread throughout the township and many had graves going back to the early 1700s. (Courtesy of the Amwell Church of the Brethren.)

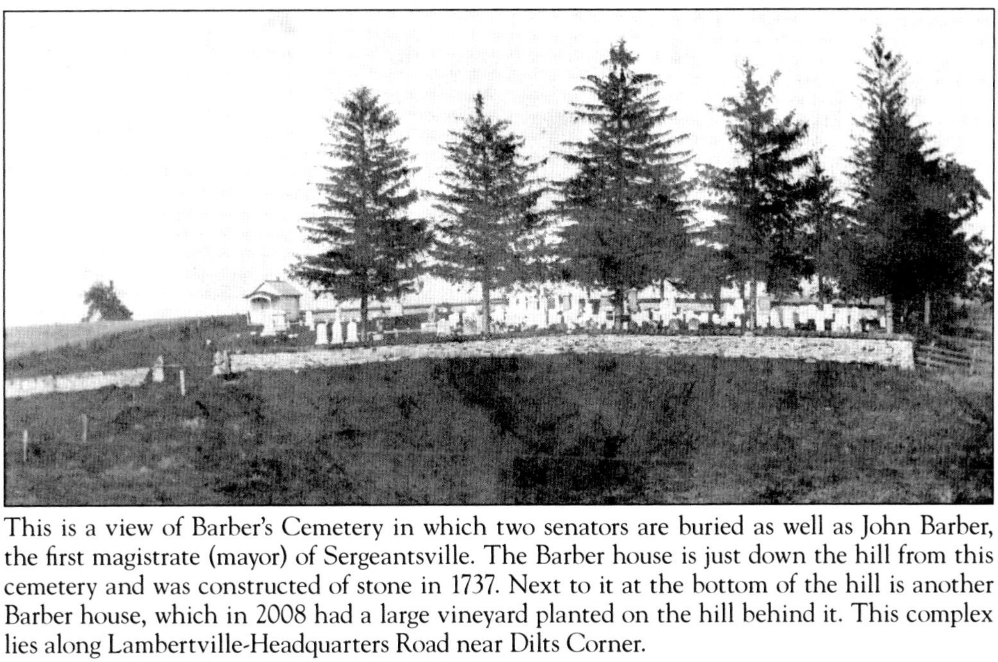

This is a view of Barber's Cemetery in which two senators are buried as well as John Barber, the first magistrate (mayor) of Sergeantsville. The Barber house is just down the hill from this cemetery and was constructed of stone in 1737. Next to it at the bottom of the hill is another Barber house, which in 2008 had a large vineyard planted on the hill behind it. This complex lies along Lambertville-Headquarters Road near Dilts Corner.

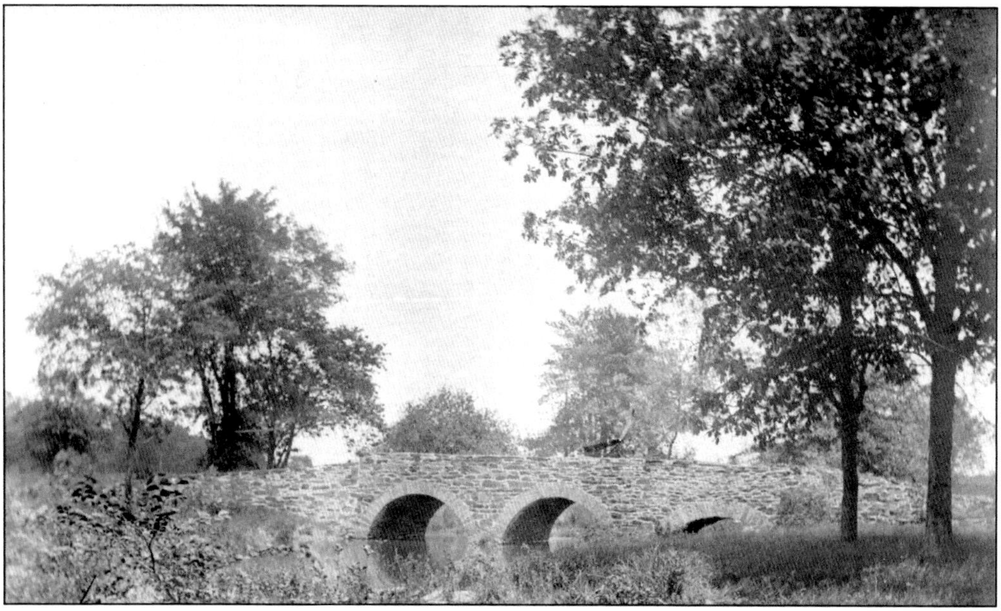

The old arch bridge along Route 579 in Croton is shown in the early 20th century. This classic three-arch bridge was replaced by a modern structure in the late 20th century. Such stone bridges are still quite abundant throughout the township. They were often originally constructed with stones from nearby streams by local farmers hired by contractors commissioned by the County Board of Freeholders. The techniques of construction and design were similar to those employed by the Romans 2,000 years ago.

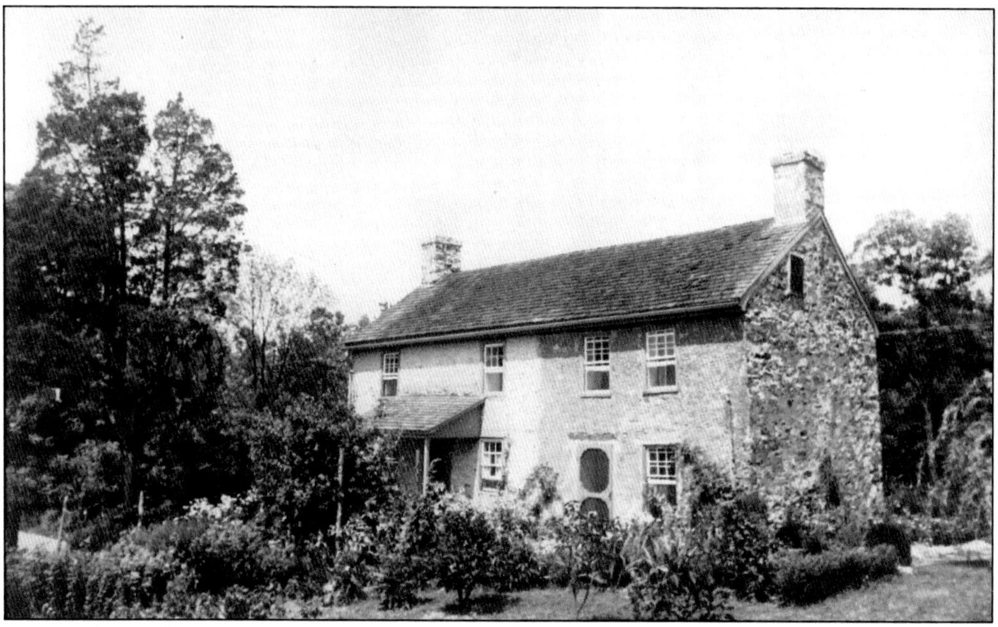

Here is the Miller's House in 1940 while it was being restored by Will Cotton, the *New Yorker* magazine cartoonist who owned it from the early 1920s through the 1940s. (Courtesy of Maggie Clare and Gary Hinesley.)

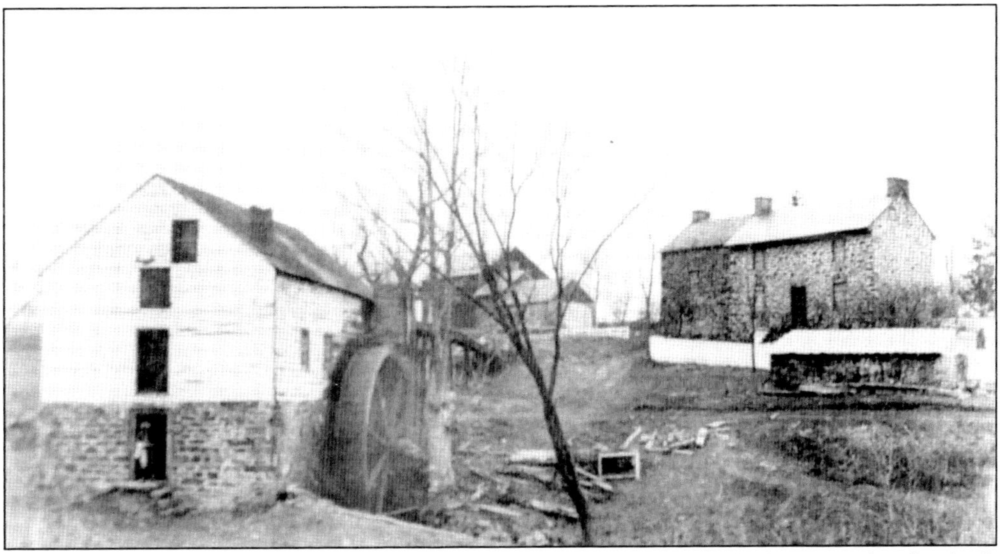

This photograph from the early 20th century shows the Samuel Opdyke house and mill, which were built in 1784. This mill and the surrounding structures were built by Opdyke, who also built a number of other mills in the area in the 1700s. This mill was located just off Route 604 near Pine Hill Road above the covered bridge.

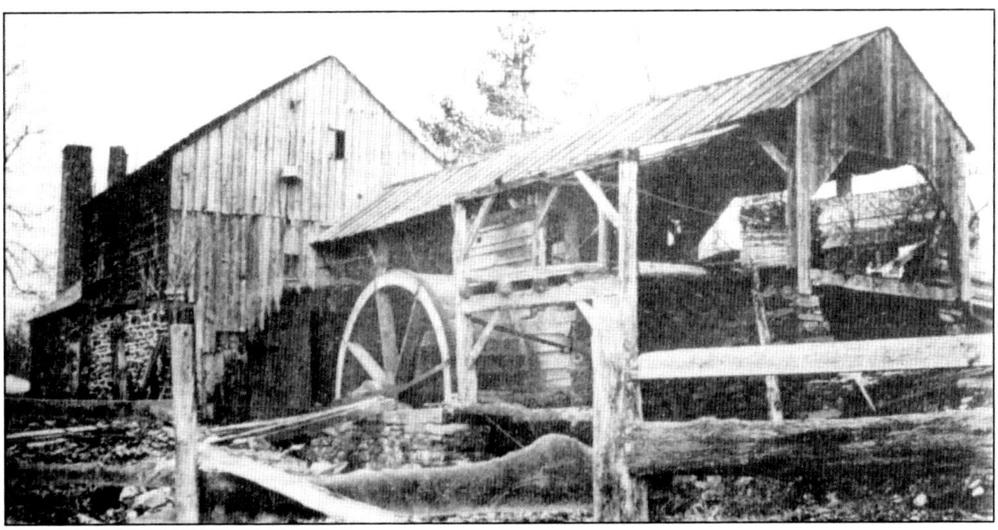

Pictured is the sawmill on Mill Road along the Wickecheoke Creek that was built in 1775 by Thomas Opdyke, son of John Opdyke. This mill was located one mile from Pine Hill Road on Mill Road.

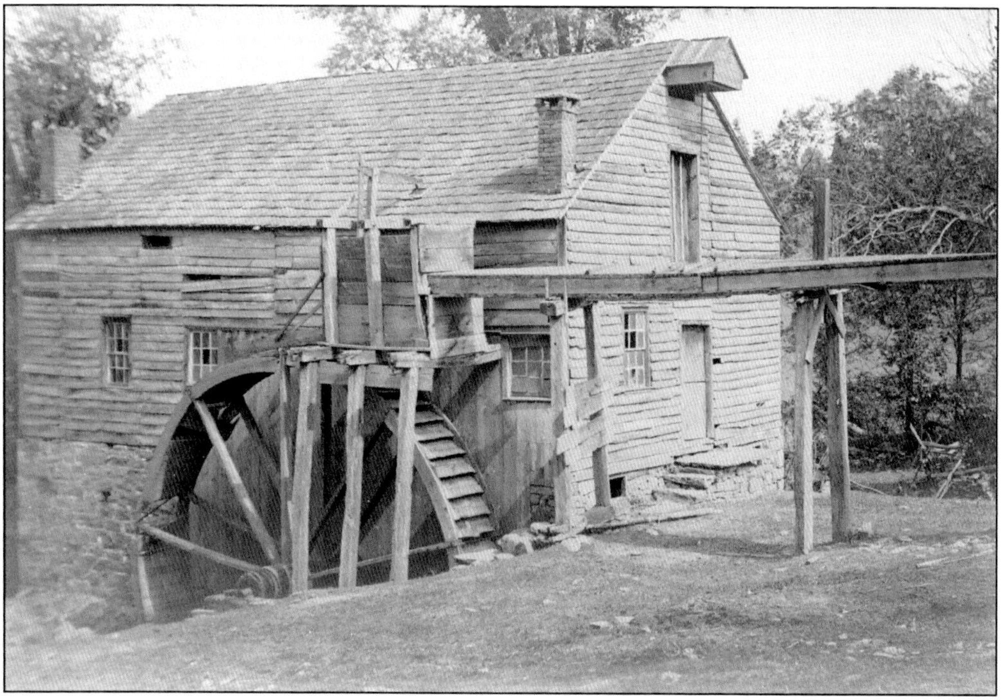

This gristmill was in operation until 1900. It stood alongside the Wickecheoke Creek and had a raceway, which brought water for the waterwheel from a pond on higher ground above it. The Miller's House stood on the corner nearby, just across from the covered bridge.

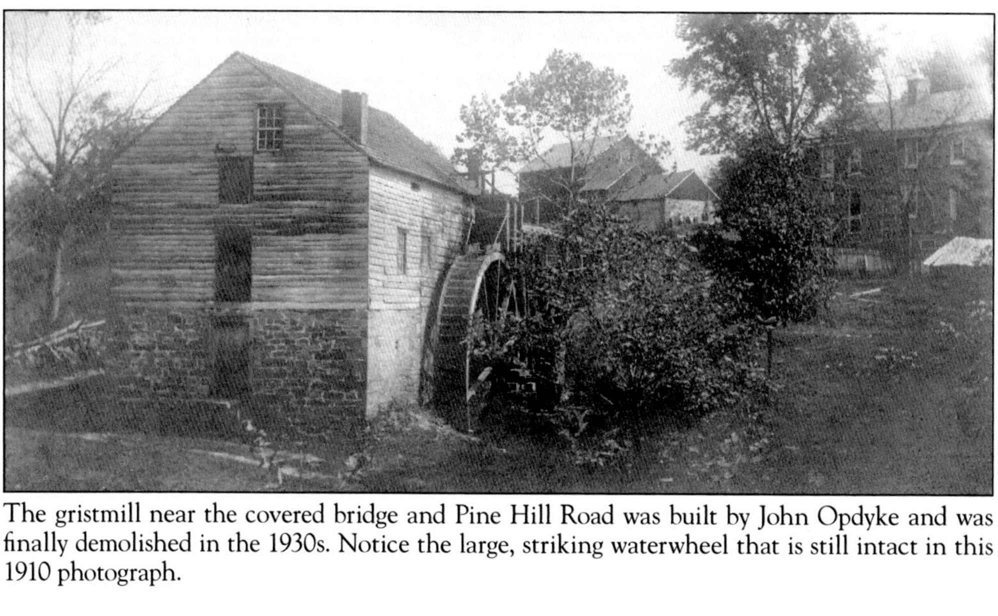

The gristmill near the covered bridge and Pine Hill Road was built by John Opdyke and was finally demolished in the 1930s. Notice the large, striking waterwheel that is still intact in this 1910 photograph.

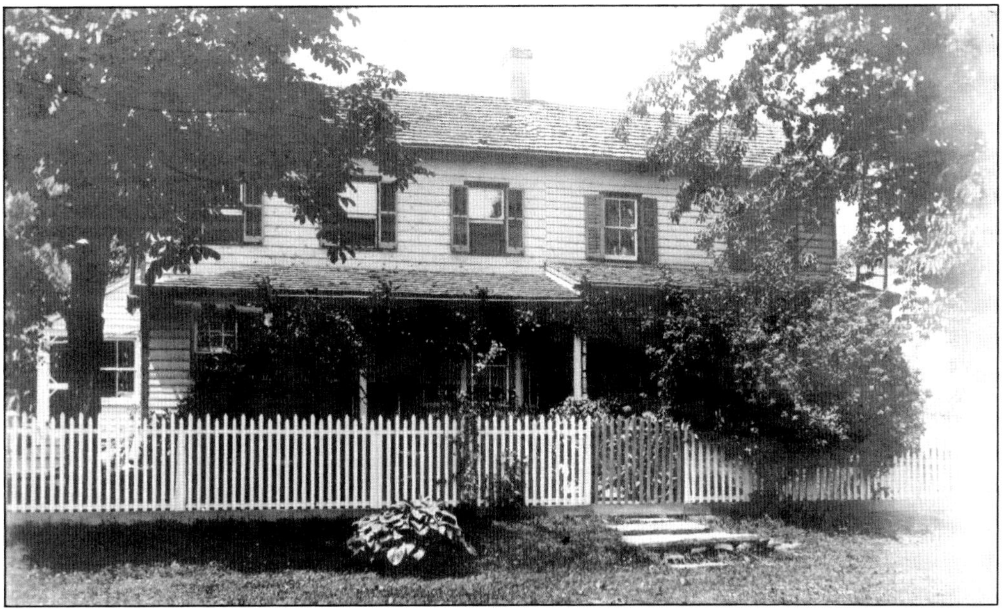

This house, shown in the early 20th century, was a hillside retreat and stood at the intersection of Routes 523 and 579 on the road between Sergeantsville and Flemington.

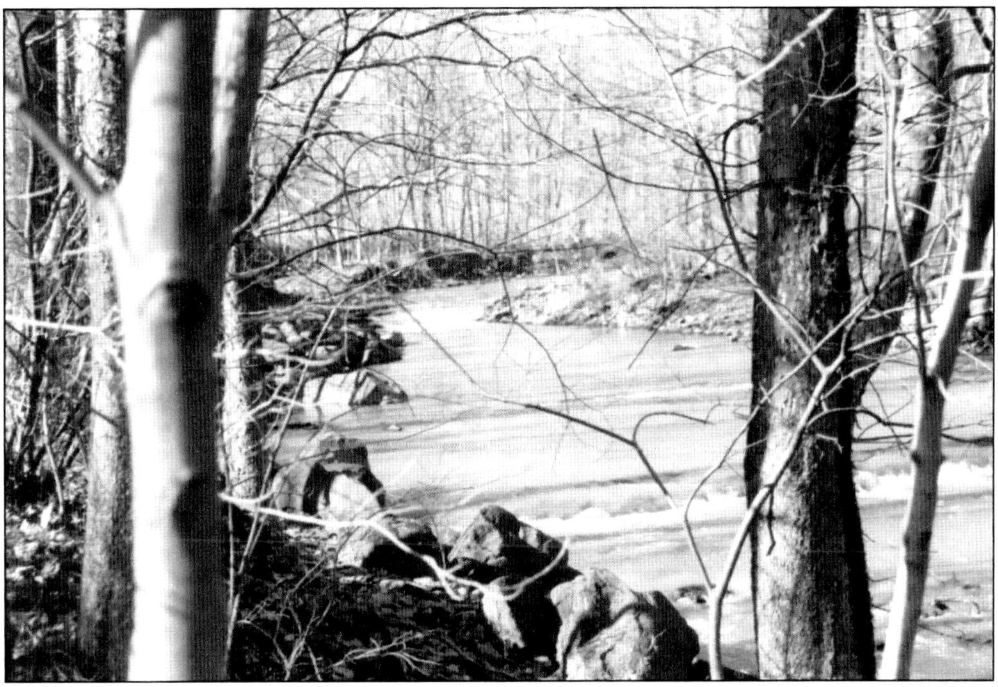

The Wickecheoke Creek, shown in 1981, can become quite swift, with white water cascading through in heavy rains and thaws.

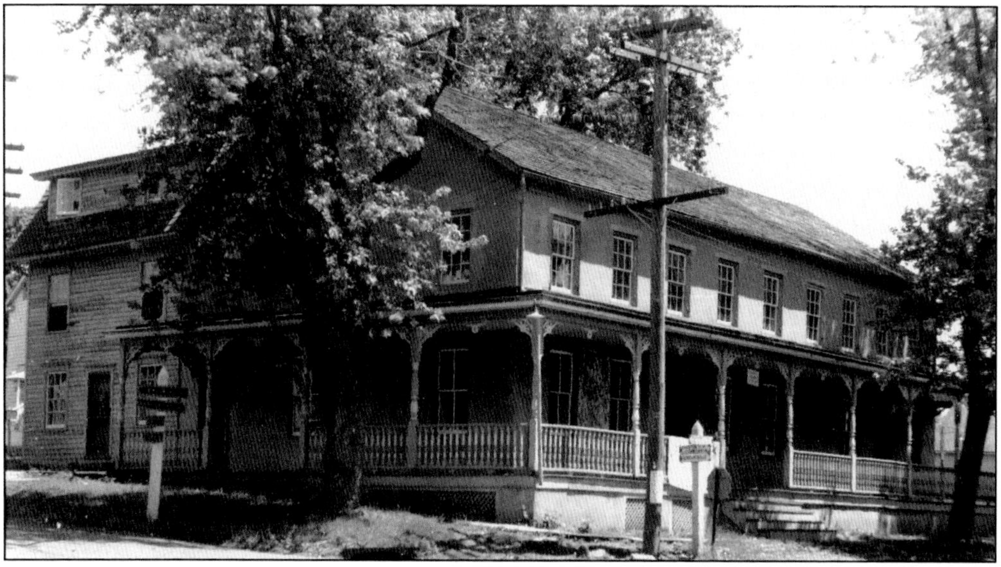

This 1930s photograph shows the hotel in Sergeantsville before it was remodeled and became today's municipal building.

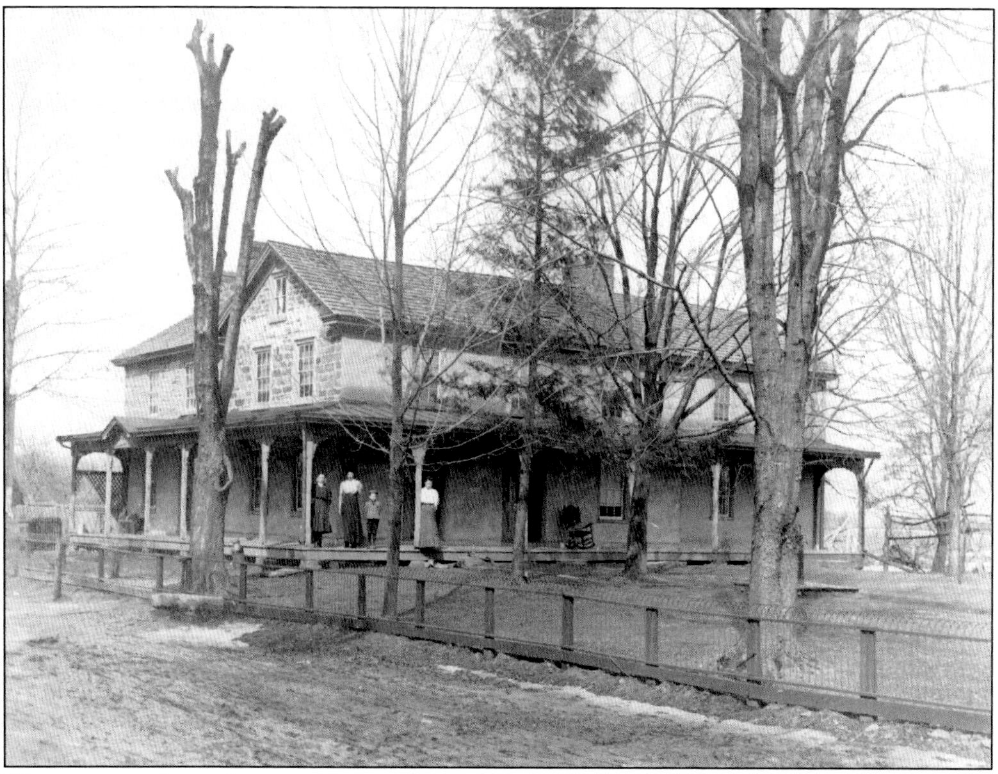

The structure shown here was originally a tavern in Rosemont, and Bill Reading lived in the house in the 20th century. This photograph was taken in the early 20th century.

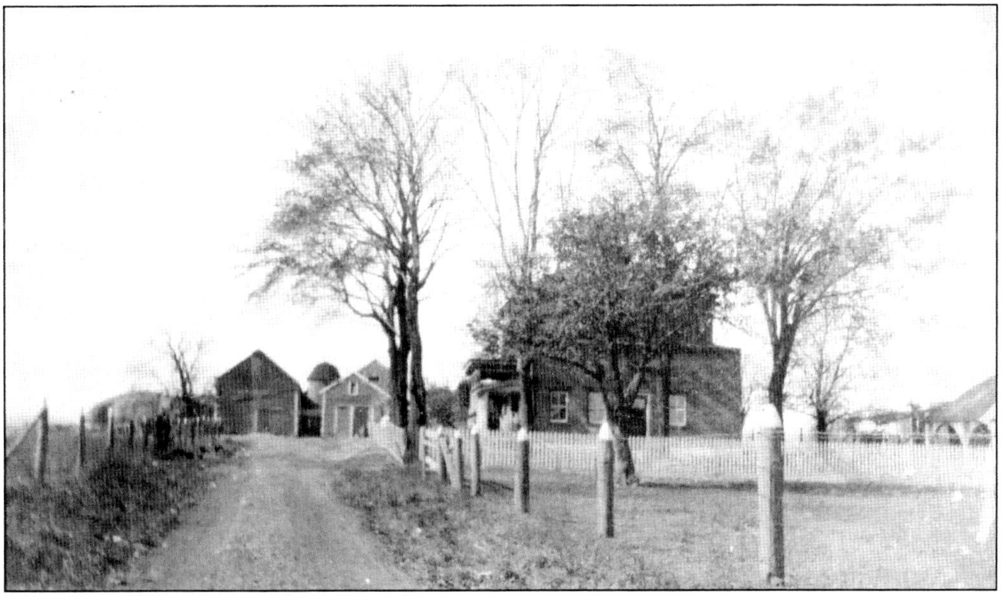

The Bond farm is shown along the farm drive in 1922. This farm complex looks very similar today, with a quite symmetrical and orderly appearance. It has "curb appeal." The barns were built in the late 1700s, and the house was built in 1849. (Courtesy of Dave Bond.)

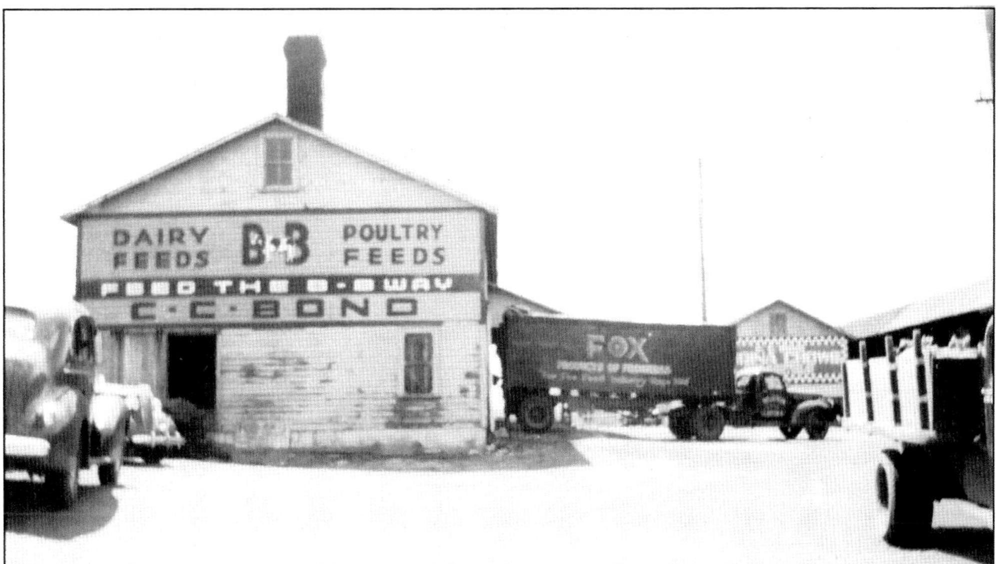

Clarence Bond operated a feed store in the former dairy collection depot in Ringoes, shown here in the late 1930s. Farmers brought their milk to this depot, and a "milk train" sent by Harbison's Dairy in Philadelphia took it to the city. Bond sold feed and grain after the dairy closed. (Courtesy of Dave Bond.)

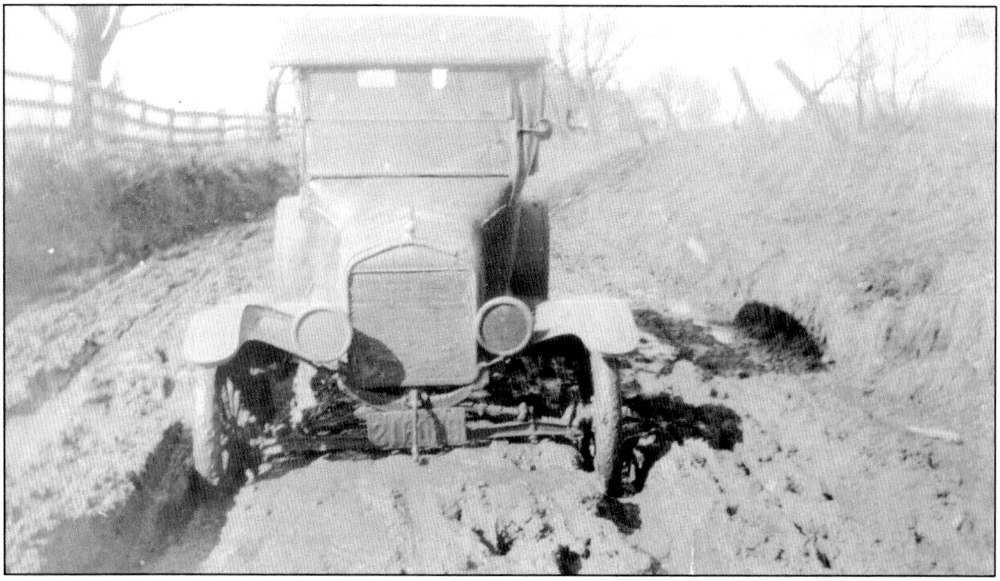

Seen in 1924 is a Model T on Route 579 near Ringoes in Delaware Township. This photograph was taken during the early spring thaw when the roads became almost impassable. (Courtesy of Dave Bond.)

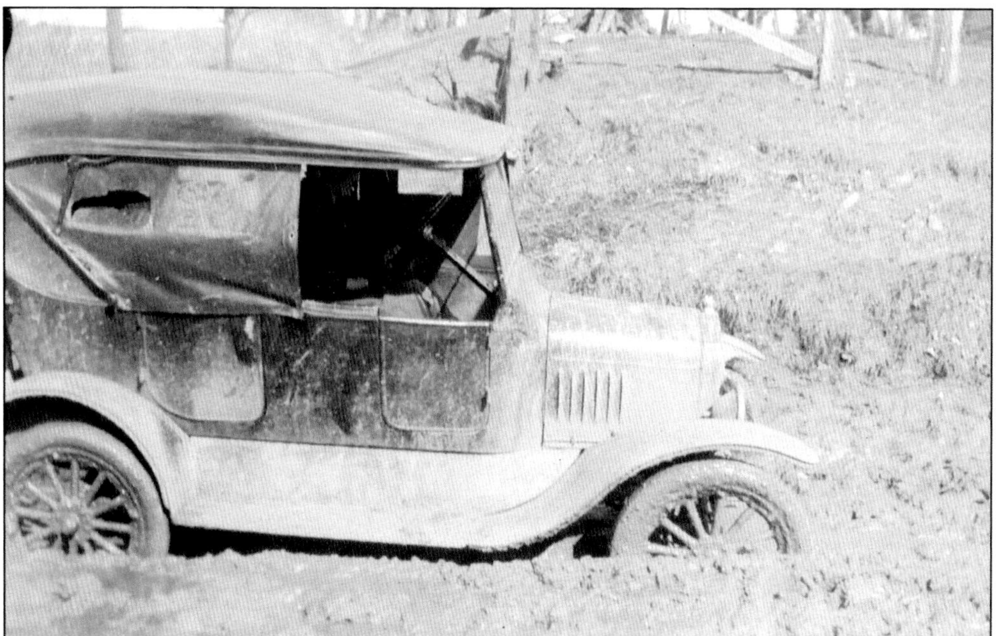

Here is a Model T moving through the mud on Route 579 just south of the Bond farm in the early 1920s. This was a major north–south route (the Old Trenton-Easton Turnpike), and yet it was typical of all the roads in the township before the late 1920s and 1930s. (Courtesy of Dave Bond.)

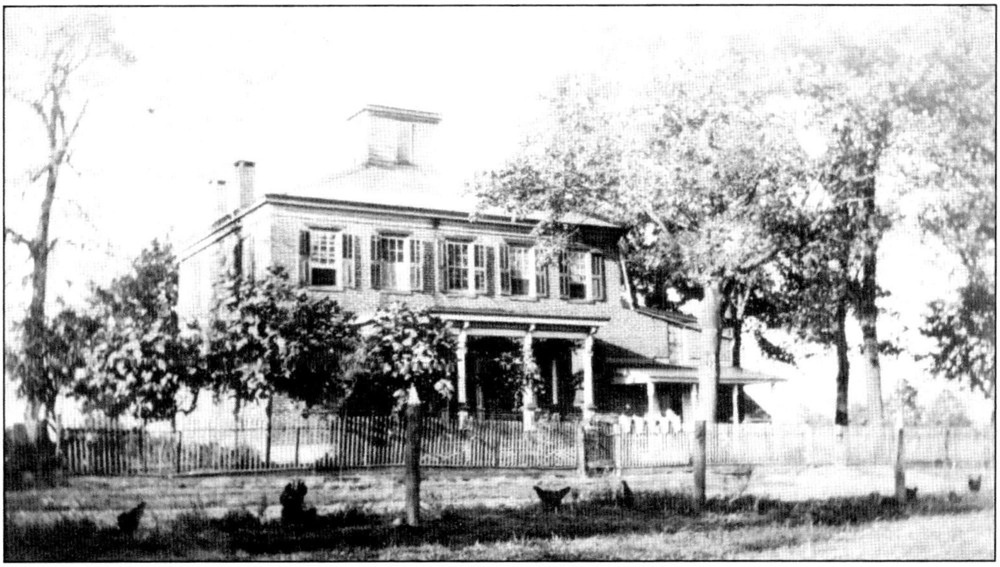

A 1921 picture shows the Bond farmhouse, which was built in the mid-19th century. The witch's watch on the peak was said to have been used to observe slaves working in the fields around the farm before the end of slavery. (Courtesy of Dave Bond.)

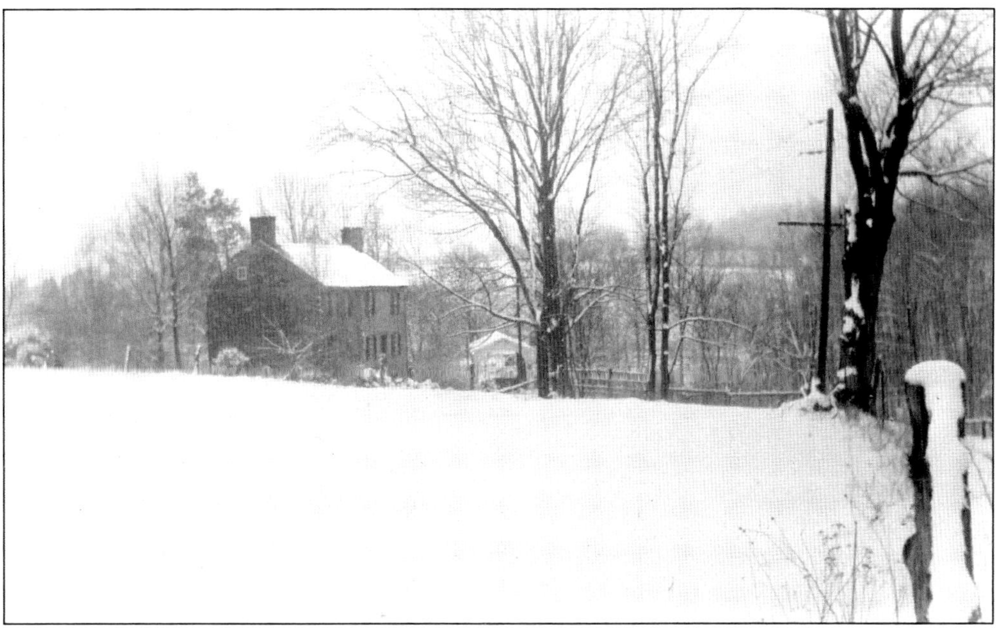

Snow covers the Miller's House in this photograph from the winter of 1940. (Courtesy of Maggie Clare and Gary Hinesley.)

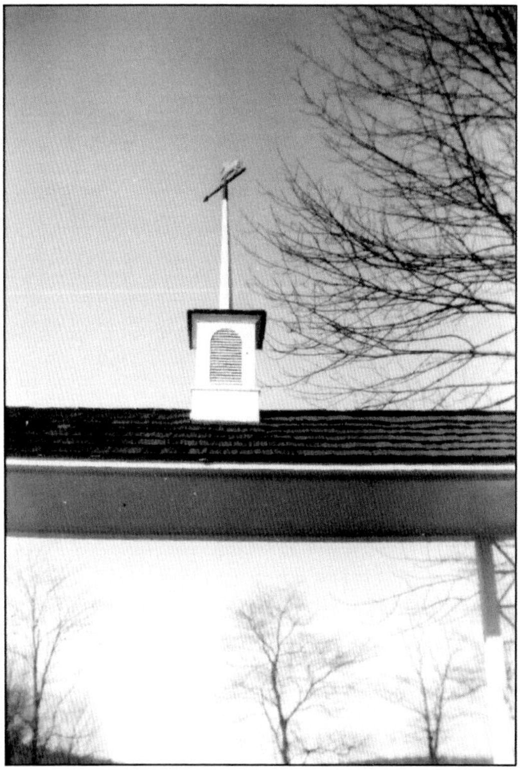

This cupola is shown on an entrance structure at the Paul Whiteman farm in the 1930s. Whiteman, the great early jazzman (called the "King of Swing"), had a farm near the Delaware River. He was said to have ridden his horse to the Stockton Inn (the "Little Hotel with a Wishing Well" of the 1930s song) for a drink or two.

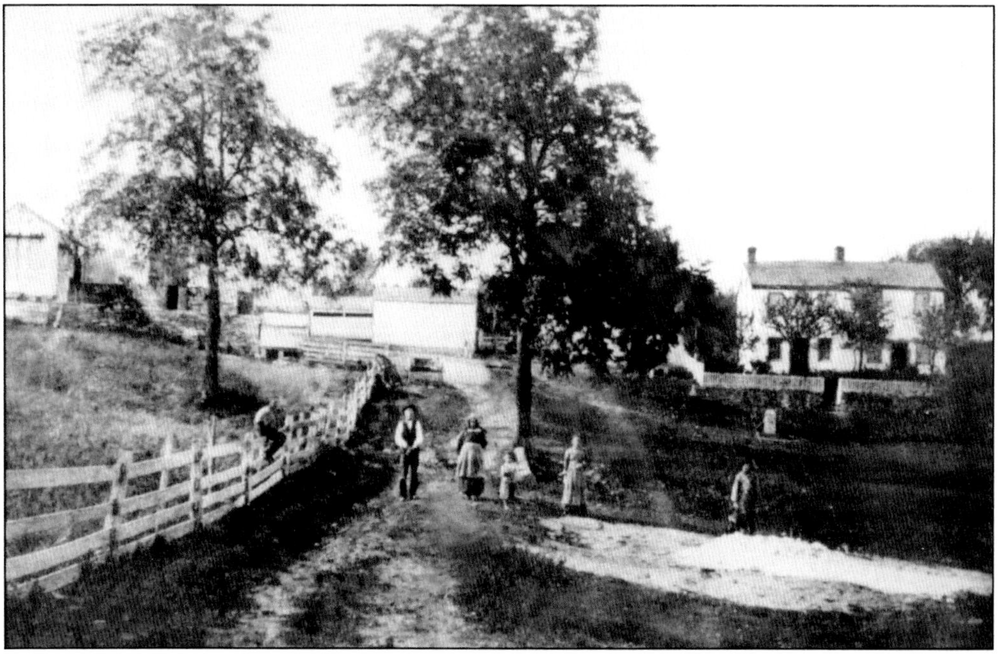

A farm scene is shown on Sanford Road in the early 20th century. Note the four-rail fence. It must always be remembered that Delaware Township has been primarily about farms and farmers, and even though it is changing to an extent, that heritage in the land and people is still the driving core of the township.

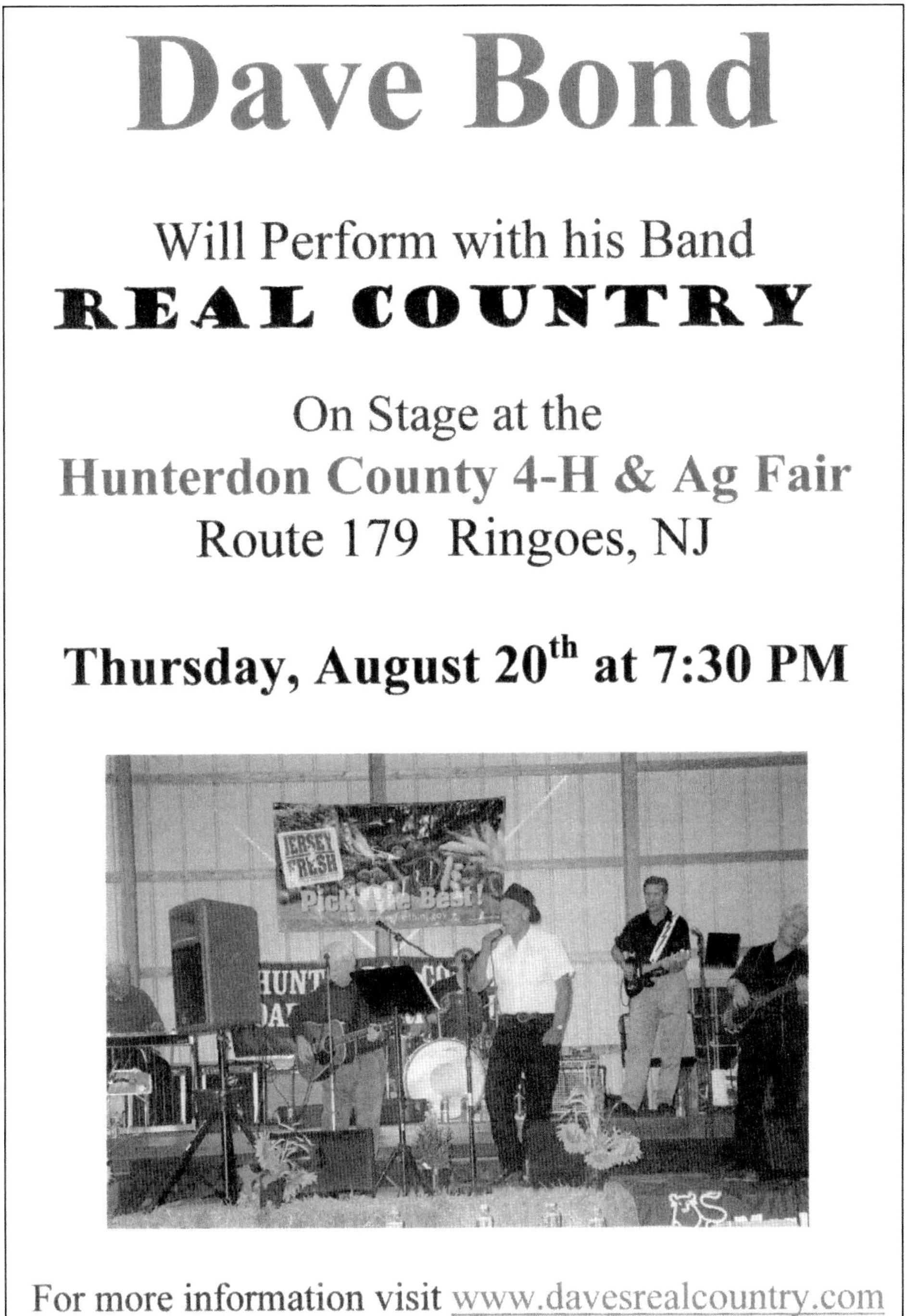

Dave Bond, who is a tractor dealer in the township today, has a band in which he performs as the main singer and farms a few hundred acres. Bond and the Real Country band perform at various venues, including a barn dance through the local radio station. The photograph on the poster above was taken at a concert held in a barn at Wood's Edge Wool Farm in the township. (Courtesy of Dave Bond.)

MADE IN THE USA

Arcadia Publishing, the leading local history publisher in the United States, is committed to making history accessible and meaningful through publishing books that celebrate and preserve the heritage of America's people and places. Consistent with our mission to preserve history on a local level, this book was printed in South Carolina on American-made paper and manufactured entirely in the United States.

This book carries the accredited Forest Stewardship Council (FSC) label and is printed on 100 percent FSC-certified paper. Products carrying the FSC label are independently certified to assure consumers that they come from forests that are managed to meet the social, economic, and ecological needs of present and future generations.

FSC
Mixed Sources
Product group from well-managed forests and other controlled sources

Cert no. SW-COC-001530
www.fsc.org
© 1996 Forest Stewardship Council